DAY HIKING

Mount
St. Helens

A hiker admires the Pumice Plain from the Boundary Trail on Johnston Ridge.

A sparkling Coldwater Lake from South Coldwater Ridge

Previous page: Wildflowers on the Pumice Plain on the Truman Trail

Mount Rainier from the summit of Badger Peak

Receiving illumination at Seminary Hill

Frozen Goat Marsh and snowy Mount St. Helens

Covel Creek Falls

Classic view of Spirit Lake and Mount St. Helens from Norway Pass

Swift Reservoir, Mount Rainier, and Mount Adams from Siouxon Peak

A misty morning at Spencer Meadow

A heron hunts at Lake Sacajawea.

A climbing party, including the two co-authors, on the summit of Mount St. Helens

DAY HIKING

Mount St. Helens

national volcanic monument · nature trails ·
winter routes · summit

by Craig Romano
& Aaron Theisen

MOUNTAINEERS
BOOKS

Mountaineers Books is the publishing division of The Mountaineers, an organization founded in 1906 and dedicated to the exploration, preservation, and enjoyment of outdoor and wilderness areas.

MOUNTAINEERS BOOKS 1001 SW Klickitat Way, Suite 201, Seattle, WA 98134
800.553.4453, www.mountaineersbooks.org

Printed in the United States of America
Distributed in the United Kingdom by Cordee, www.cordee.co.uk
First edition, 2015

Copy Editor: Erin Moore
Design and Layout: Jennifer Shontz, www.redshoedesign.com
Cartographer: Pease Press Cartography
Cover photograph: *Spirit Lake and Mount St. Helens from the Boundary Trail near Coldwater Peak*
Frontispiece: *An emerald Castle Ridge yields to a snowcapped, gray Mount St. Helens.*
All photographs © the authors unless otherwise noted.

Library of Congress Cataloging-in-Publication Data
Romano, Craig.
  Day hiking Mount St. Helens : National Volcanic Monument : nature trails, winter routes, summit / by Craig Romano and Aaron Theisen.—
First edition.
     pages cm
  Includes index.
  ISBN 978-1-59485-848-2 (trade paper)—ISBN 978-1-59485-849-9 (ebook) 1. Hiking--Washington (State)—Mount Saint Helens National Volcanic Monument--Guidebooks. 2. Washington (State)—Guidebooks. I. Theisen, Aaron. II. Title.
  GV199.42.W22M697 2015
  796.5109797)—dc23

2014039618

Background maps for the maps in this book were produced using the online map viewer CalTopo and National Geographic's TOPO! software. For more information about CalTopo, visit caltopo.com.

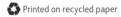 Printed on recycled paper

ISBN (paperback): 978-1-59485-848-2
ISBN (ebook): 978-1-59485-849-9

Table of Contents

Cross-Country Skiing and Snowshoe Trails

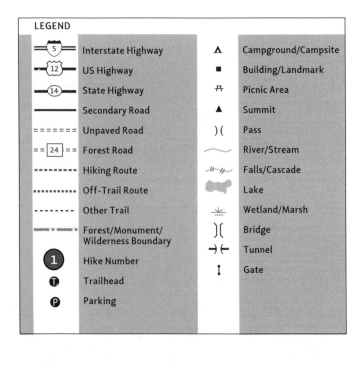

LEGEND

Symbol	Description	Symbol	Description
5	Interstate Highway	▲	Campground/Campsite
12	US Highway	■	Building/Landmark
14	State Highway	⊼	Picnic Area
	Secondary Road	▲	Summit
=======	Unpaved Road	)(	Pass
== 24 ==	Forest Road	～	River/Stream
----------	Hiking Route	⊬⊬	Falls/Cascade
••••••••••	Off-Trail Route		Lake
- - - - - -	Other Trail	☀	Wetland/Marsh
	Forest/Monument/Wilderness Boundary	)(	Bridge
1	Hike Number	→←←	Tunnel
T	Trailhead	↕	Gate
P	Parking		

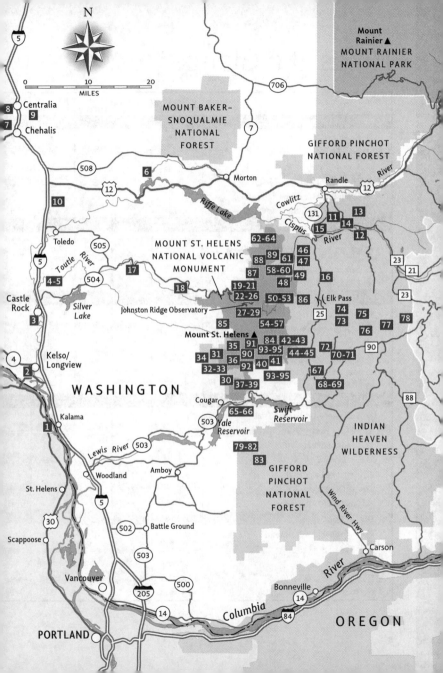

Hikes at a Glance

HIKE	DISTANCE (roundtrip)	RATING	DIFFI-CULTY	HIKABLE ALL YEAR	BIKES OKAY
COWLITZ RIVER VALLEY					
1. Kalama Marine Park	1.8 miles	*	1	•	•
2. Lake Sacajawea	3.7 miles	**	2	•	•
3. Cowlitz Riverfront East	3.6 miles	**	1	•	•
4. Seaquest State Park—Silver Lake	1 mile	**	1	•	
5. Seaquest State Park—Forest Loop	2 miles	**	3	•	•
6. Mayfield Trail (Ike Kinswa State Park)	2.8 miles	**	1	•	
CHEHALIS RIVER VALLEY					
7. Willapa Hills Trail	10.5 miles	***	2	•	•
8. Chehalis River Discovery Trail	3.6 miles	**	1	•	
9. Seminary Hill	1.3 miles	**	2	•	
10. Lewis and Clark State Park	2 miles	**	1	•	
CISPUS RIVER VALLEY					
11. Woods Creek Watchable Wildlife	2.1 miles	***	1	•	
12. Covel Creek—Angel Falls	4.9 miles	****	2		
13. Layser Cave	0.4 mile	**	1		
14. Kraus Ridge	8.8 miles	**	3		•
15. Iron Creek Old Growth	0.3 mile	**	1	•	
16. Iron Creek Falls	0.1 mile	**	1	•	
MOUNT ST. HELENS WEST					
17. Sediment Rention Dam Trail	1.4 miles	**	1	•	
18. Forest Learning Trail	0.8 mile	**	1		
19. Winds of Change Trail	0.3 mile	***	1		
20. Elk Bench Trail	2 miles	***	2		
21. Birth of a Lake Trail	0.5 mile	***	1		
22. Coldwater Lake	9 miles	***	3		•
23. South Coldwater Ridge	6.8 miles	***	3		•
24. The Hummocks	2.5 miles	***	2		
25. Johnston Ridge	9 miles	****	4		
26 Eruption Trail	0.6 mile	****	1		
27. Harry's Ridge	8.2 miles	****	3		
28. Coldwater Peak	12.8 miles	*****	5		
29. Truman Trail—Pumice Plain	10.4 miles	****	4		

KID-FRIENDLY	DOG-FRIENDLY	WILD-FLOWERS	WATER-FALLS	OLD GROWTH	BIRD-WATCHING	HISTORIC	WHEELCHAIR ACCESS
•	•						•
•	•					•	•
•	•						•
•					•		•
•	•						
•	•				•	•	
•	•				•	•	•
•	•				•		
•	•				•		
•	•			•		•	
•				•	•		
•			•	•	•		
•						•	
				•	•		
•	•		•	•			
•	•		•				
•					•	•	
•							•
•		•					•
•		•					
•						•	•
•		•	•				
•		•				•	
•		•			•		
		•				•	
•		•				•	•
		•					
		•				•	
		•					

HIKE	DISTANCE (roundtrip)	RATING	DIFFI-CULTY	HIKABLE ALL YEAR	BIKES OKAY
MOUNT ST. HELENS SOUTH					
30. Merrill Lake Nature Trail	1 mile	***	1		
31. Goat Marsh	2.8 miles	***	1		
32. Kalama River	8 miles	***	2		•
33. Cinnamon Trail	8.8 miles (one-way)	***	3		•
34. Fossil Trail	14.6 miles	***	4		•
35. Sheep Canyon	12.2 miles	*****	4		•
36. Butte Camp	7.6 miles	****	3		•
37. Trail of Two Forests	0.4 mile	**	1		
38. Ape Cave	1.5 miles/ 2.5 miles	*****	3		
39. Volcano Viewpoint Trail	1.6 miles	**	2		
40. June Lake	2.6 miles	**	1		
41. Pine Creek	2.2 miles	**	1		
42. Ape Canyon	9.4 miles	****	3		•
43. Lava Canyon	3.9 miles	****	3		
44. Smith Creek	13.6 miles	***	4		•
45. Smith Creek Butte	11.6 miles	***	5		
MOUNT ST. HELENS EAST					
46. Strawberry Mountain	8.8 miles	*****	3		
47. Strawberry Mountain Lookout Site	4.8 miles	****	3		
48. Meta Lake	0.6 mile	***	1		
49. Ghost Lake	5.2 miles	***	2		
50. Norway Pass—Mount Margaret	11.4 miles	*****	4		
51. Mount Margaret Backcountry Lakes	15 miles	****	5		
52. Mount Whittier	14.9 miles	*****	5		
53. Independence Ridge Loop	6.8 miles	****	3		
54. Harmony Falls	2.4 miles	***	2		
55. Windy Ridge Lookout	3 miles	***	2		
56. Windy Ridge and the Plains of Abraham	8.8 miles	*****	3		partia
57. Loowit Falls	8.8 miles	****	3		
MOUNT ST. HELENS NORTH					
58. Ryan Lake	0.7 mile	**	1		
59. Green River	10.0 miles	***	2		•
60. Goat Mountain and Deadmans Lake	11.2 miles	*****	4		•
61. Quartz Creek Big Trees	0.4 mile	***	1		
62. Goat Creek—Cathedral Falls	5.6 miles	***	2		•

KID-FRIENDLY	DOG-FRIENDLY	WILD-FLOWERS	WATER-FALLS	OLD GROWTH	BIRD-WATCHING	HISTORIC	WHEELCHAIR ACCESS
•	•			•			
•	•			•	•		
•	•			•			
•	•			•			
	•			•			
	•	•					
	•			•			
•							•
						•	
•	•						
•	•	•	•	•			
•	•			•		•	
	•	•		•			
partial			•				partial
	•	•	•	•			
				•		•	
•	•	•					
	•			•		•	
•					•	•	•
•	•	•			•		
		•					
		•	•				
		•					
		•					
•		•	•				
•		•					
•		•					
•		•	•				
•	•				•		
•	•		•	•			
	•	•		•			
•	•			•			
•	•		•	•			

HIKE	DISTANCE (roundtrip)	RATING	DIFFI-CULTY	HIKABLE ALL YEAR	BIKES OKAY
63. Vanson Peak	13.2 miles	****	4		•
64. Tumwater Mountain	14.4 miles	***	5		•
LEWIS RIVER VALLEY					
65. Yale Reservoir Logging Road Trail	7.5 miles	**	2	•	•
66. Cougar—Beaver Bay	2 miles	**	1		
67. Cedar Flats Research Natural Area	1 mile	***	1		
68. Curly Creek Falls	0.4 mile	**	1		
69. Lower Lewis River	5.6 miles	***	3		•
70. Middle Lewis Falls	1 mile	**	2		•
71. Upper Lewis River	5 miles	****	2		•
72. Spencer Butte	4.8 miles	***	3		•
DARK DIVIDE ROADLESS AREA					
73. Wright Meadow	3 miles	**	2		•
74. Badger Peak	10.4 miles	****	4		•
75. Craggy Peak	14.6 miles	****	4		•
76. Quartz Creek	8.2 miles	****	3		•
77. Boulder Trail—Table Mountain	2.6 miles	**	2		•
78. Council Bluff	3 miles	****	2		•
SIOUXON ROADLESS AREA					
79. North Siouxon Creek	9.2 miles	****	4		•
80. Siouxon Creek	13.8 miles	****	3		•
81. Horseshoe Ridge	11.9 miles	****	5		•
82. Huffman Peak	13.6 miles	***	4		•
83. Siouxon Peak	15.3 miles	****	5		•
BACKPACKING TRIPS					
84. Loowit Trail	32 miles	*****	5		south
85. Castle Ridge	23.8 miles	*****	4		
86. Boundary Trail	57.4 miles (one-way)	*****	5		east half
87. Lakes Trail	16.4 miles (one-way)	*****	5		west half
88. Green River—Goat Mountain Loop	21.5 miles	****	4		•
89. Tumwater Mountain Loop	19.7 miles	***	4		•
SUMMIT-CLIMBING ROUTES					
90. Mount St. Helens Summit: Monitor Ridge	9.4 miles	*****	5		
91. Mount St. Helens Summit: Worm Flows Winter Route	11.6 miles	*****	5		

KID-FRIENDLY	DOG-FRIENDLY	WILD-FLOWERS	WATER-FALLS	OLD GROWTH	BIRD-WATCHING	HISTORIC	WHEELCHAIR ACCESS
	•	•	•	•		•	
	•	•	•	•		•	
•	•		•				
•	•						
•	•			•			
•			•				•
•						•	
	•		•	•			
	•					•	
	•				•	•	
				•		•	
		•		•			
	•			•			
	•				•		
•		•				•	
	•		•				
•	•		•				
			•	•			
			•	•			
			•			•	
		•				•	
		•					
		•	•	•		•	
			•				
				•			
	•	•		•			
	•	•	•	•		•	
		•					
						•	

HIKE	DISTANCE (roundtrip)	RATING	DIFFI-CULTY	HIKABLE ALL YEAR	BIKES OKAY
CROSS-COUNTRY SKIING AND SNOWSHOE TRAILS					
92. Kalama Ski Trail	22.2 miles	***	3		
93. Swift Creek—June Lake Loop	4.9 miles	****	2		
94. Pine Marten Trails	up to 7 miles	**	1		
95. Sasquatch Loop	9.9 miles	***	3		

KID-FRIENDLY	DOG-FRIENDLY	WILD-FLOWERS	WATER-FALLS	OLD GROWTH	BIRD-WATCHING	HISTORIC	WHEELCHAIR ACCESS
•	•			•			
•	•			•			
•	•						
	•						

Acknowledgments

Researching and writing *Day Hiking Mount St. Helens* was fun, exciting, and a lot of hard work. A huge thank you to all the great people at Mountaineers Books, especially publisher Helen Cherullo, project manager Mary Metz, and editor in chief Kate Rogers.

I want to thank Aaron Theisen for agreeing to work with me on this project and for being such a great co-author and friend. I am happy to have been able to work with you on an area that we both greatly love. I look forward to working with you again in the near future. I also want to thank our editor, Erin Moore, for her attention to detail and thoughtful suggestions that help to make this book a finer volume.

I could not have hiked and researched every single mile of trail within the Mount St. Helens National Volcanic Monument without the help of the following great people. A big thanks to Kristan Carver, Peder Bisbjerg, Jay Thompson, Douglas Romano, Ryan Ojerio, Gwen Tollefson, Ted Evans, and Wendy Wheeler-Jacobs for accompanying me on so many great hikes!

A big *grazie* too to rangers Heather Latham and Gary Walker with the Mount St. Helens National Volcanic Monument for all of their invaluable help and information.

I also want to once again thank God for watching over me, keeping me safe and healthy, while I hiked all over the backcountry. And lastly, but most importantly, I want to thank my loving wife, Heather, for supporting me while I worked on yet another guidebook. Thanks for hiking with me, too, to some of the special places in this book and providing me with more precious memories. I can't wait for us to take our new son to Mount St. Helens!

—*Craig Romano*

My first foray into the guidebook world could not have gone more smoothly, thanks to the team at Mountaineers Books, in particular publisher Helen Cherullo, project manager Mary Metz, and editor in chief Kate Rogers. In addition, I thank editor Erin Moore for her keen eye and insightful comments.

I thank my co-author and friend Craig Romano for the opportunity to contribute to the *Day Hiking* series. I've enjoyed our far-reaching conversations on trail and look forward to many more—on one of these hikes we'll eventually solve all the world's problems!

Thanks, too, to my parents, Mike and Colleen, and siblings Joe and Micaela for our time spent together on trail, both during the course of research for this book and while growing up around Mount St. Helens.

Finally, I must thank my wife, Kristi, who juggled work and home obligations while I slept in a tent on the other side of the state, and my son, Owen, who dreamed up superheroes who could light my way while hiking. I simply could not have done it without their love and support.

—*Aaron Theisen*

Opposite: A sand ladder makes travel easier on steep pumiced slopes.

Much of Mount St. Helens' southern reaches, including this old-growth forest grove, survived the 1980 eruption.

Preface

Mount St. Helens is an American and Pacific Northwest icon. For many people alive on May 18, 1980, it was the only major volcanic eruption within the Continental United States in their lifetime—at least so far. You had to go back to 1917 for the last continental US eruption, when another Cascades volcano, California's Lassen Peak, spewed lava and ash all over the countryside.

Just before Mount St. Helens became a household name across America, I arrived in the Pacific Northwest on an around-the-country bike trip. It was spring of 1980, and looking out from a hillside near Longview, Washington, I saw the smoking volcano for the first time. Five weeks later Mount St. Helens erupted! I remember that day clearly. I was in DeKalb, Illinois, on my way back home to New Hampshire. If you lived in Washington and Oregon at the time, you most certainly won't ever forget it. I still hear residents tell stories of the eruption as if it was yesterday.

My co-author, Aaron Theisen, was a mere month old when St. Helens erupted. But he was born and raised in Longview within the shadows of that history- and earth-shattering mountain. He says he grew up with its lure and has had a fondness for the peak for as long as he can remember.

After I moved to Washington State in 1989, I wasted no time heading to Mount St. Helens to see it up front and personal. My hike into the Mount Margaret Backcountry that July is one of my fondest hiking memories. I had never seen before nature's force and power at such a magnitude. It looked as if an atom bomb had hit the mountain.

Today, I am still amazed. To see the sheer force of the eruption and its destruction—and then to witness the rapidity of the landscape's recovery and rejuvenation—is astounding. Every trip to this fascinating landscape blows me away (yes, pun intended). I marvel at its destructive and healing forces. And every trip I make to the mountain instills more reverence of the power and resiliency of nature.

If you have never been to Mount St. Helens, I invite you to come now to catch the show. There's still so much to be revealed. And if you've been here many times before, you know all too well that your next visit will reveal each time a changing landscape. Aaron and I love this mountain and its environs. We have thoroughly explored its trails and want to share our love for America's most famous volcano with you.

And with that, it's time once again for my "battle cry" from previous *Day Hiking* titles. As our world continues to urbanize, its denizens growing more sedentary and disconnected from the natural world, life for many has lost its real meaning. Nature may need us to protect it from becoming paved over—but we need nature to protect us from the encroaching world of vacuous consumption and shallow pursuits. So, shun the mall, turn off the TV, ditch the smart phone, and hit the trail! We've lined up 95 magnificent hikes to help you celebrate nature, life, the incredible landscapes of the Mount St. Helens National Volcanic Monument, and you. Yes, you! Go take a hike! Celebrate life and return from the natural world a better and more content person. You don't need a lot of money or fancy equipment—just a little energy, direction, and wanderlust.

Henry David Thoreau proclaimed, "In wildness is the preservation of the world." And I add: In wildness is also the salvation of our souls—the meaning of life—and the preservation of our humanness. If I'm preaching to the choir, help me then to introduce new disciples to the sacred world of nature. For while we sometimes relish our solitude on the trail, we need more like-minded souls to help us keep what little wild lands remain. Help nature by introducing your family, coworkers, neighbors, and elected representatives to our wonderful trails. I'm convinced that a society that hikes is not only good for our wild and natural places (people will be willing to protect them) but also good for people (we can all live more healthy and connective lives).

Enjoy this book. Aaron and I have enjoyed researching and writing it. We're convinced that people can change the world for the better, one hike at a time. We hope to see you on the trail. Happy hiking!

—*Craig Romano*

A NOTE ABOUT SAFETY

Safety is an important concern in all outdoor activities. No guidebook can alert you to every hazard or anticipate the limitations of every reader. Therefore, the descriptions of roads, trails, routes, and natural features in this book are not representations that a particular place or excursion will be safe for your party. When you follow any of the routes described in this book, you assume responsibility for your own safety. Under normal conditions, such excursions require the usual attention to traffic, road and trail conditions, weather, terrain, the capabilities of your party, and other factors. Because many of the lands in this book are subject to development and/or change of ownership, conditions may have changed since this book was written that make your use of some of these routes unwise. Always check for current conditions, obey posted private property signs, and avoid confrontations with property owners or managers. Keeping informed on current conditions and exercising common sense are the keys to a safe, enjoyable outing.

—*Mountaineers Books*

Introduction

A BLAST FROM THE PAST: MOUNT ST. HELENS HISTORY

On a developmental and geologic time scale, Mount St. Helens might be considered to be a volatile teen. Formed only 275,000 years ago, the volcano developed its aesthetically pleasing pre-eruption form over the past 3000 years, as multiple mountain-building eruptions deposited debris onto the peak. Before its 1980 eruption, Mount St. Helens was the fifth-highest peak in Washington at 9677 feet tall, its symmetrical conical shape earning it the moniker "the Mount Fuji of America."

However, the beautiful form hid a violent reputation. The Cowlitz Indians called Mount St. Helens *Lavelatla*, which means "smoking mountain," and the Chinook told of *skookums*, mountain devils, who lived on the summit and ate men. The first European to sight the volcano was Captain George Vancouver of the British Royal Navy, who in 1792 named the peak after countryman Alleyne Fitzherbert, the Baron St. Helens. Although neither Vancouver nor Lewis and Clark, who followed a decade later, witnessed an eruption, early European settlers recorded multiple eruptions over the course of the 1800s.

Mount St. Helens then lay quiet for a century, until, in the spring of 1980, small eruptions—as many as one per hour— began to rattle the mountain. At 8:32 AM on May 18, 1980, a magnitude-5.1 earthquake rocked Mount St. Helens. Simultaneously,

Phlox, heather, and lomatium on Horseshoe Ridge

Memorial on Johnston Ridge pays tribute to the fifty-seven people who died in the 1980 eruption.

the north side and summit of the mountain sloughed off. The slide, the largest debris avalanche in recorded history, traveled west and quickly overtook the North Fork Toutle River. The rapid disappearance of the north flank of the mountain caused the magma to depressurize and violently vent, with a lateral blast out of the north flank throwing debris at up to 300 miles per hour. Removal of the summit cone released the pressure in the volcano's ducts, which caused built-up magma to expand toward the new hole in the mountain, and a massive plume of ash began to billow out the top.

Over the course of the next nine hours, Mount St. Helens spewed more than 520 million tons of ash, causing mid-day darkness even in Spokane 250 miles away and ash to fall from the sky as far away as the Great Plains. Over the south, west, and east faces, rapidly melting snow flowing off the peak mixed with mud and ash to create destructive lahars that swept away old-growth trees, buildings, and bridges. The eruption killed fifty-seven people in its path. It wiped out nearly all the wildlife on the mountain and every tree in a six-mile radius, creating a localized "extinction-level event."

Two years later, Congress designated the 110,000-acre Mount St. Helens National Volcanic Monument a "living laboratory" for research into ongoing volcanism, the natural process of recovery from the eruption, and visitor education and recreation.

The "Smoking Mountain" stirs still: Mount St. Helens experienced eruptions from 2004 through 2008, and volcanologists claim it is the volcano most likely to erupt in the foreseeable future. But in the decades since the 1980 eruption, the recovery of the flora and fauna around Mount St. Helens—and the expansion of a glacier within the crater—has astounded scientists and wowed millions of visitors.

You'll probably notice seismic measuring equipment throughout the national monument.

WHAT'S IN THIS BOOK?

The book you are now holding focuses on the best day hikes within the Mount St. Helens National Volcanic Monument and its periphery, including the Dark Divide and Siouxon Roadless Areas and the Cowlitz, Chehalis, and Lewis river valleys. But there's more. Unlike other volumes in the *Day Hiking* series, this volume is more comprehensive, with its aim to be the best and most inclusive book on the national volcanic monument. In this book you'll also find backpacking trips, summer and winter climbing routes to St. Helens' summit, winter cross-country skiing and snowshoe trails, and information on area visitors centers and campgrounds.

Hikers makes the laborious trek up Monitor Ridge.

USING THIS BOOK

The *Day Hiking* guidebooks were developed to be easy to use while still providing enough detail to help you explore a region. They include all the information you need to find and enjoy the hikes but leave enough room for you to make your own discoveries. We have hiked every mile of trail described in *Day Hiking Mount St. Helens* so you can follow the directions and advice with confidence. However, conditions can change: more on that later in this introduction.

What the Ratings Mean

Each hike starts with two subjective assessments: a rank of 1 to 5 stars for an overall rating, and a numerical score of 1 to 5 for a route's difficulty. The overall appeal **rating** is based on our impressions of each route's scenic beauty, natural wonder, and other unique qualities, such as solitude potential and wildlife-viewing opportunities.

    ***** Unmatched hiking adventure, great scenic beauty, and wonderful trail experience

    **** Excellent experience, sure to please all

    *** A great hike, with one or more fabulous features to enjoy

    ** May lack the "killer view," but offers lots of little moments to enjoy

    * Worth doing as a refreshing walk, especially if you're in the neighborhood

The **difficulty** score is based on trail length, overall elevation gain, steepness, and trail conditions. Generally, trails that are rated more difficult (4 or 5) are longer and steeper than average. But it's not a simple equation. A short, steep trail over talus slopes may be rated 5 while a long, smooth trail with little elevation gain may be rated 2.

    5 Extremely difficult: Excessive elevation gain and/or more than 5 miles one-way

    4 Difficult: Some steep sections, possibly rough or poorly maintained trail

    3 Moderate: A good workout, but no real problems

    2 Moderately easy: Relatively flat or short route with good trail

    1 Easy: A relaxing stroll in the woods

To help explain a hike's difficulty score, you'll also find **roundtrip** mileage (unless otherwise noted as one-way), total **elevation gain**, and the hike's **high point**. While we have consulted maps and measured the hikes using GPS, a trip's distance can vary depending on how you customize the route. The elevation gain measures the *cumulative* gain and loss you'll encounter on a trip, accounting for all significant changes in elevation along the way. As for the trip's high point, it's worth noting that not all high points are at the end of the trail—a route may run over a high ridge before dropping to a lake basin, for instance.

The recommended **season** is a tool to help you choose a hike. Many trails can be enjoyed from the time they lose their winter snowpack right up until they're buried in fresh snow the following fall. But snowpacks vary from year to year, so a trail that's open in May one year may be snow-covered until July the next. The hiking season for each trail is an estimate. Contact land managers for current conditions before you go.

Hikes in this guidebook typically reference Green Trails **maps**, which are based on the standard 7.5-minute USGS topographical maps. However, we also list maps available from local groups, agencies, or national forests. Green Trails maps are available at most outdoor retailers in the state, as well as at many US Forest Service visitors centers. Under **contact** each hike lists the area's governing agency, which has information about localized maps as well as current access and trail conditions. Find agencies' phone numbers and websites in Appendix I under Contact Information. **Notes** for each trip comprise permits required, road conditions, possible hazards, and seasonal closures. Trailhead **GPS** coordinates are provided to help get you to the trail—and back to your car should you wander off-trail.

Finally, **icons** at the start of each hike give a quick overview of what each trail has to offer:

 Kid-friendly

 Dog-friendly

 Exceptional wildflowers in season

 Exceptional waterfalls

 Exceptional old-growth forest

 Bird-watching

 Historical relevance

 Interpretive trail

 Endangered trail (threatened with loss or closure)

 Saved trail (rescued from permanent loss)

Getting There includes thorough driving directions from the nearest large town or geographic feature that will get you to the trailhead. **On the Trail** route descriptions tell you what might be found on the hike, including geographic features, scenic potential, flora and fauna, and more. Options for **Extending Your Trip** round out many hikes.

Most of the hikes in this book are illustrated with reference maps: the exceptions are a handful of very short trails, often interpretive trails, for which a map would be superfluous. No maps are included for hikes 1, 13, 15, 16, 17, 18, 30, 37, 58, and 61. In addition, some hikes are close enough geographically that they share maps. You'll find shared maps for hikes 4 and 5; 19–21; 22–26; 27 and 28; 32 and 33; 38 and 39; 48 and 49; 50–52; 53 and 54; 55 and 56; 59 and 60; 62–64; 65 and 66; 68 and 69; 70 and 71; 73 and 75; and 88 and 89.

PERMITS, REGULATIONS, AND FEES

Hikers have a responsibility to know, understand, and abide by regulations governing the areas they explore. As our public lands have become increasingly popular and as both state and federal funding have continued to decline, regulations and permits have become components in managing and maintaining our natural heritage. The US Forest Service, National Park Service, Washington State Parks, and other land managers have implemented a sometimes complex set of land use rules and regulations.

Generally, most developed trailheads in Washington's national forests (including those in the Mount St. Helens National Volcanic Monument) fall under the Region 6 Forest Pass Program. To park legally at these designated national forest trailheads, you must display a Northwest Forest Pass decal in your windshield. These sell for $5 per day or $30 for an annual pass good throughout Region 6 (www.recreation.gov).

Within the Monument, two sites along State Route 504, the Coldwater Lake Recreation Area and the Johnston Ridge Observatory, require a Monument Pass. These passes are $8 per person per day (children under fifteen are free) and can be purchased on site. Interagency (see below), Senior and Access Passes (Golden Age/ Access Passes), and an annual Northwest Forest Pass are also accepted at these sites, making purchasing a Monument Pass unnecessary. Note that for the Johnston Ridge Observatory, a Northwest Forest Pass is good for only one person.

Hikers who frequent national parks and forests should consider buying the America the Beautiful Annual Pass (interagency pass; http://store.usgs.gov/pass) for $80. This pass grants the driver and three other adults in a vehicle access to all federal recreation sites that charge a day-use fee (children under sixteen are admitted free). These include national parks, national forests, national wildlife refuges, and Bureau of Land Management areas throughout the country.

State lands: Washington State Parks and other state lands adopted the Discover Pass (www.discoverpass.wa.gov) for vehicle access in 2011. This is a political solution to keep the underfunded state parks system alive. A Discover Pass costs $10 per vehicle per day or $30 for up to two vehicles annually. Purchase the pass online or at many retail outlets or, better yet, from a state park office to avoid the $5 handling fee.

Local areas: PacifiCorp parks in the Lewis River Recreation Area (e.g., Hike 66, Cougar—Beaver Bay) charge a day-use fee of $3 Friday through Sunday and on holidays between Memorial Day weekend and September 15.

A climber properly displays her climbing permit.

Backcountry Camping

Overnight camping within the Mount Margaret Backcountry within the Mount St. Helens National Volcanic Monument requires reservations and permits made with the US Forest Service online (www.recreation.gov) or in person at Monument headquarters.

Climbing Permits

Climbing permits for Mount St. Helens must be purchased for any travel above 4800 feet on the mountain. Permit fees and daily quotas vary throughout the year. For climbs between April 1 and October 31, permits ($22 as of 2015) must be purchased online

WHOSE LAND IS THIS?

Almost all of the hikes in this book are on public land. That is, they belong to you and the rest of the citizenry. What's confusing, however, is who exactly is in charge of this public trust. More than half a dozen different governing agencies manage lands described in this guide.

Most of the hikes are on land administered by the **US Forest Service**. A division of the Department of Agriculture, the Forest Service strives to "sustain the health, diversity, and productivity of the Nation's forests and grasslands to meet the needs of present and future generations." The agency purports to do this under the notion of "multiple-use." However, supplying timber products, providing grazing allotments, managing wildlife habitat, and developing motorized and nonmotorized recreation options have a tendency to conflict with each other. Some of these uses may not exactly sustain the health of the forest either.

The Forest Service also administers the 110,000-acre Mount St. Helens National Volcanic Monument, created in 1982 as a "living laboratory" for research into ongoing volcanism, the natural process of recovery from the eruption, and visitor education and recreation. As such, the Monument has several areas in which public access is restricted.

State and county park lands are managed primarily for recreation and preservation.

Washington State Department of Natural Resources lands are managed primarily for timber harvest, with pockets of natural-area preserves.

State wildlife areas, overseen by the Department of Fish and Wildlife, are managed primarily for protecting wildlife and habitat while providing access to wildlife-related recreation, including hunting and fishing.

Be aware of the agency that manages the land you'll be hiking on, for each agency has its own rules and fees. And remember, we have a say in how our public lands are managed. Agencies have periodic planning periods during which public participation carries clout.

(http://mshinstitute.org/index.php/climbing) and picked up in person at the Lone Fir Resort in Cougar. Between November 1 and March 31, climbers must self-register at either the Climber's Bivouac or Marble Mountain Sno-Park climber registers. There is no fee for the permit. Between April 1 and May 14, permits are unlimited. From May 15 to October 31, permits are restricted to one hundred a day and sell out fast, especially on weekends. For peak summer season climbs, it's wise to plan ahead.

All required permits and passes are clearly listed for each hike.

WEATHER

Mountain weather in general is famously unpredictable; but because Mount St. Helens is in southwest Washington, you can always count on a chance of precipitation, whether frozen or liquid. Mount St. Helens has a maritime climate, with Pacific Ocean currents creating a more temperate climate with a copious amount of rainfall, which is heaviest from November to April. Summers are generally mild with extended periods of no or low rainfall. July through early October is generally a delightful time to hike the region.

Low elevations in the valleys surrounding Mount St. Helens see little snow. Higher up, snow blankets the high country primarily from November through May but can occur any time of year. Be prepared. Even though they sit at lower elevations relative to many of their Cascades cousins, the forested ridges—particularly in the Dark Divide Roadless Area—tend to preserve snowpacks; hikers shouldn't be surprised to encounter snowfields as low as 5000 feet well into July.

Plan your hike according to your weather preference. But no matter where you hike in the region, always pack raingear. Being caught in a sudden rain- and windstorm with inadequate clothing can lead to hypothermia (loss of body temperature), which is deadly if not immediately treated.

Other weather-induced hazards you should be aware of result from past episodes of rain and snow. River and creek crossings can be extremely dangerous to traverse after periods of heavy rain or snowmelt. Always use caution and sound judgment when fording.

Snowfields left over from the previous winter's snowpack can be hazardous, especially for hikers who head into steep high-country slopes early in the hiking season. Depending on the severity of the past winter and the weather conditions of the spring and early summer, some trails may not melt out until well into summer. In addition to treacherous footing and route-finding difficulties, lingering snowfields can be prone to avalanches or slides. Use caution when crossing them and review techniques for self-arrest before heading out.

Strong winds can happen anywhere in the region, particularly at higher elevations and in combination with heavy rainfall. Avoid hiking during high winds and windy periods, which carry with them the hazards of falling trees and branches.

Generalities aside, short-term forecasts are the key to planning the safest and most enjoyable trip. A high-pressure system could offer a week of premier weather in May, while a low-pressure system could present a week of wetness in June. We have experienced snow in the high country in August two days after the temperatures soared into the 90s.

Plan your hike according to your weather preference. But no matter where you hike in the region, this should be standard procedure:

Check the National Weather Service forecast for the region before you go, and plan accordingly.

Pack raingear. Most hiking fatalities related to exposure and hypothermia occur during the milder months when unsuspecting hikers get caught in a sudden change of temperature accompanied by winds. Always carry extra clothing layers, including rain and wind protection.

ROAD AND TRAIL CONDITIONS

Trails generally change little year to year. But change can occur, sometimes very quickly. A heavy storm can cause a river to jump its channel, washing out sections of a trail or access road in moments. Windstorms can blow down trees across trails by the hundreds, making paths unhikable. And snow can bury trails well into the summer. Avalanches, landslides, and forest fires can damage or obliterate trails. Lack of agency funding for trail repair and maintenance also leads to trail neglect and degradation.

With this in mind, each hike included in this book lists which land manager to contact, and includes full contact information in Appendix I, so you can phone them prior to your trip and ensure that your chosen road and trail are open and safe to travel.

On the other hand, some trails are created, improved, or rerouted over the course of time. Groups such as the Washington Trails Association, Mount St. Helens Institute, Columbia Land Trust, and friends groups for state parks and federal wildlife refuges have been sources of countless hours of volunteer labor, helping local, state, and federal crews build and maintain trails in this book. These groups and more are listed at the end of the book to help you connect with them—and perhaps add some muscle power or other expertise to the cause.

Management decisions can have greater impacts even than floods and fires on our trails, including (but by no means limited to) ever-shrinking trail funding, inappropriate trail uses, and conflicting land management policies and practices. Decades ago the biggest threat to public trails was the overharvesting of timber and the wanton building of roads to access it. Ironically, as timber harvesting has all but ceased on much of our national forest land in Washington, one of the biggest threats to our trails now is access. Many roads once used for hauling timber (and by hikers to get to trailheads) are no longer being maintained. Many of these roads are slumping, growing over, and becoming downright dangerous to drive. Some have washed out completely, severing access to trails. While decommissioning of roads that go "nowhere" is economically and environmentally prudent, so is maintaining and keeping open the main trunk roads that see a lot of use for trail access. Once a road has been closed for several years, the trails radiating from it often receive no maintenance and become unhikable.

On the other end of the threat scale to many of our trails is increased motorized use. The speed and noise of motors don't mix well with horseback riders, hikers, and quiet muscle-powered modes of backcountry travel. Motorcycles and all-terrain vehicles have a heavy impact on trails. Even when users obey rules and regulations—and most do—wheels tear up tread far more than boots, and this is especially true in the fragile soils and lush meadows of the high country. The noise too that many of the machines emit is simply incompatible with Leave No Trace backcountry principles. Although the majority of motorcyclists with whom we have shared trails are decent people, motorcycles simply preclude a wilderness experience. And while we support the rights of motorized recreation users to have access to public lands, many of the trails that currently allow motorcycles should never have been opened to them.

Several of the trails in this book, particularly in the Lewis River and Dark Divide, are open to motorized vehicles. Some trails, such as Kraus Ridge (Hike 14), only allow motorcycles part of the year, to protect wildlife habitat; other trails, such as Craggy Peak (Hike 75), allow motorcycles year-round but receive little use. The value of these routes, and the importance of maintaining a hiker presence on them, overrides the possible disruption.

This guide includes several trails that are in danger of becoming unhikable because of threats from motorized use, decreased access, or other issues. These Endangered Trails are marked with a special icon in this book. Washington State has had some great trail successes in recent years, thanks in large part to a massive volunteer movement spearheaded by statewide and local organizations.

Trails frequently wash out around Mount St. Helens due to unstable conditions.

These Saved Trails are marked, too, to help show that individual efforts make a difference. As you enjoy these Saved Trails, stop to consider the contributions made by fellow hikers that helped protect trail resources. And consider getting involved.

WILDERNESS ETHICS

Ensuring the long-term survival of our trails and the wildlands they cross requires a group effort. To avoid fouling our own nest, hikers have nourished a "wilderness ethic" to leave the land as good as or better than we found it.

Instead of merely complying with no-litter rules, bring a bag and carve out time to pick up after others. Avoid creating unauthorized trails. Rest on rock and camp on bare ground when possible to avoid tramping down or killing vegetation in fragile dryland or alpine areas. Don't pollute streams or lakes with soaps or chemicals. As the adage says: take only pictures, leave only footprints.

Wilderness ethics, most of which apply when visiting all public open-space lands, rise from attitude and awareness rather than rules and regulations. The following are the accepted principles of Leave No Trace:

Plan ahead: Know the regulations of the area you plan to visit. Call ahead for current conditions. Check the weather forecast. Bring proper gear and prepare for emergencies. Consider the abilities of your group, and assure that everyone understands wilderness ethics. Protect food from bears and other critters to avoid turning wild animals into a nuisance—or dangerous beggars.

Travel and camp on durable surfaces: Stay on the trail. Avoid tramping parallel trails to talk with a companion or widening trails to avoid hiking in mud. Don't cut switchbacks. Choose rocky off-trail routes when possible

Ground squirrels help redistribute seeds and promote plant regeneration.

and avoid meadows. Picnic and camp on hard, dry surfaces such as rock, sand, gravel, or conifer-needle duff rather than on vegetation or meadows. Take special care to avoid tramping or camping within 100 feet of backcountry streams or lake shorelines.

Dispose of waste properly: Pack out everything you pack in. Human food and trash is unhealthy for animals and leads to harmful habituation by animals to human presence and food. Bury human waste at least 100 feet from water sources, trails, or campsites. Use toilet paper sparingly and pack it out. A plastic bag confines odors effectively and double bagging prevents any accidental contamination.

Leave what you find: Wildflowers, fossils, and other natural objects of beauty or interest should be left for others to discover and enjoy.

Minimize campfire impacts: Where fires are permitted, use existing fire rings if possible. Never cut live trees or branches for firewood. Most fires are unnecessary, but if you must build one, be sure it's dead out when you leave. A small, thoughtfully built fire can be completely extinguished and the ashes removed or buried to leave no trace.

Respect wildlife: Never feed wild animals or leave food available to them. This is for your own good and the protection of those who follow. Observe from a distance, for your safety as well as to prevent the animal from unnecessary exertion or danger. Keep pets under control so they don't disturb wildlife.

Be considerate of other visitors: Read on to find out how.

TRAIL ETIQUETTE

While wilderness ethics hone our respect for the land, trail etiquette steers us into balance with others we might see along the way. Many of the trails in this book are open to an array of trail users. Some trails are hiker-only, but others allow people on horseback, mountain bike, or motorcycle. Common sense and courtesy will smooth out the possible bumps in any encounter. Beyond that, here are a few guidelines:

- **Right-of-way:** When meeting other hikers, the uphill group has the right-of-way. There are two general reasons for this. First, on steep ascents, hikers heading up may be watching the trail and might not notice the approach of descending hikers until they are face-to-face. More importantly, it's easier for descending hikers to break their stride and step off the trail than it is for those who have gotten into a good climbing rhythm. But by all means, if you're the uphill trekker and you wish to grant passage to oncoming hikers, go right ahead with this act of trail kindness.
- **Moving off-trail:** When meeting other user groups (like bicyclists and horseback riders), the hiker should yield. This is because hikers are more mobile and flexible than other users, making it easier for them to step off the trail.
- **Encountering horses:** When meeting horseback riders, the hiker should step off the downhill side of the trail unless the terrain makes this difficult or dangerous. All hikers in a group should move to the same side of the trail. Remain visible and talk in a normal voice to the riders. This calms the horses. If hiking with a dog, keep your buddy very close and under control.
- **Hiking with dogs:** One of the most contentious issues in hiking circles is whether dogs should be allowed on trails. Although pets are prohibited within the restricted area of the Monument, many of the areas in this book allow dogs. Hikers who take dogs on the trails should have their dog on a leash or under strict voice command at all times. Some areas require dogs to be on-leash, such as designated pet areas within the Monument, state and local parks, and PacifiCorp recreation areas. Too many dog owners flagrantly disregard this regulation, setting themselves up for tickets, hostile words from fellow hikers, and the possibility of losing the right to bring Fido out on that trail in the future. Some people are uncomfortable with loose dogs that rush toward them—and they may have had a bad experience to justify that. Respect their right to a dog-free space. On the other hand, a well-behaved, leashed dog can help warm up these hikers to canine companions.
- **Never roll rocks off trails or cliffs:** You risk injuring someone or something below.

WATER

As a general rule, treat all backcountry water sources to avoid *Giardia*, waterborne parasites, and other aquatic nasties. Assume that all water is contaminated. Treating water can be as simple as boiling it, using an ultraviolet light purifier, chemically purifying it with iodine tablets, or pumping it through a water filter and purifier. Note: Pump units labeled as filters generally remove everything but viruses, which are too small to be filtered out. Pumps labeled as purifiers use a chemical element—usually iodine—to render viruses inactive after filtering all the other bugs out.

FISHING

Some hikers consider a fishing rod essential gear in their day packs. However, fishing is a highly regulated sport, with seasons, gear restrictions, and catch limits that can vary by fish species as well as by stream or lake. Anglers age fifteen and older must have a Washington State fishing license. Regulations and requirements are spelled out in the *Sport Fishing Rules* pamphlet available at the Washington Department of Fish and Wildlife website (www.wdfw.wa.gov).

HIKING AMONG HUNTERS

Many public lands are opened to hunting. The season dates vary, but generally big-game hunting begins in early August and ends in December. While hiking in areas frequented by hunters, it's best to make yourself visible by donning an orange cap and vest. If hiking with a dog, your buddy should wear an orange vest too. The majority of hunters are responsible, decent folks (and conservationists who provide significant support for public lands), and you should have little concern when encountering them in the backcountry. Still, if being around outdoors-people schlepping rifles is unnerving to you, stick to hiking where hunting is prohibited—within the scope of this book that means sections of the Monument, state and local parks, and county conservation areas.

Grouse blend in well in the new vegetative cover.

WILDLIFE
The Bear Essentials

Many of the regions in this book, in particular the Dark Divide Roadless Area, harbor a healthy population of black bears, and your chances of eventually seeing one are pretty good. Most hikers consider themselves lucky to catch a glimpse of a bear's bottom as it reacts normally to human contact—by running away. But occasionally a bruin may want to get a look at you. In very rare cases, a bear may act aggressively. To avoid an un-bearable encounter, heed the following advice compiled from bear experts:

- **Respect a bear's need for space.** If you see a bear in the distance, make a wide detour around it. If that's not possible, leave the area.
- **Avoid direct eye contact** if you encounter a bear at close range, and, most important, **do not run**.
- **Talk in a low, calm manner** to the bear to help identify yourself as a human.
- **Wave your arms slowly** above your head to make yourself look taller.
- **Slowly move upwind** of the bear if you can do so without crowding the bear. The bear's strongest sense is its sense of smell, and if it can sniff you and identify you as human, it may retreat.
- **Know how to interpret bear actions.** A nervous bear will often rumble in its chest, clack its teeth, and "pop" its jaw. It may paw the ground and swing its head violently side to side. If the bear does this, watch it closely (without staring directly at it). Continue to speak low and calmly.
- **Try to scare it away by clapping your hands or yelling** if you cannot safely move away from the bear, and the animal does not flee.

- **A bear may bluff-charge**—run at you but stop well before reaching you—to try and intimidate you. Resist the urge to run, as that would turn the bluff into a real charge and you will *not* be able to outrun the bear.
- **In the case of a bear attack**, a human without the benefit of bear spray should react differently depending on whether the bear is being predatory or defensive. **In the case of a predatory confrontation** (more typical of the rare black bear that's stalking you), fight back aggressively. **In the case of a defensive confrontation** (more typical of grizzly encounters, especially sows with cubs or food caches), drop to the ground and play dead if contact is about to be made. Lie on your stomach, clasp hands behind your neck, and use your elbows and toes to avoid being rolled over. If the bear succeeds in rolling you over, keep rolling until you're on your stomach. Remain still and try not to struggle or scream. A defensive bear will stop attacking once it feels it has stopped the threat. Do not move until you're sure the bear has left the area.

Where Cougars Roam

Cougars, also called mountain lions, are among the most secretive of the apex predators lurking in the wilds of western Washington. Very few hikers ever see cougars in the wild. But Washington supports a healthy population of *Felix concolor*; they're linked to virtually any habitat where deer are found in good numbers, which encompasses the entire coverage area of this book. While cougar encounters are extremely rare in the region, they do occur. To make sure the encounter is a positive one (at least for you), you need to understand a bit about these wildcats.

The view from Norway Pass is one of the most photographed.

Cougars are curious critters (after all, they're cats). They will follow hikers simply to see what kind of beasts we are, but they rarely (almost never) attack adult humans. If you do encounter one, remember that cougars rely on prey that can't, or won't, fight back. So, as soon as you see the cat, heed the following recommendations of the Washington Department of Fish and Wildlife.

While recreating in cougar habitat:

- **Hike in small groups** and make enough noise to avoid surprising a cougar.
- **Keep your camp clean** and store food and garbage in double plastic bags in vehicles.
- **Keep small children close** to the group, preferably in plain sight just ahead of you.
- **Don't approach carcasses,** especially deer or elk; they could have been cougar prey left for a later meal.

If you encounter a cougar:

- **Stop, don't run.** Running triggers a cougar's instinct to chase. Make sure to pick up and hold small children.
- **Don't approach the animal**, especially if it's near a kill or with kittens.
- **Try to appear larger than the cougar.** Never take your eyes off the animal or

turn your back. Don't crouch down or try to hide.
- **Shout, wave your arms, and throw rocks** if the animal displays aggressive behavior. The idea is to convince the cougar that you are not prey, but a potential danger.

DAY HIKING GEAR

Although gear is beyond the scope of this book (which is about where to hike, not how to hike), it's worth noting a few points. No hiker should venture up a trail without being properly equipped. Starting with the feet, a good pair of boots—and good socks—can make all the difference between a wonderful hike and a blistering affair. Keep your feet happy and you'll be happy.

For clothing, wear whatever is most comfortable unless it is cotton. Cotton is a wonderful fabric, but not the best for hiking. When it gets wet, it stays wet and lacks insulation value. In fact, wet cotton sucks away body heat, leaving you susceptible to hypothermia. Far better are synthetics or wool.

While every hiker's gear list will vary, a few items should be universal in every day pack.

Hikers who venture deep into the woods should be prepared to spend the night out, with emergency food and shelter. Mountain storms or whiteouts can whip up in a hurry, catching fair-weather hikers by surprise. And there's always the chance of an illness or injury that could delay or prevent you from returning to the trailhead. Be prepared with the Ten Essentials.

THE TEN ESSENTIALS

1. **Navigation (map and compass):** Carry a topographic map of the area you plan to visit and knowledge of how to read it. Take a compass too, and know how to use it.

2. **Sun protection (sunglasses and sunscreen):** Even on gray days, carry sunscreen and sunglasses. The burning rays of the sun penetrate the clouds. At higher elevations your exposure to UV rays is much more intense than at sea level. Burning is significantly magnified by the reflectiveness of snow and water.

3. **Insulation (extra clothing):** It may be 70 degrees Fahrenheit at the trailhead, but at the summit it can be 45 and windy. Even a summer thunderstorm can cool the air temperature by 40 degrees in minutes. Snow is possible any time at high elevations. Carry raingear, wind protection, and extra layers.

4. **Illumination (flashlight/headlamp):** If caught after dark, you'll need a headlamp or flashlight to follow the trail. If forced to spend the night, you'll need it to set up emergency camp and gather wood. Carry extra batteries too.

5. **First-aid supplies:** At the very least, your kit should include bandages, moleskin, gauze, scissors, tape, tweezers, pain relievers, antiseptics, and perhaps a small first-aid manual. Consider first-aid training.

6. **Fire (firestarter and matches):** If you're forced to spend the night, an emergency campfire will provide warmth and light. Be sure you keep matches dry. Resealable plastic bags do the trick, but a hard plastic container is better. Firestarter can be purchased commercially. One homemade version is cotton balls swabbed in petroleum jelly and stored in a container. Tip: the Vaseline-coated cotton ball will glow with a better, longer-lasting fire-starting flame if you pull tufts of greased fibers out in every direction before lighting. A candle can come in handy too.

7. **Repair kit and tools (including a knife):** A knife is helpful; a compact multitool is better, adding lightweight pliers and scissors to your options. A basic repair kit should include nylon cord, a small roll of duct tape, and a small tube of superglue. A few safety pins can work wonders too.

8. **Nutrition (extra food):** Always pack more food than what you need for your hike. Energy bars are easy options for a pick-me-up or emergency rations.

9. **Hydration (extra water):** Carry two full water bottles, unless you're hiking entirely along a water source. You'll need to carry iodine tablets or a purifying device on longer or remote hikes.

10. **Emergency shelter:** This can be as simple as a large garbage bag, or something more useful and efficient, like a reflective space blanket. A poncho can double as an emergency tarp.

Tiger lily

BEFORE YOU GO

Always tell somebody reliable—best to write it down—where you're going, what you're doing, and when you plan to be home. Also include which land manager, agency, or emergency operator to contact should you not return in a reasonable time.

TRAILHEAD CONCERNS

Sadly, the topic of trailhead and trail crime must be addressed. As urban areas continuously encroach upon our green spaces, societal ills follow along. But by and large our hiking trails are safe places—far safer than most city streets—and violent crimes are extremely rare. Common sense and vigilance, however, are still the rule. This is true for all hikers, but particularly so for solo hikers. Be aware of your surroundings at all times. Leave your itinerary with someone back home. If something doesn't feel right,

it probably isn't. Take action by leaving the place or situation immediately.

If you arrive at a trailhead and someone looks suspicious, don't discount your intuition. Take notes on the person and his or her vehicle. Record the license plate and report the behavior to the authorities. Do not confront the person. Leave and go to another trail. But remember, most hikers are friendly, decent people. Some may be a little introverted, but that's no cause for worry.

By far your biggest concern should be trailhead theft. While most car break-ins are crimes of opportunity, organized gangs intent on stealing IDs have also been known to target parked cars at trailheads. While many trailheads are rarely targeted, there's no sure way of preventing this from happening to you other than being dropped off at the trailhead or taking the bus (rarely an option). But you can make your car less of a target by not leaving anything of value in it. Take your wallet, cell phone, and listening devices with you—or better yet, don't bring them along in the first place. Don't leave anything in your car that may appear valuable. A duffle bag on the back seat may contain dirty T-shirts, but a thief may think there's a laptop in it. Save yourself the hassle of returning to a busted window by not giving criminals a reason to clout your car. And contact your government officials and demand that law enforcement be a priority in our national forests. We taxpayers have a right to recreate safely on our public lands.

ENJOY THE TRAILS

Most importantly, be safe and enjoy the thrill of discovery and exercise on the trails in this book. They exist for our enjoyment and for the enjoyment of future generations of hikers.

TRAIL GIANTS

I grew up in rural New Hampshire and was introduced to hiking and respect for our wildlands at a young age. I grew to admire the men and women responsible for saving and protecting trails and wilderness areas as I became more aware of the often-tumultuous history behind the preservation efforts.

After moving to Washington in 1989, I immediately gained a respect for Harvey Manning and Ira Spring. Their pioneering *100 Hikes* guidebooks introduced many of us to a love of the Washington backcountry. I joined the Mountaineers Club, the Washington Trails Association, Columbia Land Trust, and other local trail and conservation organizations so that I could help to protect these places and carry on this legacy to future generations.

I believe 100 percent in what Ira Spring termed "green bonding." We must, said Ira, "Get people onto trails. They need to bond with the wilderness." That green bonding is essential to building public support for trails and trail funding, for, when hikers get complacent, trails suffer.

And while Harvey Manning's legendary diatribes lambasting public officials' short-sighted land practices can often be off-putting, I tacitly agreed with him many times. And while Harvey was a bit combative, a tad too polarizing at times, sometimes you just have to raise a little hell to get results.

As you hike the trails described here, consider that many of them would have long ago ceased to exist without the phenomenal efforts of people like Ira Spring, Harvey Manning, and Louise Marshall, who wrote the first Northwest hiking book, *100 Hikes in Western Washington*, a forerunner for many of the Mountaineers Books series still in print. Thanks to the scores of unnamed hikers who joined them in protecting wilderness, funding trails, and stewarding the environment.

Consider writing a letter to your Congressional or state representative, asking for better trail and public lands funding. If you're not already a member, consider joining an organization devoted to wilderness, backcountry trails, or other wild country issues. Organizations like the Washington Trails Association, Columbia Land Trust, The Mountaineers, Mazamas, and countless others help leverage individual contributions and efforts to help ensure the future of our trails and the wonderful wilderness legacy we've inherited. (For contacts, see Appendix II, Conservation and Trail Organizations.) Buy a specialty license plate for Washington's state parks or the Washington National Park Fund and let everybody on the way to the trailhead see what you value and support.

—*Craig Romano*

If you enjoy these trails, consider stepping up to be one of their advocates. Your involvement can be as simple as picking up trash, signing up for a volunteer work party, joining a trail advocacy group, educating fellow citizens, or writing a letter to Congress or your state representatives. Introduce children to our trails. We need to continue a legacy of good trail stewardship. All of these seemingly small acts can make a big

Moonrise over Mount Adams from Council Bluff

difference. At the end of this book is a list of organizations working on behalf of trails and wildlands in the vicinity of Mount St. Helens. Several of them organize great group hikes into the areas covered by this book and beyond. Check them out.

Happy hiking!

GETTING AROUND THE MOUNTAIN

Mount St. Helens can be divided into four distinct travel regions, Mount St. Helens West, South, East, and North. This book also covers river valleys and roadless areas along the volcano's periphery.

Despite the mountain's proximity to two major metropolitan areas, services can sometimes be scarce; be sure to top off your gas tank whenever you have the opportunity.

Mount St. Helens West

Spirit Lake Memorial Highway (State Route 504) connects Interstate 5 (at Castle Rock, exit 49) to the northwest side of Mount St. Helens via the Toutle Valley.

Open year-round, **Mount St. Helens Visitor Center at Silver Lake** (www.parks.wa.gov/245/Mount-St-Helens-Visitor-Center) is six miles from the interstate on SR 504 and features several interactive exhibits, including a large step-in model of the volcano. The lodge-like **Hoffstadt Bluffs Visitor Center** (mile 27) boasts the second-largest post-and-beam construction on the West Coast. In addition to the exhibits, visitors can wander a paved path through a memorial grove commemorating the fifty-seven people killed during the eruption. The **Forest Learning Center** (mile 33)—managed by Weyerhaeuser, Washington Department of Transportation, and Rocky Mountain Elk Foundation, and open mid-May through October free of charge—explores the recovery of the economically and ecologically valuable forests surrounding Mount St. Helens. Previously managed as a visitor center, the **Science and Learning Center at Coldwater** (mile 44) re-opened in 2012 with its primary aim as a learning center for schools and science groups. However, when the center is open, on Saturdays and Sundays, volcano souvenirs and Volcano Volunteers are available, courtesy of Discover Your Northwest.

Named for David Johnston, the USGS volcanologist who died in the May 18 eruption (he famously radioed "Vancouver! Vancouver! This is it!" at the moment of the lateral blast) **Johnston Ridge Observatory**, 52 miles east of Castle Rock at the end of SR 504, sits in the heart of the blast zone. Open mid-May through October, the observatory features daily and hourly Forest Service Ranger programs discussing the 1980 eruption and the recovery of the landscape since then.

There are no campgrounds within Mount St. Helens National Volcanic Monument. Campers visiting Spirit Lake Memorial Highway should consider a base at the 55-site **Seaquest State Park** near the Mount St. Helens Visitor Center at Silver Lake. **Eco Park Resort**, in Toutle, also offers tent sites in addition to rustic log cabins and yurts.

Mount St. Helens South

The south side of the volcano is accessed by State Route 503, which leaves I-5 at Woodland (exit 21, and, alternatively, from I-205 in Vancouver at exit 30) to parallel the Lewis River. Most services can be found in Cougar,

The old Clearwater Visitors Center was converted into the Mount St. Helens Science and Learning Center at Coldwater.

Johnston Ridge Observatory at the end of the Spirit Lake Highway

29 miles from I-5; climbers must pick up their permits at the **Lone Fir Resort** in town. SR 503 becomes Forest Road 90, and nearly 20 miles from Cougar, just before FR 90's junction with FR 25, visitors can pick up information and souvenirs from the Volcano Volunteers at the **Pine Creek Information Center**.

Unlike the other sides of the mountain, which have few campgrounds, the south side of Mount St. Helens offers several nice campgrounds, some publicly managed and some managed by Pacifi-Corp as part of its licensing arrangement for its Lewis River dams. Of particular note are **Cresap Bay**, on Lake Merwin; **Cougar** and **Beaver Bay**, just east of Cougar on FR 90 on the banks of Yale Reservoir; and **Swift Forest Camp**, on the shores of Swift Reservoir. Lone Fir Resort in Cougar also has space for tents and campers, in addition to motel rooms.

Mount St. Helens East and North

From the gateway community of Randle on US Highway 12 (I-5 exit 68), Forest Roads 25 and 26 access Windy Ridge (FR 99) and popular viewpoints and trails on the northeast side of Mount St. Helens. Note that winter snows close FR 25 and FR 99 from November to late May.

The newly re-opened **Cascade Peaks** facility, managed by the Mount St. Helens Institute, serves light snacks and provides visitor information. At the end of FR 99,

visitors to **Windy Ridge Interpretive Site** can experience ranger-led stories of the devastation of the 1980 eruption and subsequent renewal.

Campers will find fine accommodations south of Randle at the large 99-site **Iron Creek Campground;** at the confluence of Iron Creek and the Cispus River on FR 25; and at **Tower Rock Campground**, a quarter mile from the Cispus River on FR 2306. West of Randle, in the Cowlitz River valley, Tacoma Power runs several nice campgrounds, including the 163-site **Taidnapam Park** on Riffe Lake, near Morton; the 152-site **Mossyrock Park,** near Riffe Lake; and the 55-site **Mayfield Lake Park**, on Mayfield Lake near Mossyrock. The **Ike Kinswa State Park** on Mayfield Lake has 101 sites and 5 cabins and is open year-round.

Periphery

US Highway 12 connects Interstate 5 to the Cowlitz, Chehalis, and Cispus river valleys on the north and west sides of the mountain. State Route 503 connects I-5 to the Lewis River and Dark Divide and Siouxon Roadless Areas on the south and east.

Opposite: Yellow flag irises flank Silver Lake.

cowlitz river valley

Flowing from Mount Rainier to its confluence with the Columbia River, the Cowlitz River carved a valley that provided an important thoroughfare for early Native Americans and for the Europeans who followed in their footsteps. The millennia-old travel route connecting the Columbia River to Puget Sound eventually became Interstate 5, but today Cowlitz river valley offers several community paths for a more leisurely pace of travel.

① Kalama Marine Park

RATING/ DIFFICULTY	ROUNDTRIP	ELEV GAIN/ HIGH POINT	SEASON
*/1	1.8 miles	70 feet/ 60 feet	Year-round

Maps: USGS Kalama, Deer Island; Cowlitz on the Move online; **Contact:** Port of Kalama; **Notes:** Wheelchair accessible. Trail open to bicycles. Fishing options; **GPS:** N 46 00.452 W 122 50.932

Stroll on, Columbia, on this short path along Kalama's waterfront. Just blocks from Kalama's quiet downtown, this path makes for a great lunchtime leg-stretch or provides an opportunity to watch steelhead anglers at work on the shore.

GETTING THERE
From I-5, take exit 30 (Kalama). (If approaching from I-5 south, turn right on Oak Street.) Turn left under the overpass and bear right onto the Frontage Road, continuing for 0.8 mile. Turn left onto Oak Street. At 0.1 mile, bear right onto Hendrickson Drive and continue 1 mile to the Port of Kalama boardwalk entrance and boardwalk on the right (elev. 60 ft).

Sandy spelling practice on the Kalama waterfront

ON THE TRAIL
Beginning at the Port of Kalama boardwalk, pass the 222-slip Port of Kalama marina. Named for John Kalama, a Hawaiian-born Hudson's Bay Company fur trapper who settled at the mouth of the river that eventually took his name, Kalama briefly boasted one of the largest communities in the Washington and Oregon territories owing to its enviable location on the Columbia—deep, ice-free, and close to Portland. Briefly the original Pacific terminus for the transcontinental Northern Pacific rail line, Kalama still serves as a busy river-and-rail port.

The path turns to asphalt at 0.1 mile and parallels Louis Rasmussen Park. Flanked by beach volleyball players on the portside and spring steelhead anglers to the starboard, wander past three impressive totem poles, including one of the largest single-log specimens in the world. The path ends at a river access, should you care to cast a fishing line yourself.

2 Lake Sacajawea

RATING/ DIFFICULTY	LOOP	ELEV GAIN/ HIGH POINT	SEASON
**/2	3.7 miles	130 feet/ 97 feet	Year-round

Maps: USGS Kelso, Cowlitz on the Move online; **Contact:** City of Longview Parks Department; **Notes:** Wheelchair accessible. Open to bicycles. Fishing options; **GPS:** N 46 08.456 W 122 57.067

The crescent-shaped crown jewel of Longview, "The Lake" attracts dog walkers, joggers, anglers, and amblers to its historic shores.

GETTING THERE

From I-5 North, take exit 30, heading west on SR 432. At 2.4 miles, continue straight on Tennant Way. At 1 mile, turn right on 15th Ave. At 0.1 mile, turn left on Douglas St. Merge onto E. Kessler Blvd and continue 1 mile to the parking area on the left. From I-5 south, take exit 40 toward Longview and State Route 4. Turn right on North Kelso Avenue, which becomes North Pacific Avenue, and continue 0.8 mile to Cowlitz Way. Turn right and continue 0.6 mile to SR 4 (Ocean Beach Highway). Drive 1.1 miles to 24th Avenue. Turn left and then immediately bear right onto West Kessler Boulevard. Continue 0.3 mile, past Louisiana Street, to a parking area on the right (elev. 70 ft).

ON THE TRAIL

Although the city center of Longview—at its founding the largest privately funded planned city in the United States—lies nearby, Lake Sacajawea is the de facto

Bridge to the Japanese Garden at Lake Sacajawea

LONGVIEW, PLANNED CITY

The fertile land at the confluence of the Cowlitz and Columbia rivers has a history of nurturing bold civic planning. In the early 1850s, at a settlement named Monticello, close to what is now the Longview city center, nearly two thousand citizens gathered at the Monticello Convention to make a plea for statehood, beginning the legislative process that led to the creation of the state of Washington.

Nearly seventy years later, the president of Long-Bell Lumber Company, Robert Alexander Long, eyed the forests strategically located on the banks of the Columbia for a set of new timber mills. Historically, timber companies built mills and let the settlements supporting them spring up organically—and often haphazardly. Realizing that the two mills he intended to build would require about 14,000 workers and would overwhelm the infrastructure of the tiny town of Kelso next door—and perhaps inspired by the "City Beautiful" civic movement *en vogue* at the time—Long stumped for his company to purchase the land and construct a ready-made logging town bearing his name.

At the time of its inception, Longview was the only planned city of its size to have been completely conceived and built entirely using private funds. And the concept was indeed complete: Kansas City–based architecture firm Hare & Hare, hired to design Long's eponymous city, planned Longview down to the last sidewalk and street name before construction even began. The designers called for a shallow slough in the center of town to be dredged and converted into a picturesque lake (Hike 2, Lake Sacajawea). Long personally donated several local landmarks, including the Monticello Hotel, R. A. Long High School, the YMCA, and Longview Public Library—all monuments to an era of civic pride and private investment in the public good.

heart of the timber-and-port town. Lake Sacajawea, created by the same landscape architecture firm that drew up the plans for the city of Longview, was once a shallow marsh. The city dredged five-foot-deep Fowler's Slough to make an urban garden in the style of the early twentieth century City Beautiful Movement. And it's still a looker.

From the Louisiana Street parking area, follow the gravel path left (south) past cherry blossoms, rhododendrons, and towering maples, which enliven spring, summer, and fall, respectively. Historic homes on West Kessler Boulevard harken back to Longview's past. Immediately pass a large playground and popular duck-feeding

spot. Here, a footbridge crosses the lake to Nichols Boulevard and R. A. Long High School and allows for an abbreviated loop. Otherwise, continue past Lions Island—site of the city's Fourth of July fireworks display—and under bridges at Washington Way (0.5 mile) and 20th Avenue (0.9 mile). Round the south end of the lake and scope your surroundings for the Solar System Walk, with granite markers representing the Sun and its orbiting planets. Continue to circumnavigate the lake to cross under a bridge at Louisiana Street at 2.7 miles. At 3.3 miles pay a visit to the recently restored Botanical Japanese Garden at the north end of the lake before returning to your car.

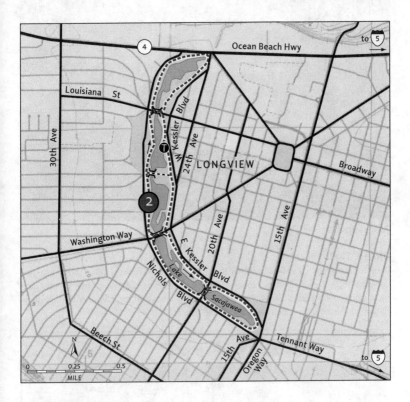

EXTENDING YOUR TRIP
Cross the footbridge or the bridges at Washington Way, 20th Avenue, or Louisiana Street for figure-eight configurations.

3 Cowlitz Riverfront East

RATING/ DIFFICULTY	ROUNDTRIP	ELEV GAIN/ HIGH POINT	SEASON
**/1	3.6 miles	120 feet/ 140 feet	Year-round

Maps: USGS Castle Rock, Cowlitz on the Move online; **Contact:** City of Castle Rock Parks; **Notes:** Wheelchair accessible. Trail open to bicycles; **GPS:** N 46 16.806 W 122 54.497

Amble alongside the Cowlitz River on an award-winning community trail that belies the town's size.

GETTING THERE
From I-5, take exit 49 (Castle Rock), heading west on State Route 411 (Huntington Avenue North) for 0.3 mile to the trailhead on the right (elev. 110 ft).

The Cowlitz River

ON THE TRAIL

Once a prosperous steamboat port on the Cowlitz, Castle Rock's riverfront today is a great place to work up a sweat. The Association of Washington Cities awarded the Cowlitz Riverfront Trail its highest honor, and rightfully so: wide, level, and well lit, this trail receives community use by everyone from after-work dog-walkers to BMX daredevils.

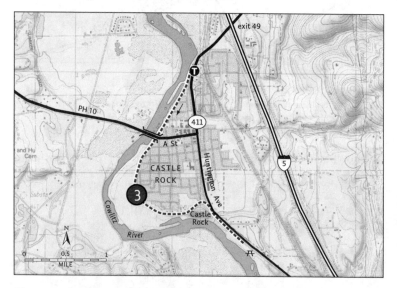

From Lions Pride Park, stroll south along the slow-flowing Cowlitz. At 0.4 mile, bear right under a bridge. Pass an impressive BMX park (0.8 mile) and skate park (1 mile). Ahead the community's namesake lords over the Cowlitz. Where the path curves around Castle Rock at 1.3 miles, a steep side path accesses the top. Although there is no view, it's a worthy diversion nonetheless: the turret-shaped landmark that guided the First Peoples and fur trappers up the Cowlitz River merits firsthand inspection. Otherwise, continue the last quarter mile to the south trailhead, which features picnic area and privy.

EXTENDING YOUR TRIP

Cross the Cowlitz for the west-shore counterpart, which begins at Fairgrounds Park. More an anglers' access point than true trail, this route is nonetheless good for burning a few extra calories.

4 Seaquest State Park— Silver Lake

RATING/ DIFFICULTY	LOOP	ELEV GAIN/ HIGH POINT	SEASON
**/1	1 mile	20 feet/ 520 feet	Year-round

Maps: USGS Silver Lake, Seaquest State Park online; **Contact:** Seaquest State Park; **Notes:** Discover Pass required. Wheelchair accessible; **GPS:** N 46 17.684 W 122 49.433

A sliver of its former self, seven-foot-deep Silver Lake is gradually receding. But the lake's loss is wetlands' gain—and a boon for bird-watchers, too, on this mile-long interpretive trail.

GETTING THERE

From I-5, take exit 49 (Castle Rock). Head east on State Route 504 for 6 miles, through

Walkers admire the buckbean and other bog plants of Silver Lake.

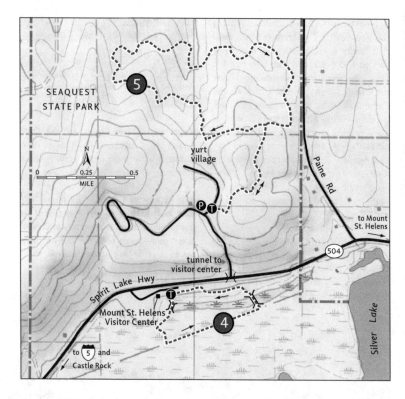

the town of Castle Rock, to the Mount St. Helens Visitor Center entrance on the right (elev. 510 ft).

ON THE TRAIL

To the west of Mount St. Helens, hikers can examine a lake newly born (see Hike 21). In contrast, the Silver Lake loop showcases a lake at the end of its lifespan; the part of the "lake" this hike explores is now more of a wetland. Ironically, Silver Lake formed when a previous eruption dammed Silver Creek. Today, a dam controls the lake's slowly receding waters for the use of boaters and anglers.

From Mount St. Helens Visitor Center—the first visitors center built after the 1980 eruption, and thus placed well outside the blast zone—follow the interpretive signs of the Wetland Haven Trail over boardwalk and dike as they describe the history of the wetland and the community of flora and fauna gradually reclaiming receding Silver Lake. Thick mats of buckbean stretch out into the lake, and several species of sedges fan out from the edges. Water lilies, stream violets, and yellow flag reap the benefits of lower water levels, and with them come ducks, birds, and the insects on which they feast.

Flowering shrubs frame the short dike connecting the boardwalks on either end, with several benches situated for bird-watching. Although the lack of water movement through the lake has dramatically altered nutrient levels and allowed invasive plants to intrude, citizen groups are ensuring there's life yet in Silver Lake's golden years.

5 Seaquest State Park— Forest Loop

RATING/ DIFFICULTY	LOOP	ELEV GAIN/ HIGH POINT	SEASON
**/3	2 miles	430 feet/ 670 feet	Year-round

Maps: USGS Silver Lake, Seaquest State Park online; **Contact:** Seaquest State Park; **Notes:** Discover Pass required. Open to horses and bicycles; **GPS:** N 46 17.894 W 122 48.996

Wander the wooded periphery of one of the best base campgrounds for exploring the north side of the Monument.

GETTING THERE
From I-5, take exit 49 (Castle Rock). Head east on State Route 504 for 6 miles, through Castle Rock, to the Seaquest State Park entrance on the left (elev. 470 ft).

ON THE TRAIL
Owing to the dearth of camping on the north side of the Mount St. Helens National Volcanic Monument, Seaquest serves as a popular base of exploration. But its miles of perimeter trails—and the old-growth forests that escaped both saws and scalding-hot pyroclastic flows—also entice passers-through.

From the day-use parking area, find the signed nature trail. Ambling among ancient Douglas-firs, leave the nature trail at 0.1

Hikers negotiate a moist lowland forest.

mile and turn left on the park's perimeter trail. Although nominally a year-round route, several spots get waterlogged; avoid this trail early in the spring or after a hard rain. The large-diameter Douglas-fir impress, but so too does the parade ground of soldier-straight western hemlock, a forest rapidly recovering from past logging. On the ground, salal and sword fern compete for the scant sunlight—and so too does the western wahoo, a state-listed plant. In the trees roost bald eagles, western tanagers, and evening grosbeaks, along with a wealth of woodpecker species.

At 0.2 mile, bear left at a trail junction—you'll be returning from the right. At 0.4 mile, turn right at a second junction; to the left lie several yurts that are available as rentals (see Extending Your Trip). Now on true single track, admire the serene forest setting. Cross a footbridge over a tiny creek at 0.5 mile and at 0.7 mile bear right at a junction. The tread descends into a (frequently waterlogged)

depression before gradually working its way out. At 1.8 mile, turn right onto wider tread, and immediately afterward bear left to close the cherry stem loop.

EXTENDING YOUR TRIP

Consider a stay in one of Seaquest State Park's yurts. A modern spin on the accommodations the nomadic Mongolian people have been using on the windblown central Asian steppe for more than three thousand years, the yurts consist of a weatherproofed canvas tarpaulin skin stretched over a wooden skeleton. Consider it a happy medium between a tent and hotel room.

6 Mayfield Trail (Ike Kinswa State Park)

RATING/ DIFFICULTY	ROUNDTRIP	ELEV GAIN/ HIGH POINT	SEASON
**/1	2.8 miles	minimal/ 475 feet	Year-round

Quiet shoreline along Mayfield Lake

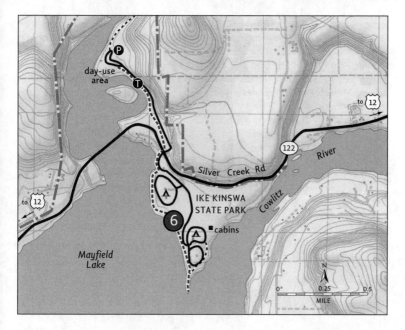

Map: USGS Mayfield Lake; **Contact:** Washington State Parks; **Notes:** Discover Pass required. Dogs permitted on-leash. Fishing options; **GPS:** N 46 33.702 W 122 32.091

Amble along the shoreline of a man-made lake to pebbled beaches and forested coves. This nature trail skirting campsites and fishing holes can be busy in the warmer months. But come here in fall or winter and you might just be sharing the way with resident geese, osprey, and eagles.

GETTING THERE

From I-5, take exit 68, heading east on US Highway 12 for 13.8 miles to the junction with State Route 122. Turn left and follow SR 122 for 4.2 miles to a park road's junction in Ike Kinswa State Park. Turn left and proceed 0.6 mile to the day-use area (elev. 450 ft). Privy and water available.

ON THE TRAIL

Start by walking back down the park road you just drove on. At 0.2 mile reach a trailhead on your right. Now follow this nice path under arching vine maples reaching SR 122 at 0.6 mile. Carefully cross the state highway and then walk along the campground access road reaching at 0.7 mile the trailhead for the Mayfield Lake Trail close to the entrance station. There's no parking here, hence the start from the day-use area.

Head right on the well-trodden path, skirting private campsites and coves. In summer, expect lots of company—but weekdays in autumn are usually quite peaceful. Come upon plenty of pebbly coves perfect for casting a line or taking a dip. Enjoy nice views out to the highway bridge and the low hills surrounding Mayfield Lake. The 2200-acre lake was formed in 1963 when Tacoma Power built the Mayfield Dam on the Cowlitz River near its confluence with the Tilton River. The state park derives its name from a Cowlitz Indian who lived here in the 1880s. Many old native village sites and graves were flooded with the construction of the dam.

At 1.3 miles, come to an old woods road. The trail continues right following the road and skirting more camps to come to a junction. Left leads 0.25 mile to the state park's cabins. You want to continue straight a short distance coming to a point in the lake at 1.4 miles. Here enjoy a great view of the lake and obscure peaks to the east known as the Rockies. Return the way you came when ready.

EXTENDING YOUR TRIP
From the day-use area, follow a level trail along the Tilton River through a thick forest of maples and cottonwoods. The trail leaves the park at 0.9 mile connecting to a series of private horse trails.

Opposite: The Willapa Hills wetlands are a vital wildlife oasis between the Cascades and the coast.

chehalis river valley

Unlike other western Washington rivers, which run into the Columbia or Puget Sound, the slow-moving Chehalis River drains from its sources—four small sub-ranges in southwest Washington—directly into the Pacific Ocean. Along the way, it forms a broad and biologically diverse flood-plain. A combination of working agricultural land and natural areas preserved through prudent public planning, the Chehalis River valley boasts several lovely flatland and foothills hikes.

7 Willapa Hills Trail

RATING/ DIFFICULTY	ROUNDTRIP	ELEV GAIN/ HIGH POINT	SEASON
***/2	10.5 miles	minimal/ 280 feet	Year-round

Maps: USGS Centralia, Adna; **Contact:** Lewis County Community Trails; **Notes:** Wheelchair accessible. Open to bicycles. Dogs permitted; **GPS:** N 46 38.739 W 122 58.376

Walkers take in the rail-trail trestles.

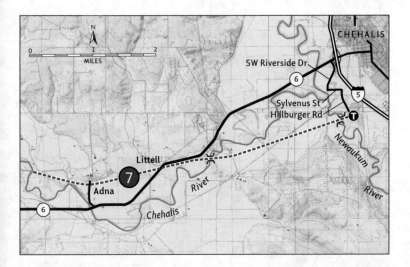

The Willapa Hills rail trail travels 56 miles from Chehalis to South Bend over century-old trestles and through idyllic farmland. The first 5 miles, from Chehalis to Adna, are paved and perfect for joggers, dog-walkers, cyclists, and the occasional cow that wanders onto the path.

GETTING THERE

From I-5, take exit 77 (Chehalis) to head west on State Route 6. At the light, turn left onto SW Riverside Drive. At 0.2 mile, bear left on SW Newaukum Avenue. Continue 0.3 mile to Southwest Sylvenus Street. Turn left and continue 0.5 mile (road becomes Hillburger Road) to the road's end and trailhead (elev. 280 ft).

ON THE TRAIL

The lowest uplands in the entire Pacific Coast Range, the rich volcanic bottomlands of the Willapa Hills stretch from the Chehalis to the Pacific Ocean. It's been decades since the last train whistled across the Willapa Hills, and since then Washington State Parks has converted the rail line into one of western Washington's best rail trails.

From the new eastern terminus, cross trestles over the Chehalis and Newaukum rivers through rich agricultural bottomland—cattle and tractor tracks mark this as a working farmland. At 1 mile, pass a private man-made lake that once hosted barefoot water-skiing competitions. A couple of busy road crossings beg caution, particularly SR 6 at Stearns Road. At 3 miles, the trail bisects a wetland—scope for birds from the small trestle—before passing Adna High School and reaching the Adna trailhead.

The path continues another 0.7 mile through a broad valley, to the Adna bridge at 5.25 miles. Flooding in 2007 damaged the span, although it's slated to be repaired soon. In the meantime, consider this a Willapa appetizer. Turn around here for a 10.5-mile roundtrip. Your return trip features an increasingly rare pastoral view of Mount Rainier from the Puget lowlands.

8 Chehalis River Discovery Trail

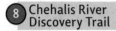

RATING/ DIFFICULTY	ROUNDTRIP	ELEV GAIN/ HIGH POINT	SEASON
**/1	3.6 miles	210 feet/ 265 feet	Year-round

Map: USGS Rochester; **Contact:** Lewis County Community Trails; **Notes:** Dogs permitted on-leash; **GPS:** N 46 45.448 W 123 01.318

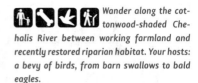

Wander along the cottonwood-shaded Chehalis River between working farmland and recently restored riparian habitat. Your hosts: a bevy of birds, from barn swallows to bald eagles.

GETTING THERE

From I-5, take exit 82 (Centralia). Head west on Harrison Avenue. Continue 2.4 miles to Goodrich Road. Turn left and continue 1.1 miles, past the wastewater treatment plant to the road's end and parking area (elev. 265 ft).

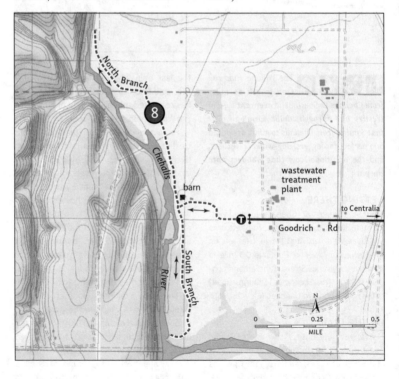

WANT TO PROTECT LAND AROUND MOUNT ST. HELENS? BUY IT!

What's the fastest, most surefire, and often least-controversial way to protect land? Buy it yourself! And that is exactly what land trusts across the country do. It's a concept that began in Massachusetts in the late 1800s, and today thousands of land trusts exist from coast to coast—nearly all of them nonprofit organizations whose primary purpose is to buy land and secure development rights in order to protect natural areas, farmlands, shorelines, wildlife habitat, and recreational lands. After the areas are secured, trusts usually transfer the lands with legally bound stipulations to government agencies to be managed for the public. Many trusts also maintain their own preserves, and most of these are open to the public.

There are several land trusts operating in the Mount St. Helens area, including the Columbia Land Trust. Based in Vancouver, Washington, the 2000 member Columbia Land Trust began in 1990 and has protected more than 18,000 acres of land. Their Mount St. Helens Forest Conservation Project is a multiphase conservation initiative designed to protect from development 20,000 acres of forest lands and wildlife habitat centered on the Pine Creek watershed. Located south of the volcano and surrounding the Swift Reservoir, Pine Creek is prime habitat for bull trout, a protected species under the federal Endangered Species Act. The Trust is not only working to conserve this watershed for wildlife habitat, but together with the Washington State Department of Natural Resources, also to keep some of the land in timber production. Without the trust's intervention, much of this watershed was slated for subdivision for seasonal homes. Consider joining them (see Appendix II, Conservation and Trail Organizations).

ON THE TRAIL

From the parking area, walk the gated access road past working farms and an old barn—notice the nesting barn swallows?—to a T-junction at 0.3 mile. Pick up an interpretive guidebook and follow the signposts, first right, then back. Trees and shrubs along the riverbank were planted in a partnership between the City of Centralia and the Chehalis River Basin Land Trust to protect salmon habitat. As they grow, cottonwood, red-osier dogwood, and willow will restore eroded riverbanks and create spawning grounds for threatened char. In the meantime, they provide superb birdwatching, including bald eagles, a pair of which resides here year-round. Note, too,

Streamside willows make a fine bird perch.

the mature black cottonwood forest across the river. The largest such grove remaining along the Chehalis, this ribbon of riparian woodland is protected in perpetuity under a conservation easement.

At 1.2 miles, reach the end of the north branch of the route. Note the expansive agricultural fields: they soak up water from the treatment plant and act as a filter before it reaches the river. Follow the path back past the T-junction to the south branch at 2 miles. Continue on the south branch to its terminus at 2.6 miles, where a thick grove of Douglas-fir and western red cedar towers

over a 90-degree bend in the river. Relax on the shaded shoreline before returning the way you came.

9 Seminary Hill

RATING/ DIFFICULTY	LOOP	ELEV GAIN/ HIGH POINT	SEASON
**/2	1.3 miles	290 feet/ 590 feet	Year- round

Map: USGS Centralia; **Contact:** Lewis County Community Trails; **Notes:** Dogs permitted on-leash; **GPS:** N 46 42.807 W 122 56.902

Rhododendrons and ferns compete for dappled sunlight.

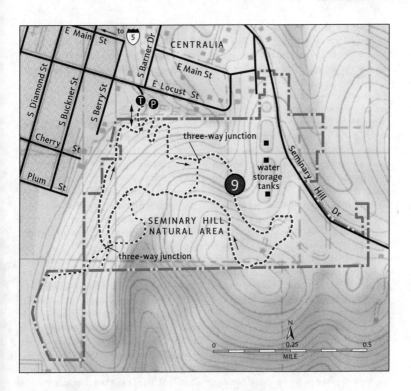

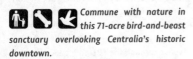 Commune with nature in this 71-acre bird-and-beast sanctuary overlooking Centralia's historic downtown.

GETTING THERE

From I-5, take exit 82 (Centralia). Head east on Harrison Street and follow it 0.7 mile. Continue onto East Main Street 0.7 mile to Gold Street. Turn right and drive one block to East Locust Street. Turn left and drive 0.2 mile to the trailhead on the right (elev. 340 ft).

ON THE TRAIL

In 1884, George Washington, an African American pioneer who established the town of Centralia, donated $10,000 to the Northwest Convention of Missionary Baptists to construct a seminary on the hill overlooking the community. Although the building burnt down in 1938, the name remains. And thanks to the Friends of Seminary Hill, residents of Centralia have this wonderful natural area in their backyard, which overlooks the Chehalis and Skookumchuck River valleys. Dozens of short, interconnecting trails crisscross the preserve; the route described below prods the periphery.

Beginning by the wooden trail map, climb the stairs to the left. Trillium, geranium, and myriad ferns flank the trail. At 0.2 mile, bear left. Note the invasive ivy that threatens to overtake the natural area; volunteers have stepped forth to stem the spread. At 0.3 mile, go straight at a three-way junction under a forest canopy that illuminates woodland blooms and rhododendron. At 0.4 mile, bear right. To the left, a water storage tower; to the right, warblers.

At 0.5 mile, bear left onto an old roadbed and in 200 feet turn into a tangle of thick alder. Weave among creeping Oregon-grape and doghair western hemlock, returning to the old roadbed at 0.8 mile. Turn left; ignoring side trails, continue under towering timber. At 1.1 miles, turn right at a three-way junction and begin a gradual descent back to the trailhead.

EXTENDING YOUR TRIP

Consult the map board at the trailhead for more loop options. It's difficult to get lost in the Seminary Hills, so take a leap of faith!

10 Lewis and Clark State Park

RATING/ DIFFICULTY	LOOP	ELEV GAIN/ HIGH POINT	SEASON
**/1	2 miles	125 feet/ 525 feet	Year-round

Map: USGS Jackson Prairie; **Contact:** Lewis and Clark State Park; **Notes:** Discover Pass required. Dogs permitted on-leash. Main park entrance closed in winter; **GPS:** N 46 31.333 W 122 48.834

Explore one of the last intact stands of old-growth forest remaining in the Cowlitz Valley in this Civilian Conservation Corps–constructed state park.

GETTING THERE

From I-5, take exit 68 and drive 2.5 miles east on US Highway 12 to Mary's Corner. Turn right onto Jackson Highway, entering the state park in 0.7 mile. Turn right at the park entrance and park in the day-use area (elev. 410 ft). Privy available. (Note: the main park entrance is closed in winter. Winter visitors should park in the parking area across the Jackson Highway and walk up the main park roadway to the trailhead.)

ON THE TRAIL

Lewis and Clark State Park—interestingly, not on the Lewis and Clark Trail—protects one of the last remaining old-growth stands of trees in the Cowlitz Valley. Although most of the old-growth Douglas-fir and western red cedar blew down in the 1962 Columbus Day Storm, the remainder predate Columbus. Built in 1922 as a camp for auto tourists, the park took shape under the Civilian Conservation Corps, the Depression-era public works program whose structures still stand on the grounds. Up to five miles of trails weave through the 621-acre park; the route described here provides a fine introduction.

Begin at the Trail of the Deer trailhead, the trail meandering among the massive Roman columns of western red cedars and Douglas-firs, ferns at their feet. Vine maples and rhododendrons wreathe the route; nurse logs sprout the next generation of giants. In the canopy, take note of woodpeckers,

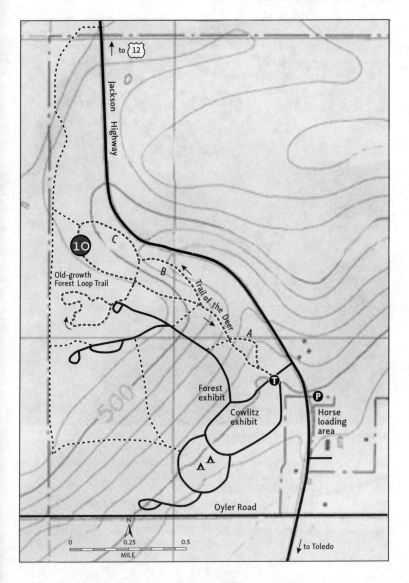

Riotous growth of miner's lettuce on a nurse log

Steller's jays, and great horned owls. A series of marked loops make a pearl necklace loop. Bear right at the first junction then stay right at signed Loop B and, shortly after, Loop C. Detour into the Old-growth Forest Loop to admire the ancient cedars before returning to the main loop. Continue, bearing right at each loop junction, to return to the trailhead.

EXTENDING YOUR TRIP

Three more miles of hiking trail trace the perimeter of the park, through thick timber and wet meadows.

Opposite: Sun-dappled hemlock forest on Kraus Ridge

cispus river valley

ts name derived from the Sahaptin-language *ci'cpac* or *shishpash*, the Cispus River valley was a primary west-of-the-Cascades travel route for the Upper Cowlitz tribe and a key source of game and fish. Today it's a major route for tourists visiting Windy Ridge and the east side of the monument. Although its fog-enshrouded valleys and forested hills lack the majesty of the mountain to the west, the Cispus will delight travelers looking for family-friendly hikes with history, waterfalls, and wildlife.

11 Woods Creek Watchable Wildlife

RATING/ DIFFICULTY	LOOP	ELEV GAIN/ HIGH POINT	SEASON
***/1	2.1 miles	130 feet/ 1210 feet	Year-round

Map: Green Trails McCoy Peak 333; **Contact:** Gifford Pinchot National Forest, Cowlitz Valley Ranger District; **Notes:** NW Forest Pass or interagency pass required. Pond Loop is barrier-free; **GPS:** N 46 27.668 W 121 57.541

 *Birders flock to this stop on the Audubon Society's Washington State Birding Trail, thanks to its mix of five fauna-friendly habitats. Those with flocks of their own will enjoy this family-friendly figure-eight with plenty to touch, see, and hear.*

A dense tangle of aspen woodland

GETTING THERE
From Randle, drive south 1 mile on State Route 131 to a junction with Forest Road 23. Bear right (south) on SR 131, which becomes FR 25, and proceed 4.7 miles to the trailhead, on the left (elev. 1140 ft). Privy available.

ON THE TRAIL
Begin on the Pond Loop. On a wide, near-level compacted-gravel trail, wander among a mixed-hardwood and conifer forest crowned by cottonwoods, one of the continent's tallest trees. Listen for the staccato tap of sapsuckers.

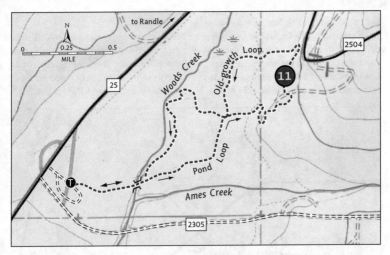

At 0.2 mile under a thickening canopy, cross Woods Creek on a sturdy footbridge. Stay right at an unmarked junction and at 0.6 mile intersect the Old-growth Loop. Bear right. Hemlocks gradually replace hardwoods as you amble onward, flanked by creeping Oregon-grape, salal, vanilla leaf, and ferns. The trail begins to gently climb among furrowed old Douglas-firs, whose boughs have shaded the ground for centuries.

At 1 mile, the trail crests near a wooden bench then begins descending through ever-younger forest. Vine maples garland the trail. At 1.3 miles, skirt the edge of a meadow, and at 1.5 miles, reach the intersection with the Pond Loop. This time, bear right. Break out onto a broad meadow. Homesteaders cleared but never occupied the forest here, and birds have since occupied the space. A viewing platform at 1.7 miles offers the best binocular spot.

At 2 miles close the loop near the first bridge you encountered; turn right for the trailhead.

12 Covel Creek—Angel Falls

RATING/ DIFFICULTY	ROUNDTRIP	ELEV GAIN/ HIGH POINT	SEASON
****/2	4.9 miles	1280 feet/ 2210 feet	Apr–Nov

Map: Green Trails McCoy Peak 333; **Contact:** Gifford Pinchot National Forest, Cowlitz Valley Ranger District; **Notes:** Dogs permitted; **GPS:** N 46 26.309 W 121 51.112

Hike to—and through—two captivating cataracts high above the Cispus River valley. Although 140-foot Angel Falls is the taller and more awe-inspiring, it's Covel Falls and its behind-the-veil trail that will delight children of all ages.

GETTING THERE

From Randle, drive south 1 mile on State Route 131 to a junction with Forest Road 23. Bear left (east) on FR 23 and proceed 8.1 miles to Cispus Road (FR 29). Turn right and drive 1.3 miles, crossing the Cispus River, then turn right again to stay on Cispus Road (now FR 76). Drive 0.7 mile to the entrance to Cispus Learning Center. Park on the side of the road or at camp headquarters (elev. 1350 ft).

ON THE TRAIL

Begin at the Cispus Learning Center. Established by the Association of Washington School Principals, the learning center has since its inception in 1981 introduced thousands of schoolchildren to "green bonding."

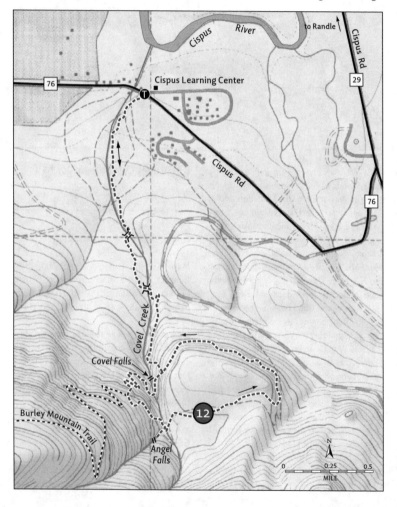

The kid-friendly cascade of Covel Falls

Carefully cross the road and immediately enter an even-aged forest, the result of massive forest fires in the Cispus Valley in the early 1900s. Pass the roped Cispus Braille Trail. At 0.2 mile and again at 0.3 mile, bear right at an unmarked junction. Ascend through fern fronds, and at 0.6 mile cross a bridge over Covel Creek. The platter-sized leaves of thimbleberry and devil's club usually shelter a chorus of frogs.

At 0.8 mile, turn left at an intersection, crossing a narrow bridge and climbing steep stone stairs. To the right, Covel Creek tumbles over a series of short cascades.

At 1.2 miles, turn right on a junction; you will return via the trail to the left. Covel Falls beckons, with a trail that goes behind the cataract. A rope guiderail comes in handy on a wet day.

Admire the falls from all angles then scramble up a creek-slickened slope through open fir forest. Bear left at a trail junction and

drop to the base of Angel Falls, which drapes over 140 feet from a mossy ledge overhead. Slick rocks and logs at the outlet complicate close viewing; kids will want to admire from a distance.

Continue on the trail through a tangle of maples to a trail junction at 2.2 miles. Turn left onto a rocky tread. From this granite grotto—surely the escape of many a Cispus student over the years—gaze upon the Cispus River valley. Keep an eye out for wildlife, too: the Cispus is one of the best rivers in the region for viewing elk, black bear, bald eagle, and spotted owl.

EXTENDING YOUR TRIP
From the intersection near Angel Falls, Burley Mountain Trail tacks gently upward through huckleberries and ferns 3 miles to a saddle below the summit of Burley Mountain, on which sits one of three fire lookouts remaining in the Gifford Pinchot National Forest.

Layser Cave

RATING/ DIFFICULTY	LOOP	ELEV GAIN/ HIGH POINT	SEASON
**/1	0.4 mile	110 feet/ 2390 feet	Apr–Nov

Map: Green Trails McCoy Peak 333; **Contact:** Gifford Pinchot National Forest, Cowlitz Valley Ranger District; **Notes:** NW Forest Pass or interagency pass required; **GPS:** N 46 27.686 W 121 51.607

View one of western Washington's most significant archaeological sites, complete with a cave-front view over the Cispus Valley's cloud-catching crags. And since it's less than half a mile, the whole clan can enjoy this trek!

GETTING THERE

From Randle, drive south 1 mile on State Route 131. At the junction, bear left (east) on Forest Road 23 and proceed for 6 miles to FR 83. Turn left on FR 83 and drive 1.5 miles to the trailhead on the right (elev. 2390 ft). A wide parking area on the left side of the road will accommodate several vehicles.

ON THE TRAIL

From the roadside trailhead, descend wooden steps into a thick hemlock forest. Stop to read the interpretive sign. The Taidnapum or "Upper Cowlitz" tribe, who were likely constituents of the Yakama Nation east of the Cascades, occupied the upper Cowlitz and Cispus River basins, and Taidnapum hunters used the steep canyons to corner game.

Mount Adams and the upper Cispus Valley

Keep right at the loop to reach the cave entrance. Discovered in 1982 by Forest Service employee Tim Layser, the sixty- by forty-foot clam-shaped cave had lain unoccupied for several thousand years. Animal bones and stone tools on the cave floor allowed archaeologists to date the earliest human use of the cave to around 7000 years ago—the oldest known upland human settlement in western Washington and Oregon.

Return to the main trail to descend onto a rock shelf. From a small viewing platform, scan the Cispus River valley and the fir-cloaked ridges beyond and in the distance, Mount Adams. View also Tower Rock, Burley Mountain, Juniper Ridge, and Tongue Mountain, a Sehaptin-language synechdoche for the mountain goats hunted on its peak. Not a bad cave-front view, eh?

Linger at your leisure before closing the cherry-stem loop back to the trailhead.

14 Kraus Ridge

RATING/ DIFFICULTY	ROUNDTRIP	ELEV GAIN/ HIGH POINT	SEASON
**/3	8.8 miles	1570 feet/ 2370 feet	Apr–Nov

Map: Green Trails McCoy Peak 333; **Contact:** Gifford Pinchot National Forest, Cowlitz Valley Ranger District; **Notes:** Open to bicycles. Open to motorcycles April 1–November 30; **GPS:** N 46 27.896 W 121 53.843

This low ridge overlooking the Cispus River lacks views, but bring binoculars anyway: birds and small critters can often be spotted in this mixed-age low-elevation forest. Although open to motorcycles part of the year, you're far more likely to see the tracks of elk than those of tires.

GETTING THERE

From Randle, drive south 1 mile on State Route 131 to a junction with Forest Road 23. Bear left (east) and continue on FR 23 for 5 miles. Turn right on FR 2306 and drive 1 mile to the trailhead on the right (elev. 1780 ft). Limited parking; park on the side of the road.

ON THE TRAIL

From the trailhead, ascend under towering Douglas-firs. The canopy shades a panoply of woodland flowers: trillium, yellow wood violet, native raspberry, and calypso orchid.

Fern frond, moss, and criss-cross cedar bark

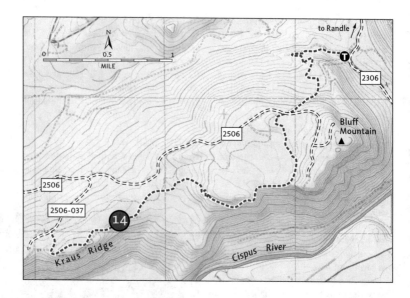

Below the trail grows a gully full of younger maples and hemlocks. Pass a small marsh and a few old-growth Douglas-firs bearing century-old fire scars. At 1 mile the grade switches from gentle to grueling, but know that your sweat will soon be rewarded with relaxing ridgeline walking.

At 1.4 miles, cross an overgrown spur road into open alder forest. On nearly level tread, devote some time to bird-watching: sapsuckers in particular seem to favor this forest. Find a short side path at 2.5 miles to a small overlook of the Cispus River valley. Although alder trees obscure most of the view, the dramatic stone faces of Tower Rock and Burley Mountain, just across the Cispus River, stand out.

Back on the trail, negotiate a gauntlet of stinging nettles and devil's club before descending across elk beds in a grassy forest opening at 2.9 miles. Cross a trickling stream at 3 miles and amble along the forest edge, alternating between thick screens of young trees and old Douglas-firs, wizened survivors of the Cispus fires a century ago. The tread gradually descends to the trail's end at a forest spur road at 4.4 miles. Turn around here and see what wildlife you might have missed the first time.

15 Iron Creek Old Growth

RATING/ DIFFICULTY	LOOP	ELEV GAIN/ HIGH POINT	SEASON
**/1	0.3 mile	minimal/ 1260 feet	Year-round

Map: Green Trails McCoy Peak 333; **Contact:** Gifford Pinchot National Forest, Cowlitz Valley Ranger District; **Notes:** Wheelchair accessible. Dogs permitted; **GPS:** N 46 25.591 W 121 59.027

A green and lively old-growth understory

Wander through a grand grove of old-growth Douglas-fir, western red cedar, and hemlock on a quiet flat where Iron Creek meets the Cispus River. Along the loop, marvel at the forest regeneration cycle, where stalwart firs and cedars provide shade and sun-dappled open-canopy forest spurs on new life.

GETTING THERE

From Randle, drive south 1 mile on State Route 131 to a junction with Forest Road 23. Bear right (south) to continue on SR 131, which becomes FR 25, and proceed 8.5 miles to the trailhead on the left immediately past the Iron Creek Campground (elev. 1260 ft). Privy available.

ON THE TRAIL

From the parking area, pass through the cut log of a downed fir some five feet in diameter. The massive trunks of western red cedar, Douglas-fir, and hemlock inspire awe. But be sure to scan the ground around the

trunk, too: sun-shunning Indian-pipe and a variety of mushrooms thrive in the moist, shady environs. As you walk, notice too the mixed canopy thanks to the natural processes of age, disease, and wildfires, which touch even wet forests.

Drop gently down to a gully lush with ferns and vigorous vine maples; the open canopy here allows these chlorophyll-craving colonizers to thrive.

Amidst the riotous undergrowth, parallel the gully. The intersection of Iron Creek and the Cispus River, a Wild and Scenic River candidate, chatters just out of sight. Closer at hand, note the nurse logs spiked with hemlock saplings. The forest is continually changing, old trees giving life to young, nothing wasted.

EXTENDING YOUR TRIP

Connect with the 1.5-mile Iron Creek Campground Trail near the picnic area for further forest roaming around the campground perimeter, including a pair of Douglas-firs

High spring flow at Iron Creek Falls

that have stood sentinel over the Cispus River for six centuries.

16 Iron Creek Falls

RATING/ DIFFICULTY	ROUNDTRIP	ELEV GAIN/ HIGH POINT	SEASON
**/1	0.1 mile	100 feet/ 2860 feet	Year-round

Map: Green Trails McCoy Peak 333; **Contact:** Gifford Pinchot National Forest, Cowlitz Valley Ranger District; **Notes:** Dogs permitted; **GPS:** N 46 19.841 W 121 58.234

Iron Creek Falls is no less impressive for being so easy to reach. A favorite of photographers, the falls make a great foot-soaker for anyone traveling on the east side of the national volcanic monument.

GETTING THERE
From Randle, drive south 1 mile on State Route 131 to a junction with Forest Road 23. Bear right (south) to continue on SR 131, which becomes FR 25, and proceed 18.5 miles to the trailhead on the left (elev. 2860 ft).

ON THE TRAIL
From a large roadside pullout, the trail descends steeply through cool forest fanned by the powerful falls. Steps built into the tread ease the steepest stretches. The trail ends about 100 feet downstream of the falls, but take one of the user-maintained paths for a closer look. Iron Creek Falls arcs off a broad basalt shelf into a shallow pool 30 feet below, framed by a lush greenscape of cedar and miner's lettuce. Cross the outlet stream to the small rocky shore to soak the pumice from your feet after a day at Windy Ridge.

Opposite: Mount Adams and St. Helens Lake seen from Coldwater Peak

mount st. helens west

Mount St. Helens' west side is graced with excellent road access via a state highway, several exceptional visitors' centers, the Coldwater Lake Recreation Area, and a wide array of well-maintained trails. It is one of the more popular areas of the national volcanic monument, as folks can (and do) drive to the end of the 52-mile Spirit Lake Highway (State Route 504), enjoying some of the finest views of the blast zone and summit crater without ever leaving their car. The road, completed in 1994, is indeed one of the prettiest highways in the state; but miles of hiking trails leading to Coldwater Lake, the Pumice Plain, and the Mount Margaret Backcountry should have no trouble wrestling you from your vehicle.

17 Sediment Retention Dam Trail

RATING/ DIFFICULTY	ROUNDTRIP	ELEV GAIN/ HIGH POINT	SEASON
**/1	1.4 miles	minimal/ 1040 feet	Year-round

Map: USGS Toutle Mountain; **Contact:** US Army Corps of Engineers, Portland District; **Notes:** Dogs permitted on-leash. Stay on trail and dam walkway; **GPS:** N 46 21.838 W 122 33.563

Walk through a lush, mossy forest to a massive earthen dam built to prevent downriver flooding. Then walk upon the 184-foot-high dam, enjoying views up the North Fork Toutle River valley to rounded green hills and the ashen Mount St. Helens. Bird- and small-mammal-watching is good in the wetlands behind the dam.

GETTING THERE

From Castle Rock (exit 49 on I-5), follow State Route 504 east for 21 miles, turning right onto SR 504-Spur (Sediment Dam Road). Follow the spur for 1 mile to its end at the trailhead (elev. 1020 ft). Privy available.

ON THE TRAIL

This is an interesting trail that sees little activity despite its proximity to SR 504 and a large sign announcing its presence. Follow an old road into a young, uniform forest draped in mosses and soon come to a platform with a view of the dam in the near distance.

Turn right following a pleasant trail winding across a forest floor carpeted in oxalis and bleeding heart (*Dicentra*) that adds dabs of color come springtime. The way makes a few ups and downs and crosses a small creek before reaching the southern end of the dam at 0.4 mile. Now turn left and walk atop the nearly 1900-foot-long earthen structure built in 1989 by the US Army Corp of Engineers to prevent sedimentation from the blast zone upriver from increasing flood risks downriver. Because sedimentation exceeded projections, the dam was raised higher in 2012.

Look upriver to nearby forested hills, Castle Ridge, and Mount St. Helens. Scan the still waters behind the dam for eagles, osprey, waterfowl, beavers, and other critters. Don't be discouraged by the fence hindering your sightline as you'll soon reach a platform allowing for unobstructed viewing. Just beyond the platform however, at 0.7 mile, is a gate prohibiting viewing of the spillway and further walking. Return the way you came.

Oxalis lines the way to the Sediment Dam.

18 Forest Learning Trail

RATING/ DIFFICULTY	LOOP	ELEV GAIN/ HIGH POINT	SEASON
**/1	0.8 mile	250 feet/ 2650 feet	May–Oct

Map: Green Trails Mt St. Helens 332S; **Contact:** Charles W. Bingham Mount St. Helens Forest Learning Center; **Notes:** Wheelchair accessible. Dogs permitted on-leash. Trail open 10AM to 5PM, May through October; **GPS:** N 46 18.533 W 122 23.732

Don't overlook this trail and learning center on one of the best overlooks along the Spirit Lake Highway (SR 504). Learn about forest and wildlife recovery in the blast zone as you walk through a thick, cool forest replanted soon after the 1980 eruption.

GETTING THERE

From Castle Rock (exit 49 on I-5), follow State Route 504 east for 33 miles to the Charles W. Bingham Mount St. Helens Forest Learning Center and trailhead (elev. 2650 ft). Privy available.

Good view of the Toutle River valley from the Elk Viewpoint path

ON THE TRAIL

The learning center—developed through a partnership with Weyerhaeuser, the Washington Department of Transportation, and the Rocky Mountain Elk Foundation—focuses primarily on forest and wildlife management practices. Hike the Forest Learning Trail to see how Weyerhaeuser, which owned over 68,000 acres of timberlands within the blast zone, salvage-logged, and replanted much of it after the eruption.

The paved trail immediately enters a cool forest of noble fir. Planted in 1983, these evergreens are now over 70 feet tall. At 0.1 mile take the graveled side spur leftward. The way descends 200 feet, making a bridged crossing over a nice cascading creek before ending at what used to be a nice viewpoint, now overgrown. Perhaps it's time for a little forest thinning? Retrace your steps and complete the loop by heading left at the junction.

For a truly spectacular view over the Toutle River valley be sure to walk the center's 0.1-mile Elk Viewpoint path. The view of St. Helens is good and there's an excellent chance of seeing herds of elk below in the valley. Be sure to check out the Forest Learning Center too.

19 Winds of Change Trail

RATING/ DIFFICULTY	LOOP	ELEV GAIN/ HIGH POINT	SEASON
***/1	0.3 mile	50 feet/ 3100 feet	May–Nov

Map: Green Trails Mt St. Helens 332S; **Contact:** Mount St. Helens National Volcanic Monument; **Notes:** NW Forest Pass or interagency pass required. Trail open when science center is open (see Appendix I, Contact Information). Wheelchair accessible; Dogs prohibited; **GPS:** N 46 17.918 W 122 15.966

Sit a spell to enjoy the sweeping views of a changing landscape.

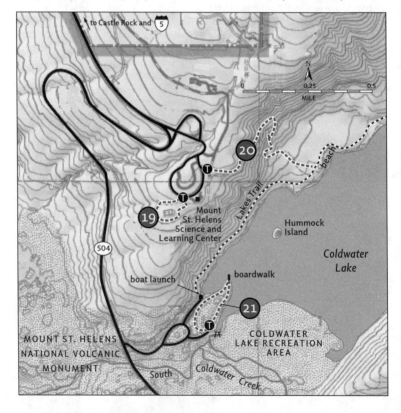

While it's only a third of a mile long, the Winds of Change Trail is one of the most scenic interpretive trails in the state. Mosey high above Coldwater Lake, admiring a stunning landscape and learning about the amazing forces that created it.

GETTING THERE

From Castle Rock (exit 49 on I-5), follow State Route 504 east for 43 miles to the Mount St. Helens Science and Learning Center (formerly the Coldwater Visitors Center) and trailhead (elev. 3100 ft). Privy available.

ON THE TRAIL

After you've visited the excellent Mount St. Helens Science and Learning Center, continue your education outside on this easy loop. Aside from the many informative panels and displays along the way, you'll have excellent photo opportunities too. When not admiring the recovering vegetation and brilliant summer wildflowers, cast your attention to Mount St. Helens standing boldly over the North Fork Toutle River valley. Marvel, too, at Castle and Coldwater lakes, two big bodies of water created by the 1980 eruption. Then be sure to go out and do some more exploring and hiking upon finishing your walk here!

20 Elk Bench Trail

RATING/ DIFFICULTY	ROUNDTRIP	ELEV GAIN/ HIGH POINT	SEASON
***/2	2 miles	600 feet/ 3100 feet	May–Nov

Map: Green Trails Mt St. Helens 332S; **Contact:** Mount St. Helens National Volcanic Monument; **Notes:** NW Forest Pass or interagency pass required. Dogs prohibited. Off-trail travel prohibited; **GPS:** N 46 17.918 W 122 15.966

It's a reverse climb to Coldwater Lake via this lightly traveled (by humans, not elk) trail. From the Mount St. Helens Science and Learning Center perched high on an open ridge, hike down to the grassy elk bench on Coldwater Lake. Views of the nearly four-mile-long lake and to the mountain that created it are stunning; and in season, the wildflowers are prolific.

GETTING THERE

From Castle Rock (exit 49 on I-5), follow State Route 504 east for 43 miles to the Mount St. Helens Science and Learning Center (formerly the Coldwater Visitors Center) and trailhead (elev. 3100 ft). Privy available.

Elk Bench Trail offers good views of Coldwater Lake.

ON THE TRAIL

While it's easier to reach the beach on Coldwater Lake via the Lakes Trail (see Hike 22), the Elk Bench Trail gives you a quieter and more scenic approach. It's more of a workout too. This is a reverse climb, so make sure the youngsters don't tucker themselves out before the return.

Locate the trailhead just north of the science center to begin your descent to Coldwater Lake. The trail loses elevation quickly, but there's no hurry to get to the lake, and you'll want to savor the sweeping views along the way. You can see Coldwater Lake almost in its entirety: from its eastern end shadowed by Minnie and Coldwater Peaks to its western end and the lake's broad emerald outlet. Admire the diverse landscape surrounding the lake, from the jagged Mount Margaret Backcountry peaks to cratered Mount St. Helens to the gently sloping, deciduous-tree-shrouded slopes along Coldwater's eastern shore.

The trail makes a sweeping switchback through an alder forest before delivering you to the cottonwood-lined grassy elk bench. You're sure to see plenty of elk sign—hoof prints and droppings—if you don't see the big deer themselves. Pass a couple of people benches and reach the Lakes Trail (elev. 2500 ft) at 0.8 mile. Right heads 0.8 mile to the Coldwater Recreation Area. You'll want to go left 0.2 mile to a lovely beach on the lake. Stay awhile before making the climb back to your vehicle.

EXTENDING YOUR TRIP

Hike as far as you want up the Lakes Trail (Hike 22), or arrange for a pickup at the Coldwater Recreation Area and save yourself a return climb.

21 Birth of a Lake Trail

RATING/ DIFFICULTY	LOOP	ELEV GAIN/ HIGH POINT	SEASON
***/1	0.5 mile	minimal/ 2510 feet	Mar–Nov

Map: Green Trails Mt St. Helens 332S; **Contact:** Mount St. Helens National Volcanic Monument; **Notes:** NW Forest Pass or interagency pass required. Wheelchair accessible. Dogs prohibited; **GPS:** N 46 17.450 W 122 15.910

Follow a delightful nature trail along Coldwater Lake's marshy outlet to a handsome dock protruding into the four-mile-long lake. On this scenic path, learn about the lake's birth in the fiery eruption of Mount St. Helens and discover its remarkable rejuvenation since then.

GETTING THERE

From Castle Rock (exit 49 on I-5), follow State Route 504 east for 45 miles, turning left into the Coldwater Lake Recreation Area. Continue 0.4 mile, bearing right, to the picnic area and trailhead (elev. 2510 ft). Privy available.

ON THE TRAIL

Take the paved path from the picnic area following alongside Coldwater Lake's outlet. The second largest lake within the national volcanic monument, Coldwater was formed in 1980 when Mount St. Helens sent an avalanche of rock and earth into the narrow valley damming Coldwater Creek. The valley before you rapidly filled with water after the eruption, prompting concern among government officials that if the damming debris

On this trail, learn how St. Helens created massive Coldwater Lake.

were to breach, a catastrophic flood could occur. In response they dug a wide channel here to help maintain a constant outtake flow and minimize the threat of flooding.

The lake's surroundings have changed radically in the past three decades, transforming from gray denuded slopes to lush young hardwood forests and fields of flowers. Just to the east of the outlet, water from South Coldwater Creek (diverted from Spirit Lake) has formed a rich delta teeming with amphibians, small mammals, and birds. The lake—thanks to wind, birds, and inlet streams—has been recolonized by a myriad of living organisms. Humans reintroduced fish to the lake.

At 0.2 mile, come to a long wooden dock extending into the sparkling lake. Take it and pause to read more interpretive panels and to admire the spectacular views of Mount St. Helens to the south and Minnie Peak to the north hovering above the lake valley. Note, too, Hummock Island and, on a high bluff above it, the Mount St. Helens Science and Learning Center.

Retrace your steps back to the trail and continue right, arriving at a boat ramp and parking area. Then follow a sidewalk to a connector path leading you back to the parking lot where you began—or retrace your steps, savoring the lake's beauty once more and reflecting upon this remarkable natural community formed in the aftermath of the 1980 eruption.

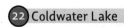 22 Coldwater Lake

RATING/ DIFFICULTY	ROUNDTRIP	ELEV GAIN/ HIGH POINT	SEASON
***/3	9 miles	550 feet/ 2625 feet	Apr–Nov

Map: Green Trails Mt St. Helens 332S; **Contact:** Mount St. Helens National Volcanic Monument; **Notes:** NW Forest Pass or interagency pass required. Trail open to bicycles the first 4.5 miles. Off-trail travel prohibited; Dogs prohibited; **GPS:** N 46 17.530 W 122 15.979

Wander through new forest glades and carpets of dazzling wildflowers along the shoreline of the monument's second-largest lake. Formed when debris and earth from the 1980 eruption dammed Coldwater Creek, Coldwater Lake is now over four miles long and 200 feet deep. Wildlife is prolific, views are nonstop, and breezes often funnel across the lake's surface, rippling mountain reflections.

GETTING THERE

From Castle Rock (exit 49 on I-5), follow State Route 504 east for 45 miles, turning left into the Coldwater Lake Recreation Area. Continue 0.4 mile, bearing left to the boat launch and trailhead (elev. 2510 ft). Privy available.

ON THE TRAIL

Locate the Lakes Trail just west of the boat launch and begin your journey along massive Coldwater Lake. Through former clear-cuts and across the blast zone, what was a stark environment in the early 1980s is now a vibrant recovering ecosystem. The resiliency of nature is on full display here, from flowered slopes to shady emerald groves of alder, willow, and cottonwood. The way gains no net elevation, but plenty of cumulative elevation is racked up along the way, rolling up and down bluffs and ledges.

From the lake's west end, take in good views of Mount St. Helens and little Hummock Island. Throughout the hike enjoy good viewing of surrounding Coldwater Peak

The Lakes Trail travels for more than 4 miles along Coldwater Lake.

and the stark southern face of Minnie Peak. At 0.8 mile pass the Elk Bench Trail (Hike 20), which climbs left to the Mount St. Helens Science and Learning Center. Continue right, reaching a wonderful lakeside spot at water's edge at 1.1 miles. This is a perfect spot to call it a hike if out with young children or if you're interested in whiling away the afternoon.

Otherwise keep hiking, passing a backcountry compost toilet and some fallen giant firs, reminder of the grand conifer forest that once grew here. Cross the first of many creeks too, eventually coming to one at 2.1 miles donning a pretty waterfall. Next skirt some cliffs before climbing across some steep ledges (elev. 2600 ft) high above the lake. Use caution here as the drop-off is steep.

Descend and cross another series of creeks (guaranteeing wet feet in the spring), reaching at 3.4 miles a wide rocky outwash. Follow cairns across the open rocky and sandy terrain, eventually coming to a daisy-dotted flat at lake level. At 4 miles, a side trail branches right to the lake where a sandy shoreline invites you to take a dip. Look for nesting spotted sandpipers here.

The trail continues, reaching the lake's marshy eastern end. Look for beaver activity among the alder thickets. Now following Coldwater Creek, the way begins to climb. After passing beneath some massive fallen firs, reach a junction (elev. 2625 ft) with the Coldwater Trail at 4.5 miles. This is a good spot to turn around—but before doing so walk a short distance south on the Coldwater Trail to a sturdy bridge spanning the thundering creek. Admire it cascading through a tight chasm—then cast your eyes upward to stone gargoyles peering down upon you from stark-faced Minnie Peak.

EXTENDING YOUR TRIP

Continue up the Lakes Trail to Snow Lake (Hike 87) or consider a long and satisfying loop back to your start via the Coldwater and South Coldwater Trails. Cross the bridge and begin climbing. The tread is good, but the trail tends to get brushy in spots as feisty deciduous growth continues to colonize this heavily logged ridge within the blast zone. Enjoy exceptional views of Coldwater Lake and the Coldwater Creek valley. At 2 miles from the bridge and after passing a small creek reach a junction (elev. 3825 ft) with the South Coldwater Ridge Trail (Hike 23). Take this trail right, following it for another 3.4 miles to SR 504. Then walk the road east 1.2 miles to the Coldwater Road, where it's 0.4 mile back to your start.

23 South Coldwater Ridge

RATING/ DIFFICULTY	ROUNDTRIP	ELEV GAIN/ HIGH POINT	SEASON
***/3	6.8 miles	1525 feet/ 3950 feet	late May–Nov

Map: Green Trails Mt St. Helens 332S; **Contact:** Mount St. Helens National Volcanic Monument; **Notes:** NW Forest Pass or interagency pass required. Open to bicycles. Off-trail travel prohibited. No water along trail; Dogs prohibited; **GPS:** N 46 17.140 W 122 15.227

Hike along a ridge above the sparkling waters of Coldwater Lake admiring Nature's reclamation of a ravaged landscape. Marvel at the deciduous forests rapidly re-greening clear-cuts and blown down trees from past logging and the 1980 blast. Let fields of wildflowers woo you and stand in awe inspecting toppled and

Mangled logging equipment: testaments of the force and fury of the 1980 eruption

mangled logging equipment that proved no match for Mother Nature's volcanic fury.

GETTING THERE

From Castle Rock (exit 49 on I-5), follow State Route 504 east for 46.2 miles to the trailhead (elev. 2550 ft), located on your left (trailhead is 1.2 miles beyond Coldwater Lake Recreation Area turnoff).

ON THE TRAIL

The way starts in a stand of fast-growing big cottonwoods. Wind up South Coldwater Ridge traversing fields of flowers and emerald forests a mere three decades old rapidly transforming a formerly bleak landscape. Much of this ridge was logged in the 1970s. St. Helens blew down the remaining big trees in May of 1980 to join the big stumps.

Enjoy good views of the South Coldwater Creek valley and Coldwater Lake delta as you lumber upward. After passing through a thickly forested spot, crest an open shoulder of the ridge. Here Coldwater Peak, Johnston Ridge, Castle Lake, the Hummocks, and Mount St. Helens all come into view—and mainly stay in view as you march forward. Coldwater Lake increasingly reveals more of its sparkling mass too.

At 1.6 miles come to the first (elev. 3500 ft) of numerous heaps of scattered, toppled, and mangled tractors and logging equipment left behind in the wake of the blast. Weyerhaeuser lost tons of equipment and 12 million board feet of timber (over 2600 logging trucks' worth) in the eruption. The rusted and contorted logging vestiges surrounded by feisty new greenery create wonderful post-apocalyptic themed photographing and drawing opportunities. *Hayduke's Dream* could be the title of these works.

The trail continues to climb, albeit more gently now as it follows a former logging road. Resplendent flowers line the way and views down to Coldwater Lake are breathtaking. Coldwater Peak provides a nice backdrop to the east. At a small saddle, stop to admire St. Helens. Keep your senses tuned for elk too—they are prolific in this part of the Monument.

Continue along the broad open ridge, basking in wondrous views. At about 2.9 miles, crest a 3950-foot high point and slowly descend, rounding a hanging valley frequented by elk. Soon a half-submerged sure-to-intrigue toppled tractor greets you. Just beyond, at 3.4 miles, is the junction (elev. 3825 ft) with the Coldwater Trail—your turnaround point. Continue the way you came.

EXTENDING YOUR TRIP
You can follow the Coldwater Trail left 2 miles down to the Lakes Trail (Hike 22) and a short road walk to make an 11.5-mile loop back to your start. Or—follow the Coldwater Trail right for a challenging ascent of Coldwater Peak (Hike 28). In 0.2 mile reach a dusty designated backcountry camp, which may be dry by late summer. The trail then wraps around a cliffy ridge above the Coldwater Creek valley. Continuing on rough-at-times tread, the way crests a saddle to traverse south-facing slopes granting excellent views of Mount St. Helens. Still climbing, the trail reaches a 5200-foot gap before descending to reach the Boundary Trail (elev. 5080 ft; see Hike 25) at 2.5 miles. From here it's 1.3 miles more to Coldwater Peak's summit.

24 The Hummocks

RATING/ DIFFICULTY	LOOP	ELEV GAIN/ HIGH POINT	SEASON
***/2	2.5 miles	250 feet/ 2550 feet	Apr–Nov

Map: Green Trails Mt St. Helens 332S; **Contact:** Mount St. Helens National Volcanic Monument; **Notes:** NW Forest Pass or interagency pass required. Dogs prohibited. Off-trail travel prohibited; **GPS:** N 46 17.183 W 122 16.303

Stroll through a series of steep-sided hills formed by debris avalanche deposits from the 1980 eruption. The Hummocks is a fascinating landscape of towering and colorful gravel mounds and lush wildlife-rich pocket ponds. What was once an unbroken old-growth forest is now a plain of jumbled rock and ash deposits up to 500 feet high, nascent wetlands, and pioneer forest.

GETTING THERE
From Castle Rock (exit 49 on I-5), follow State Route 504 east for 45.2 miles, turning right into a large parking area at the trailhead (elev. 2550 ft).

ON THE TRAIL
Locate the trailhead kiosk and begin this loop clockwise. Soon come to the first of several interpretive signs. The wide and well-groomed trail goes up and down the lumpy landscape skirting lots of ponds and marshes in the folds. Bugs, birds, and amphibians are prolific, contributing to an ensemble of soothing outdoor melodies. Try to imagine how this land appeared

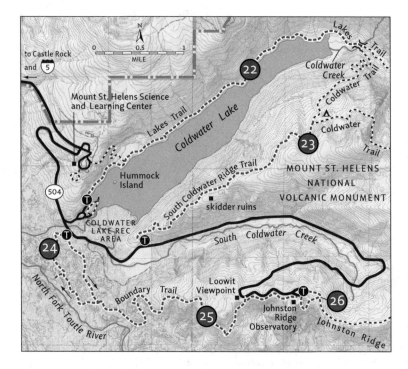

before it changed so radically. When Mount St. Helens erupted, its north face collapsed into an immense avalanche sending parts of the mountain down the valley. You are now standing on the former heart of the volcano.

At 0.7 mile reach a junction with the Boundary Trail (Hike 25) in a grassy and flowery plain beneath the watchful eye of St. Helens. Continue right across a landscape remarkably resembling a badlands, descending to a big wetland pool flanked with shade-granting alders.

The way then travels over a bluff on the North Fork Toutle River. Enjoy excellent views of the wide-channeled river and of

the mountain that altered this valley. Then cross and follow a monkey-flower-lined creek coming to a junction (elev. 2360 ft) at 1.5 miles. The short spur trail down to the river leads left to a good river-bluff-top view out to Elk Rock. Watch for nesting swallows along the river's banks.

The loop continues right, now following a creek uphill. Make a couple of bridged crossings of it and come to a big marshy area. Look for beaver activity among the bulrushes. Then keep hiking, passing a grassy flat and coming to another large wetland before ascending through an alder forest. At 2.5 miles, return to the large parking lot just north of your start.

The Hummocks were created when Mount St. Helens' north face collapsed.

EXTENDING YOUR TRIP
Combine with the Boundary Trail to the Johnston Ridge Observatory (Hike 25).

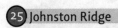
25 Johnston Ridge

RATING/ DIFFICULTY	ROUNDTRIP	ELEV GAIN/ HIGH POINT	SEASON
****/4	9 miles	1750 feet/ 4180 feet	June– mid-Nov

Map: Green Trails Mt St. Helens 332S; **Contact:** Mount St. Helens National Volcanic Monument; **Notes:** Dogs prohibited. Off-trail travel prohibited; **GPS:** N 46 17.183 W 122 16.303

🌼🏠 *Forget driving to the Johnston Ridge Observatory when you can hike to it instead! Follow part of the Boundary Trail through wildflower-shrouded hummocks and across volcano-blasted pumice hills.*

Pause along the way, admiring sweeping views of St. Helens' massive crater and the altered and continually evolving landscape surrounding it.

GETTING THERE
From Castle Rock (exit 49 on I-5), follow State Route 504 east for 45.2 miles, turning right into the large parking area and trailhead for the Hummocks (elev. 2550 ft).

ON THE TRAIL
Begin by following the Hummocks Trail (Hike 24) starting from the kiosk. On an up-and-down route, traverse the hummocks, skirting wetland pools and ponds within the folds. At 0.7 mile reach a junction (elev. 2550 ft) in a grassy and flowery plain above the North Fork Toutle River.

Head left here onto the Boundary Trail. More than 50 miles long in its entirety (Hike 86), this ridgeline trail travels west to east along what used to be the boundary between

Wildflowers and sweeping views greet hikers along Johnston Ridge.

the Rainier and Columbia National Forests, offering breathtaking views of Mount St. Helens, the Dark Divide, and Mount Adams. In 1949, the Rainier and Columbia National Forests were amalgamated into the Gifford Pinchot National Forest.

After about a half-mile of easy going across a flowered flat, begin climbing out of the hummocky valley. Traverse an old clear-cut, passing a lone cherry tree, to take in excellent views of Mount St. Helens and the sprawling hummocks of the North Fork Toutle River valley. Attain the ridge crest crossing fields of ferns and flowers. At about 2.3 miles the way steepens, switchbacking up a shoulder. The river roars below looking like something out of southwest Utah. The way eventually eases, entering a grassy slope of resplendent wildflowers, spreading ground-hugging strawberries, and regenerating fir forest. At 3 miles, cross an intermittent creek (elev. 3600 ft) and continue across young forest full of wildlife evidence. The views get even better! Stare into St. Helens' crater and out across the channeled valley to hard-to-get-to Castle Lake in the distance.

The way wraps around the ridge, skirting ledges and traversing steep south-facing slopes above the roaring river. Mount Adams and Spirit Lake suddenly come into view—the Johnston Ridge Observatory too. At 3.8 miles, reach the Loowit Viewpoint (elev. 3950 ft), a popular pullover for motorists heading to the observatory. Here you'll be greeted by tourists who drove up the ridge via SR 504. Share the lookout with them, reading interpretive panels and admiring and photographing Loowit, the aboriginal name for Mount St. Helens.

This is a good spot to turn around. But if you don't mind sharing the trail with other St. Helens–admiring folks, resume hiking on the Boundary Trail, picking it up east of the paved viewpoint loop path. Remaining on the south side of Johnston Ridge, out of view from nearby SR 504, enjoy an easy hike through swaying flowers and silver stumps, with majestic St. Helens in full view.

At 4.5 miles reach the massive parking lot (elev. 4180 ft) for the Johnston Ridge Observatory. Time to turn around—unless you plan on visiting the observatory, which can be reached by following a short, well-traveled sidewalk. You'll need your Northwest Forest

Pass (good for one visitor) or interagency pass (good for up to four adults) to enter. Otherwise you'll need to purchase a Monument Pass (see Introduction).

EXTENDING YOUR TRIP
Combine with the Eruption Trail (Hike 26).

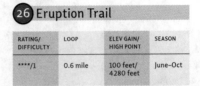

26 Eruption Trail

RATING/ DIFFICULTY	LOOP	ELEV GAIN/ HIGH POINT	SEASON
****/1	0.6 mile	100 feet/ 4280 feet	June–Oct

Map: Green Trails Mt St. Helens 332S; **Contact:** Mount St. Helens National Volcanic Monument; **Notes:** Monument Pass, NW Forest Pass, or interagency pass required. Wheelchair accessible. Dogs prohibited. Off-trail travel prohibited; **GPS:** N 46 16.648 W 122 13.086

The Eruption Trail overflows with alpine scenery, flower-gazing opportunities, natural and historical interpretation, and stunning Mount St. Helens views. You'll have a blast on this short paved path providing one of the best panoramic views of the famous volcano's crater.

GETTING THERE
From Castle Rock (exit 49 on I-5), follow State Route 504 east for 52 miles to its end at a large parking area for the Johnston Ridge Observatory (elev. 4180 ft). Privy available.

ON THE TRAIL
Judging by the size of the parking lot, you can assume that this is one of the most popular places within the national volcanic

The Eruption Trail provides excellent views of St. Helens' crater and the Pumice Plain.

monument. It was on this on ridge on May 18, 1980, that David Johnston, a young volcanologist working with the United States Geological Survey, perished while observing St. Helens' cataclysmic eruption. The first person to report this event, Johnston radio transmitted back to the survey's office: "Vancouver! Vancouver! This is it!" Those would be his last words as the mountain's lateral blast spewed pyroclastic debris over much of the surroundings. This ridge and the observatory sitting prominently upon it were named to commemorate Johnston.

Begin by walking 0.1 mile to the Johnston Ridge Observatory. By all means spend some time at the observatory visiting the displays and perhaps attending a guided walk or talk. Whether you go inside or not you'll need to get your monument pass wristband to hike the adjacent trails. Pay admission ($8 age sixteen and up; free up to age fifteen); or show your Northwest Forest Pass (good for one admission) or interagency pass (good for up to four adults).

Then head outside and follow the paved and railed trail as it winds through flowered and pumice patches to a knoll above the observatory. The path is short but you'll linger reading the engaging interpretive signs and soaking up the stunning scenery. Mount

St. Helens is less than six miles away, across pumiced plains and hillocks of pyroclastic debris. Ponder how radically this landscape changed between March 27, 1980—when the volcano produced its first steam and ash since 1857—and May 18, 1980, when the mountain's north face gave way. The lateral eruption reduced the mountain's elevation by 1300 feet and altered much of the surrounding topography.

At 0.3 mile reach a knoll top (elev. 4280 ft) adorned with a compass rose, which will have you doing a 360-degree turn identifying all of the surrounding peaks and landmarks. Then begin descending, coming to a beautiful and sobering memorial to the fifty-seven people who lost their lives in the 1980 eruption, the deadliest volcanic eruption in US history.

Shortly afterward come to a junction with the Boundary Trail. Turn left and continue on the paved path, enjoying good views north to Coldwater Peak, to reach the large parking lot at 0.6 mile and close the loop.

EXTENDING YOUR TRIP

Combine with a trip to Harry's Ridge and Coldwater Peak (Hikes 27 and 28).

VULCAN 101

Sorry, *Star Trek* fans, we're not talking Klingon here. We're talking volcanism, and we think it might be a good idea for you to become a little familiar with many of the volcanic terms you will see in this book. For starters, the word "**volcano**" is derived from Vulcano, a volcanic island in Italy's Aeolian Islands named for Vulcan, the Roman god of fire.

Ash : Volcanic ash consists of pulverized rock and mineral fragments (less than 0.1 inch in diameter) blown from an eruption.

Basalt: Dark volcanic rock (usually containing nearly 50 percent silica) formed after hot liquid rock solidifies.

Composite Volcano: A steep volcano built by both lava flows and pyroclastic eruptions.

Crater: Usually a steep-sided circular depression formed when a volcanic vent collapses or laterally explodes.

Dome: Rounded steep-sided mounds formed by viscous magma.

Fumerole: A vent in the volcano where steam and gasses escape.

Lahar: A volcanic mudflow of rapidly flowing debris originating on the volcano's slopes.

Lava: Magma (both liquid rock and, later, solidified) erupted onto the earth's surface.

Magma: Molten or partially molten rock beneath the earth's surface.

Obsidian: Black or dark-colored dense volcanic glass composed of rhyolite.

Pumice: Light-colored and porous volcanic rock formed by the expansion of gas in erupting magma.

Pyroclastic Flow: A ground-hugging flow of hot gasses, ash, and volcanic fragments that can move down the slopes of a volcano at high speeds (up to 100 mph).

Stratovolcano: A steep, conical volcano built by viscous lava and pyroclastic flows.

Tephra: Various materials that are erupted from a volcanic crater or vent and deposited from the air.

27 Harry's Ridge

RATING/ DIFFICULTY	ROUNDTRIP	ELEV GAIN/ HIGH POINT	SEASON
****/3	8.2 miles	970 feet/ 4752 feet	mid-June– Oct

Map: Green Trails Mt St. Helens 332S; **Contact:** Mount St. Helens National Volcanic Monument; **Notes:** Monument Pass, NW Forest Pass, or interagency pass required. Dogs prohibited. Off-trail travel prohibited. Dry trail—pack water; **GPS:** N 46 16.681 W 122 12.896

Harry's Ridge hovers high above Spirit Lake, and the spirit of Harry Truman, a curmudgeonly lodge keeper, rests in this wickedly beautiful area within the blast zone. Traverse lofty Johnston Ridge en route to Harry's Ridge and its sweeping Spirit Lake views. Dazzling wildflowers help soften this harsh landscape.

GETTING THERE
From Castle Rock (exit 49 on I-5), follow State Route 504 east for 52 miles to its end at a large parking area for the Johnston Ridge Observatory (elev. 4180 ft). Privy available.

ON THE TRAIL
You'll need to purchase a Monument Pass (available at the Johnston Ridge Observatory) before beginning your hike. If starting before the observatory is open, be sure to carry your Northwest Forest Pass or interagency pass with you in lieu of the Monument Pass wristband. You can be fined for hiking here without a pass.

Locate the trailhead for the Boundary Trail (carrying the distinction of being trail "No. 1") at the northeast end of the parking

lot. Hike a little over 0.1 mile to a junction (elev. 4220 ft). The paved Eruption Trail (Hike 26) continues right—you want to go left on nicely groomed, natural tread heading downhill along Johnston Ridge. The views are amazing: Mount St. Helens to the right, ever watchful, and Coldwater Peak to the left with its blocky summit. A brilliant array of flowers—penstemon, lupine, paintbrush, pearly everlasting, and more line the way. And young noble firs colonize the ridge's northern slopes. There is however little shade along this route.

Shortly after passing a kiosk and bench used for outdoor programs, reach a saddle (elev. 4020 ft) at 0.8 mile. Continue on narrower tread, cutting across patches of mountain alder and regaining some lost elevation. At 1.6 miles, the way reaches another saddle (elev. 4150 ft) before traversing a very steep and somewhat exposed slope. Families with young children or people skittish of heights may want to turn around here. Otherwise continue on carefully, hugging ledges and scooting below cliffs as you cut across an airy slope high above the Pumice Plain to the south (Hike 29).

At 2 miles, come to an excellent viewpoint of Harry's Ridge with Spirit Lake and Mount Adams in the distance. Then continue on a less intimidating course coming to a junction (elev. 4075 ft) at 2.5 miles with the Truman Trail (Hike 29). The trails meet up in a saddle (elev. 4075 ft) in the Spillover, where landslide debris from the 1980 eruption spilled over the ridge.

Remaining on the Boundary Trail, you will cross a hummocky landscape cloaked with alders and willows and home to scads of ground squirrels and thousands of grasshoppers. Not long after crossing a bridge spanning a gully, reach another junction

Mount Adams looks over a "water-logged" Spirit Lake.

(elev. 4400 ft) at 3.5 miles. The Boundary Trail continues left to Coldwater Peak (Hike 28). You want to go right, continuing 0.6 mile on a gentle ascent of Harry's Ridge, reaching seismic measuring equipment (don't disturb) at the highpoint (elev. 4752 ft).

Savor sweeping views from here to the Mount Margaret Backcountry peaks, Johnston Ridge, Mount St. Helens, and Mount Adams. Directly below is Spirit Lake with its ever-shifting flotilla of floating logs. Government officials worried that there could be a catastrophic flood if the waters of Spirit Lake, left without an outlet by the eruption, were to break through the damming debris. In 1985 they dug an outlet tunnel beneath Harry's Ridge, discharging water into South Coldwater Creek and maintaining Spirit Lake's surface level.

The ridge is named for Harry Truman, owner of the Mount St. Helens Lodge on the south shore of Spirit Lake, where he lived with his sixteen cats. Truman gained folk-hero status when he refused to leave

the area after being warned of the dangers of the imminent eruption. "If the mountain goes, I'm going with it," he said in a newspaper article. On May 18, after living fifty-two years at the lodge, Truman was buried under a pyroclastic flow, his lodge destroyed, and his body never recovered. Return the way you came.

EXTENDING YOUR TRIP

Combine with Coldwater Peak (Hike 28).

28 Coldwater Peak

RATING/ DIFFICULTY	ROUNDTRIP	ELEV GAIN/ HIGH POINT	SEASON
*****/5	12.8 miles	1900 feet/ 5727 feet	July–Oct

Map: Green Trails Mt St. Helens 332S; **Contact:** Mount St. Helens National Volcanic Monument; **Notes:** Monument Pass, NW Forest Pass, or interagency pass required. Dogs prohibited. Off-trail travel prohibited.

Dry trail—pack water; **GPS:** N 46 16.681 W 122 12.896

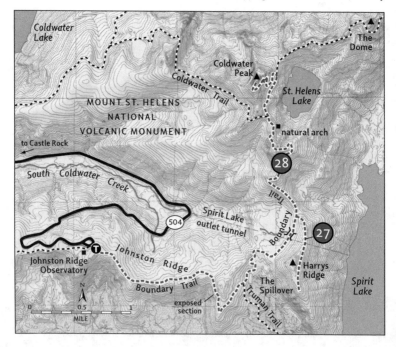 *Stand upon this anvil-shaped peak and behold one of the finest views within the entire national volcanic monument. Look down flowered slopes to sparkling St. Helens Lake ringed with Christmas trees in a high bowl above sprawling Spirit Lake. Reflect on the rock arch perched on a narrow ridge you passed through to get here. It's a tough hike—but one of the most exhilarating in the state.*

GETTING THERE

From Castle Rock (exit 49 on I-5), follow State Route 504 east for 52 miles to its end at a large parking area for the Johnston Ridge Observatory (elev. 4180 ft). Privy available.

ON THE TRAIL

You'll need to purchase a Monument Pass (available at the Johnston Ridge Observatory) before beginning your hike. If starting before the observatory is open, be sure to carry your Northwest Forest Pass or interagency pass with you in lieu of the Monument Pass wristband. You can be fined for hiking here without a pass.

Locate the trailhead for the Boundary Trail at the northeast end of the parking lot and follow this trail, marked "No. 1," east. After dropping 200 feet to a saddle, the way

A hiker peers out at St. Helens Lake, Spirit Lake, and Mount St. Helens.

gradually climbs to traverse a steep and exposed slope (use caution). At 2.5 miles, stay left at a junction with the Truman Trail and pass through a gap at the Spillover, where landslide debris spilled over the ridge during the 1980 eruption.

At 3.5 miles, reach a junction (elev. 4400 ft) with the short trail leading right up Harry's Ridge (Hike 27). From here, crowds thin, the terrain gets rougher, the trail gets steeper, the views get better, and the overall hiking experience intensifies. Pass a saddle and then begin steeply climbing up a ridge lined with blueberries, thimbleberries, and a brilliant array of wildflowers.

Views of Spirit Lake expand. Mounts Adams, Hood, and Rainier come into view. Mount St. Helens never leaves the view. Work your way through fern boughs and clusters of big silver snags—remnants of the grand forest that once shrouded these slopes. Feisty firs are busily recolonizing these volcano-blasted ridges.

Attaining the ridge crest (elev. 5200 ft), capture your first view of gorgeous St. Helens Lake set in a remote bowl beneath the steep slopes of Coldwater Peak and above the stark slopes surrounding Spirit Lake. Post-eruption, trout still thrive in the lake. Their ancestor stock survived thanks to protection from deep layers of ice and snow at the time of the eruption. Look for elk below among the grassy benches and clusters of young trees along the shoreline.

The trail now continues along the narrow ridge crest, where it darts through a dramatic natural arch. Continue on a small catwalk blasted into a ledge, taking in jaw-dropping views of St. Helens Lake below. The way then gently descends, reaching a junction in a saddle (elev. 5070 ft) at 5.2 miles.

The Coldwater Trail to the left offers a longer and more challenging approach to this peak (Hike 23) and an alternative return if you can arrange for a pick up. For Coldwater Peak, continue right on the Boundary Trail for a nearly level, enjoyable half-mile across grassy slopes and lupine patches. At 5.7 miles, bear left at a junction and start climbing steeply on the summit spur.

MOUNT ST. HELENS INSTITUTE

Based in Amboy, the Mount St. Helens Institute was founded in 1996 by a group of passionate proponents of the unique geology and ecology of Mount St. Helens. Since then, volunteers have logged over 20,000 hours a year assisting more than 100,000 volcano visitors with field seminars, work parties, and other outings. "Volcano Volunteers" stationed at Johnston Ridge, Cascade Peaks, and Pine Creek visitors centers assist with tourist queries, as do volunteer interpreters at sites around the volcano. The Institute also hosts monthly public evening lectures on geology and ecology called "Volcanic Views and Brews." If you've stopped in at a visitors center, hiked on one of the national volcanic monument's new trails, or gone on a guided climb, chances are you have a Mount St. Helens Institute volunteer to thank.

Darting beneath cliffs and switchbacking across emerald slopes adorned with blueberries, anemones, and spiraea, reach the 5727-foot precipitous summit of Coldwater Peak at 6.4 miles. Once the site of a fire lookout, some volcano-monitoring equipment now sits upon its narrow summit. The views are bedazzling! Look down upon Coldwater, St. Helens, and Spirit lakes. Look out at impressive volcanoes—St. Helens, Hood, Rainier, Adams—and the Goat Rocks, the remains of a once great 12,000-foot volcano. Let marmots and ravens and whistling breezes provide a beautiful background score to this amazing natural canvas. Return as you came and when you must.

29 Truman Trail— Pumice Plain

RATING/ DIFFICULTY	ROUNDTRIP	ELEV GAIN/ HIGH POINT	SEASON
****/4	10.4 miles	1075 feet/ 4200 feet	late June– Oct

Map: Green Trails Mt St. Helens 332S; **Contact:** Mount St. Helens National Volcanic Monument; **Notes:** Monument Pass, NW Forest Pass, or interagency pass required. Dogs prohibited. Off-trail travel prohibited; **GPS:** N 46 16.681 W 122 12.896

Hike across the lonely Pumice Plain deep into the heart of the blast zone. Once desolate, the plain now teems with wildflowers, willows, and other flourishing flora, and birds and mammals too. Cross creeks and hummocks and skirt wetland pools, enjoying unique views of Spirit Lake and Mount St. Helen's growing and smoldering crater dome.

GETTING THERE

From Castle Rock (exit 49 on I-5), follow State Route 504 east for 52 miles to its end at a large parking area for the Johnston Ridge Observatory (elev. 4180 ft). Privy available.

ON THE TRAIL

You'll need to purchase a Monument Pass (available at the Johnston Ridge Observatory) before beginning your hike. If starting before the observatory is open, be sure to carry your Northwest Forest Pass or interagency pass with you in lieu of the Monument Pass wristband. You can be fined for hiking here without a pass.

Starting on the Boundary Trail, head east across Johnston Ridge. After climbing a tad, drop 200 feet to a saddle. The way then gradually climbs, traversing a steep and exposed slope (use caution). Enjoy great views of St. Helens nearby and Adams in the distance. At 2.5 miles, come to a junction (elev. 4075 ft) with the Truman Trail in an area known as the Spillover, where landslide debris spilled over the ridge during the 1980 eruption.

Now turn right and start hiking down off the ridge on the lightly traveled Truman Trail, named for Harry Truman, the colorful curmudgeon and World War I vet who owned the Mount St. Helens Lodge at Spirit Lake. Truman refused to evacuate his property in the spring of 1980 and perished at age eighty-three with his sixteen cats during the May 18 eruption. The trail and nearby ridge above Spirit Lake are nice memorials to this man who loved Mount St. Helens.

Gradually descending, traverse a fascinating landscape of hummocks, small creeks, pocket wetlands, willow thickets, and alder groves. The surroundings are harsh yet soft: gray, green, and colorful. Approaching the Pumice Plain you'll hike along ground that could be right out of South Dakota's Badlands or California's Mojave Desert. It's an incredibly diverse topography that pre-eruption contained (but contains no longer) the North Fork Toutle River.

Trek across sandy terrain carpeted with wildflowers and pass a seismic measuring station before coming upon a couple of ponds teeming with bird, insect, and amphibian life. At about 4.4 miles, cross a couple of wide alluvial fans (elev. 3500 ft) created by creeks draining into Spirit Lake. With no outlet after the eruption, engineers bored a tunnel under Harry's Ridge (Hike 27) allowing water to escape into Coldwater Creek.

The trail continues through wet pockets and willow thickets and past several creeks. Pass a lone volcanic boulder and cross more creeks. From the open pumice flats, enjoy excellent views into St. Helens' crater and over to Loowit Falls cradled there. Be sure to

Wildflowers and wetlands add color and life in the Pumice Plain.

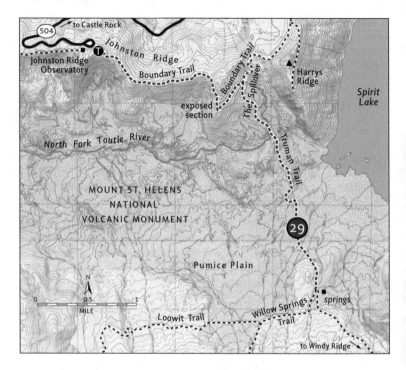

look around to take in the Mount Margaret peaks, which form an imposing wall over Spirit Lake.

At 5.2 miles, reach a junction with the Willow Springs Trail (elev. 3700 ft). This is a good point to turn around and return the way you came—but if energy and wanderlust persist, read on.

EXTENDING YOUR TRIP

The Truman Trail continues left, dropping into a gully to a creek that periodically takes part of the trail with it. Cross the boot-soaking creek and, following some large cairns, relocate the trail in a thick willow thicket. The trail then uses an old roadbed (used to bore Spirit Lake's tunnel outlet) to reach the Windy Trail (elev. 4050 ft) in 1.4 miles. The Truman Trail continues left, reaching the Windy Ridge trailhead in 2 miles.

Strong day hikers can visit Loowit Falls (Hike 57) by hiking right on the Willow Springs Trail for 0.9 mile to the Loowit Trail (elev. 3860 ft). Then hike left on the Loowit, climbing 0.8 mile to a junction (elev. 4300 ft), followed by another 0.6 mile to the falls (elev. 4575 ft).

Opposite: Mount St. Helens provides a nice backdrop to McBride Lake on the Toutle River Trail.

mount st. helens south

St. Helens' southern flank is a popular destination that's close to the Vancouver–Portland metropolitan area and easy to reach by good paved Forest Service roads. Because the area was out of the 1980 blast zone, it contains large tracts of old-growth forest and old lava flows. You'll find here well-used and -maintained trails cherished not only by hikers but by mountain bikers and equestrians too. The popular Ape Cave, Ape and Lava Canyons, and the summit climbing routes are located here as well. In winter, snowshoers, cross-country skiers, and snowmobilers take to the region's excellent network of maintained trails. But despite this area's popularity, there are still plenty of miles of trails here where you can venture out and not see another human soul.

30 Merrill Lake Nature Trail

RATING/ DIFFICULTY	LOOP	ELEV GAIN/ HIGH POINT	SEASON
***/1	1 mile	125 feet/ 1700 feet	Mar–Dec

Map: Green Trails Mt St. Helens 332S; **Contact:** Washington Department of Natural Resources, Pacific Cascade Region; **Notes:** Discover Pass required. When campground is closed for season, access trail at gate. Fishing options; **GPS:** N 46 05.687 W 122 19.181

A new trail through an old forest, the Merrill Lake Nature Trail invites quiet contemplation and outdoors admiration. Stroll along the east shore of big, undeveloped Merrill Lake through groves of ancient towering trees. A great hike if camping at the lake or as a nice quiet getaway.

GETTING THERE

From Woodland (exit 21 on I-5), follow State Route 503 east for just shy of 28 miles before turning left onto Forest Road 81 (turnoff is 1 mile west of the town of Cougar). Follow this good road for 4.7 miles, turning left into the Merrill Lake Campground. Continue 0.2 mile to the day-use parking area (elev. 1600 ft). Privy available.

ON THE TRAIL

Walk on a path through the picnic area to the boat launch and locate the trailhead to the south of the privy. The wide and well-built trail—constructed in 2013—soon comes to a creek and a junction near some monstrous trees. Take the path right to travel along placid Merrill Lake's shoreline.

The trail and campground lie within Washington State Department of Natural Resources' 114-acre Merrill Lake Natural Resource Conservation Area (NRCA). The NRCA was established to protect the lakeshore's exceptional old-growth forest and habitat for bald eagle and Cascade torrent salamander. The northern half of this undeveloped lake remains unprotected, but hopefully not for long. The Rocky Mountain Elk Foundation, Columbia Land Trust, and others are working with the state to negotiate a deal with the current landowner to secure permanent protection of more than 1400 acres along Merrill Lake.

The delightful trail crosses several creeks on well-built bridges and passes by some incredibly large old Douglas-firs, noble firs, and big-leaf maples. After about a half mile, the way turns left and heads upslope to eventually parallel FR 81. You'll pass a spur leading to the campground entrance (use this spur when gate is locked) before briefly but steeply descending back to the

Giant old-growth Douglas-fir

junction near the streamside giants. Return to your vehicle or consider a little fly fishing or paddling in the lake.

31 Goat Marsh

RATING/ DIFFICULTY	ROUNDTRIP	ELEV GAIN/ HIGH POINT	SEASON
***/1	2.8 miles	180 feet/ 2930 feet	May–Nov

Map: Green Trails Mt St. Helens 332S; **Contact:** Mount St. Helens National Volcanic Monument; **Notes:** National research area—stay on trail. Mosquitoes can be fierce in early season; **GPS:** N 46 09.267 W 122 16.146

Explore a sprawling mosaic of wetlands cradled beneath the blocky plug dome Goat Mountain. Goat Marsh was created three to five hundred years ago by pyroclastic flows (fast-moving currents of *hot gas and rock) from Mount St. Helens blocking the flow of Coldspring Creek. Beaver colonies created the two small lakes within the marsh. An excellent hike for nature study—the view of St. Helens isn't too bad either.*

GETTING THERE
From Woodland (exit 21 on I-5), follow State Route 503 east just shy of 28 miles before turning left onto Forest Road 81 (turnoff is 1 mile west of Cougar). Follow this good road (pavement ends at 11.1 miles) for 11.6 miles to a junction. Continue straight onto FR 8123. In 0.5 mile, reach the trailhead (elev. 2880 ft) and parking for a couple of vehicles on the left.

ON THE TRAIL
Start by following the Kalama Ski Trail (Hike 92) through lodgepole pine forest along the edge of an old lahar (volcanic mudflow). At 0.2 mile, after crossing a small creek, reach the junction (elev. 2830 ft) with the Goat Marsh Trail. Take it right, heading past an old gravel pit and coming soon to a split-rail fence marking the entrance to the Goat Marsh Research Area.

The research area was established in 1974 to study an array of natural communities, including one of the finest stands of noble fir in the Cascades. Wander over a small rise (elev. 2930 ft), admiring handsome Douglas-firs and noble firs. The marsh soon comes into view through the trees. Shortly after, the trail skirts one of two stretches of open water within the marsh. Here 4965-foot Goat Mountain, a plug dome volcano, can be seen hovering to the west over the marsh.

Continue hiking, skirting a marshy cove and rounding the small lake of open water as you come to a point above a long beaver

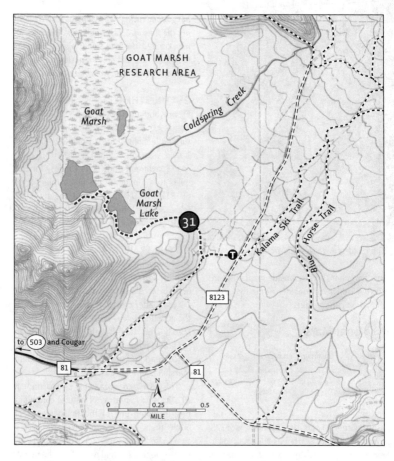

dam. The trail continues a short distance, eventually reaching water's edge at the second lake (elev. 2900 ft) at 1.4 miles. Definitely hike to trail's end—but the view from the point is where you'll want to take your lunch break. Gaze out across golden sedges to massive Mount St. Helens. Admire the double-peaked Butte Camp Dome, which, like Goat Mountain, is also a plug dome

volcano (its roof composed of a "dome" of solid lava). Come late in the fall and stay late in the day to witness the evening light dance off of St. Helen's massive snowy facade. It's breathtaking. Return the way you came.

EXTENDING YOUR TRIP

Walk the Kalama Ski Trail (Hike 92) west 0.8 mile to FR 81 (an alternative start) or

St. Helens hovers over a chilly Goat Marsh in late November.

3.3 miles to the Kalama Horse Camp. The Kalama Ski Trail can be walked east too. It's 3.2 miles across pine forests and an old lava flow to the Toutle Trail, and from there, another 0.6 mile to the trailhead at Redrock Pass (see Hike 33).

32 Kalama River

RATING/ DIFFICULTY	ROUNDTRIP	ELEV GAIN/ HIGH POINT	SEASON
***/2	8 miles	680 feet/ 2700 feet	May–Nov

Map: Green Trails Mt St. Helens 332S; **Contact:** Mount St. Helens National Volcanic Monument; **Notes:** NW Forest Pass or interagency pass required. Trail open to horses and bicycles; **GPS:** N 46 08.586 W 122 19.437

Hike alongside the tumbling Kalama River, traveling atop high bluffs and through impressive stands of primeval forest. Pause to watch dippers flitting from water to river rocks, and admire Mount St. Helens rising above the remnants of McBride Lake. An excellent hike on an overcast day, this trail is also a good choice when snows begin to bury the nearby higher grounds.

GETTING THERE

From Woodland (exit 21 on I-5), follow State Route 503 east for just shy of 28 miles. Turn left onto Forest Road 81 (turnoff is 1 mile west of the town of Cougar). Follow this good paved road for 8.9 miles to the Kalama Horse Camp. Proceed 0.2 mile to the day-use parking area and trailhead (elev. 2040 ft). Privy available.

ON THE TRAIL

Four trails diverge from this spot. The Toutle Trail, which you'll be following along the Kalama River, is the most popular of the lot. Horse use can be heavy, and mountain bikers like this trail too, so be prepared to share. And if you're hiking with a furry friend, be sure your pooch is kept under strict control.

Following the Toutle Trail, drop slightly to cross a small creek and immediately come to a junction with the Cinnamon Trail (Hike 33). Continue left and soon afterward, at 0.2 mile, come to another junction. The Kalama Ski Trail splits off (blue diamonds mark this winter ski trail, see Hike 92). Continue right, crossing a washed-out gully to arrive at the Kalama River in a dark grove of old timber. The river is named for John Kalama, a Hawaiian who worked for the Hudson's Bay Company and later drowned in this Columbia River tributary bearing his name.

After some riverside walking, you begin switchbacking to climb a high sandy bluff above the river and merge onto the Kalama Ski Trail at 0.9 mile. Continue right, hiking through open forest, along the steep and eroded bluff top. At 2.1 miles, the Kalama Ski Trail diverts left. Stay right on the Toutle Trail, hiking through attractive forest, coming to a nice campsite and FR 8122 at 2.4 miles.

Cross the road to eventually reach river level and commence a delightful near-level walk through attractive old-growth forest. Meander along the churning river, listening to soothing water music. At 3.6 miles reach an old logging road (elev. 2680 ft). Left leads 0.3 mile to FR 81 and the Blue Horse trailhead, offering a shorter option to reach McBride Lake.

Now turn right on the old road, cross the Kalama River, and immediately turn left, picking up the trail again. Pass a few campsites and soon come to the marshy edge of McBride Lake (elev. 2700 ft) at 4 miles. Formed by mudflows damming the Kalama River, recent mudflows have altered the area once again, leaving not much of a lake behind. While the lake isn't much of a body of water, the old-growth surroundings and

A large mushroom takes up residence on the Toutle Trail.

wildlife-rich flats are gorgeous—especially with Mount St. Helens providing a stunning backdrop. A seasonal waterfall near the lake's west end adds to the area's allure. Stay awhile to savor this serene scene. Then return the way you came.

EXTENDING YOUR TRIP

Continue hiking east on the Toutle Trail, climbing above McBride Lake and traversing beautiful groves of old growth. The trail then travels through an old harvested area, crossing several spring-generated streams and the headwaters of the Kalama River. At 5.7 miles, arrive at a junction (elev. 3125 ft) near a massive lone silver fir and contemplate your options.

Option A: Return to your start via the Cinnamon Trail (Hike 33) for a 14.4-mile loop. Option B: Continue on the Toutle Trail

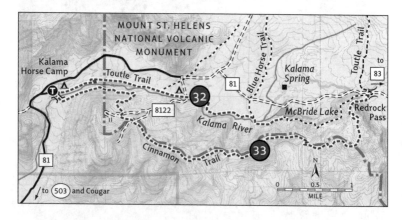

0.1 mile to Redrock Pass and the trailhead for Butte Camp (Hike 36) and arrange a pickup for a one-way hike. Or continue on the Toutle Trail for another 3 miles to the Blue Horse Trail (elev. 3300 ft). Then follow the Blue Horse Trail 2.8 miles back to the Toutle Trail for a 15.0-mile-long lollipop loop.

33 Cinnamon Trail

RATING/ DIFFICULTY	ONE-WAY	ELEV GAIN/ HIGH POINT	SEASON
***/3	8.8 miles	2600 feet/ 4000 feet	mid-June– Nov

Map: Green Trails Mt St. Helens 332S; **Contact:** Mount St. Helens National Volcanic Monument; **Notes:** NW Forest Pass or interagency pass required. Trail open to horses and bicycles; **GPS:** N 46 08.586 W 122 19.437

The Cinnamon Trail offers sweet views of Mount St. Helens. Follow a ridgeline above the Kalama River undulating between former clear-cuts and stands of primeval forest. Enjoy good views south to Mount Hood and north to blocky Goat Mountain—and captivating close in-your-face views of Mount St. Helens.

GETTING THERE
From Woodland (exit 21 on I-5), follow State Route 503 east for just shy of 28 miles before turning left onto Forest Road 81 (turnoff is 1 mile west of Cougar). Follow this good paved road for 8.9 miles to the Kalama Horse Camp. Proceed 0.2 mile to day-use parking area and trailhead (elev. 2040 ft). Privy available.

ON THE TRAIL
You'll want to start off on the most trodden of the radiating paths—the Toutle Trail. Take it, descending slightly to cross a creek before reaching a junction in about 0.1 mile. The Kalama Ski Trail (Hike 92) and Toutle Trail along the Kalama River (Hike 32) veer left. You want to go right on the Cinnamon Trail, crossing the spring-fed Kalama River (elev. 2000 ft) on a sturdy bridge.

The path now turns east, following the churning river through gorgeous old-growth forest. At 0.4 mile, bear left at a junction (elev.

2080 ft) with a bootleg path to Kalama Falls. The falls, which can be legally reached via an old logging road, are located on former commercial timberlands purchased by the Rocky Mountain Elk Foundation in 2013. Continue straight, gradually climbing to cross a couple of side creeks and pass by some big trees. At about 1.9 miles the way switchbacks and ascends more aggressively up the ridge, reaching an old logging road spur.

Continue up the old spur, passing your first views of Goat Mountain and Mount St. Helens. Better views are on the way. At 2.6 miles, cross FR 8122 and soon afterward cross another logging road. Then wander along the crest of what author Craig Romano calls Cinnamon Ridge, straddling the national volcanic monument boundary and oscillating between old cuts and old growth. Enjoy good views along the way, from the nearby Kalama River valley below to Mount Rainier in the distance.

At 4 miles reach an unmarked junction on the ridge's 4000-foot high point. Cinnamon Peak south of here is actually 100 feet lower. The path left leads 0.1 mile to a clearing and logging road. You want to continue right, slowly descending and making three crossings of a logging road.

The way then plods through huckleberries and beargrass, angling up the north side of the ridge to reach, at 4.9 miles, a breathtaking view of Goat Mountain, McBride Lake, Mount St. Helens, and Mount Adams. Continue on, reentering mature forest and, after crossing a creek (elev. 3480 ft), start climbing again. Angling now along the ridge's south side, skirt beneath a knob reaching an elevation of 3650 feet. Take in excellent views of Mount Hood, the Siouxon peaks, and Silver Star Mountain from old clearings along the way.

A hiker enjoys a sweet view of St. Helens from the Cinnamon Trail.

Then descend, reaching a 3300-foot saddle at 6.5 miles and start climbing once more. Traverse attractive old-growth groves and pass more good viewpoints before circling around a small wetland. At 8 miles, reach an opening (elev. 3730 ft) providing an exceptional up-close view of Mount St. Helens above Redrock Pass and of Mount Adams on the eastern horizon.

Then start a short and steep descent through groves of monstrous trees and slopes of slide alder to reach the Toutle Trail at 8.7 miles. Head right 0.1 mile to Redrock

Pass (elev. 3100 ft) and trailhead and your shuttle, if arranged: or consider the loop option below.

EXTENDING YOUR TRIP
For a 14.4-mile loop, return to the Kalama Horse Camp by turning left and following the Toutle Trail (Hike 32) for 5.7 gentle miles.

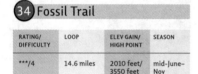

34 Fossil Trail

RATING/ DIFFICULTY	LOOP	ELEV GAIN/ HIGH POINT	SEASON
***/4	14.6 miles	2010 feet/ 3550 feet	mid-June– Nov

Map: Green Trails Mt St. Helens 332S; **Contact:** Mount St. Helens National Volcanic Monument; **Notes:** NW Forest Pass or interagency pass required. Trail open to horses and bicycles; **GPS:** N 46 08.586 W 122 19.437

You're sure to dig up a surprise or two on the Fossil Trail. Follow this lightly traveled path through primeval forest high on Goat Mountain and around sprawling Goat Marsh. Built primarily by the Backcountry Horsemen of Washington, this trail ties together old logging roads and new tread through a seldom-visited corner of the Monument.

GETTING THERE
From Woodland (exit 21 on I-5), follow State Route 503 east just shy of 28 miles before turning left onto Forest Road 81 (turnoff is 1 mile west of Cougar). Follow this good paved road for 8.9 miles to the Kalama Horse Camp. Proceed 0.2 mile to day-use parking area and trailhead (elev. 2040 ft). Privy available.

ON THE TRAIL
Several trails branch out from this campground trailhead. You'll be returning on the Toutle Trail (Hike 32) on your right. Locate the Fossil Trail to the left—take it. Ignoring a side trail back to the campground, soon come to FR 81. Cross the road and continue through old-growth hemlocks, reaching an old road at 0.5 mile. Go left and start climbing, following old skid roads and new trail tread.

Pass through beautiful old-growth noble firs as you make your way up a steep ridge radiating from Goat Mountain. Then travel along the edge of a regenerating clear-cut where excellent views can be had of the steep cliffs on Goat Mountain's south face. A bulky peak, 4965-foot Goat Mountain is a lava dome volcano, formed from the slow extrusion of lava.

At about 2.5 miles, crest the ridge (elev. 3450 ft) and begin traversing northern slopes through cool, dark primeval forest. Cross an avalanche slope providing good views out to the remote Fossil Creek valley and industrial forests of the Toutle Mountain Range. Then continue on an easy grade through ancient forest, crossing a tributary of Fossil Creek and cresting another ridge (elev. 3550 ft).

Now start descending, entering the Monument at 3.4 miles and reaching an avy chute shortly afterwards providing views out to Castle Ridge. After passing a monster cedar, enter an old cut providing a glimpse of St. Helens. At 4.2 miles reach a decommissioned road transformed into trail. Follow it to reach Coldspring Creek (elev. 2875 ft) draining Goat Marsh at 4.6 miles. This is a tricky ford: plans are moving forward to have a bridge constructed here by 2015.

Now, slowly ascend the creek valley

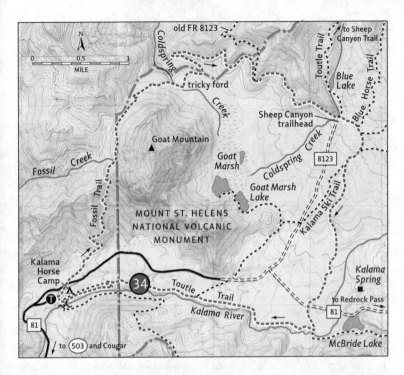

through old forest to reach the abandoned north section of FR 8123 (elev. 3175 ft) at 6.7 miles. The abandoned road can be followed left 4 miles to the old Sheep Canyon trailhead. You want to go right on this former road, gradually climbing to about 3300 feet and passing some excellent views of Goat Mountain and Goat Marsh.

At 7.7 miles, come to the beginning of a large gravelly mudflow. Here Coldspring Creek channels through large heaps of debris that periodically come down from Mount St. Helens. In the late 1990s, FR 8123 was severely damaged here, prompting monument managers to abandon much of the road. Look for cairns across the rocky landscape. Small foot logs across the channels may be in place—otherwise count on wet feet. Enjoy excellent views of Mount St. Helens through ghost forest.

At 7.9 miles reach a junction. Right leads 0.1 mile to the Sheep Canyon/Blue Lake trailhead (elev. 3225 ft) (Hike 35). For the loop, go left, immediately coming to a junction with the Toutle Trail. Then head right through open lodgepole pine forest, reaching a junction with the Blue Horse Trail (elev. 3300 ft) at 8.1 miles.

Turn right coming to the Kalama Ski Trail at 8.4 miles. For a more direct, shorter loop option, the ski trail can be followed by continuing to the right to arrive at the Kalama

The Fossil Trail wraps around Goat Mountain.

Horse Camp in 4.5 miles. For the Fossil Trail loop, continue straight (the path splits en route—either way works, as they soon meet up again), enjoying easy walking through attractive pine and hemlock forests. Reach an intersection with FR 81 (elev. 2700 ft) at 10.7 miles. Cross the road and continue on a revegetating roadbed, reaching the Toutle Trail at 11 miles. Turn right and follow it along the Kalama River (Hike 32) to return to your start at 14.6 miles.

35 Sheep Canyon

RATING/ DIFFICULTY	LOOP	ELEV GAIN/ HIGH POINT	SEASON
*****/4	12.2 miles	2645 feet/ 4725 feet	late June– Nov

Map: Green Trails Mt St. Helens 332S; **Contact:** Mount St. Helens National Volcanic Monument; **Notes:** Trail open to horses and bicycles. Backpacking opportunities; **GPS:** N 46 10.024 W 122 15.712

Hike along and above dramatic canyons scoured deep by lahars from the 1980 eruption. Savor stupendous volcanic views and marvel at a mosaic of majestic alpine wildflowers. Pass a small mudslide-formed emerald pool and wander through some of the oldest trees in the Monument. This lollipop loop at the edge of the blast zone abounds with surprises.

GETTING THERE

From Woodland (exit 21 on I-5), follow State Route 503 east just shy of 28 miles to turn left onto Forest Road 81 (turnoff is 1 mile west of Cougar). Follow this good road (pavement ends at 11.1 miles) for 11.6 miles, continuing straight at a junction onto FR 8123. Continue 1.5 miles to the trailhead (elev. 3200 ft) at road's end.

ON THE TRAIL

The trail starts on the former roadbed of FR 8123 and winds its way through a rocky outwash, compliments of Coldspring Creek's frequent flooding. FR 8123 used to continue another 5.1 miles to end at the Sheep Canyon trailhead. That stretch of road has since been converted to trail and it's best now to reach the Sheep Canyon Trail via the Toutle Trail as described here. Heavy rains in the winter of 1996–97 washed out the road here, and the creek continues to flood seasonally, prompting trailhead and trail alignment adjustments.

After about 0.1 mile, come to a junction. The way straight ahead crosses several channels of Coldspring Creek, continuing to the Fossil Trail (Hike 34) and to the old Sheep Canyon trailhead. Head right and soon come to a junction with the Toutle Trail. (The way right leads 0.2 mile to the Blue Horse Trail and, from there, 3 miles to Redrock Pass.) Head left following the Toutle Trail north. The route parallels

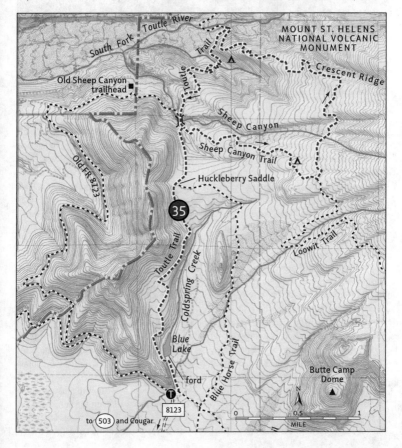

An excellent volcanic view from Crescent Ridge

Coldspring Creek along gravelly and rocky channels, providing glimpses of Mount St. Helens and Goat Mountain.

At 0.5 mile make a tricky crossing of the creek before reaching Blue Lake (elev. 3400 ft). Like June Lake (Hike 40), Blue Lake was formed by past mudflows impounding a creek to form a pool. "Lake" is an exaggeration. Good campsites can be found along this pretty little body of water set in tall timber.

From here the trail enters an exceptional old-growth forest of noble fir, Douglas-fir, and western red cedar, traversing slopes above Coldspring Creek where it flows through a tight canyon. Vine maples adding autumn colors and St. Helens' snowy summit seen through the trees break the monotony of the emerald cloak. At 2.3 miles reach a junction with the Blue Horse Trail (an alternative return) in meadows in 3960-foot Huckleberry Saddle.

Continue straight to soon descend through magnificent ancient forest and reach a junc-tion (elev. 3650 ft) at 3 miles. The trail left leads 0.6 mile to the old Sheep trailhead; and the way straight ahead on the Toutle Trail is the return of your loop to Sheep Canyon. You want to head right on the Sheep Trail. Immediately cross a small creek on a small bridge and begin climbing. The trail winds through old timber and patches of beargrass along the southern edge of the deeply trenched Sheep Canyon. Formed from mudflows triggered by the 1980 eruption, the sandy rocky canyon is quite dramatic with Mount St. Helens hovering above it. A couple of good viewpoints into the canyon are passed along the way.

The forest cover transitions from fir to mountain hemlock to lodgepole pine. At 4.7 miles reach the round-the-mountain Loowit Trail (elev. 4575 ft). Now head left for some of the most sensational scenery in the Monument, including the upper reaches of Sheep Canyon. The way drops about 100 feet to cross the rocky, gravelly, and ash-laden trench. Tread may be poor, making for a tricky crossing.

Once past that challenge, you will enjoy pleasurable hiking across wildflower flats of lupine, paintbrush, aster, gentian, harebell, and many more blossoms. Cross a couple more small trenches and round a grassy ridge punctuated with silver snags. Pass through a pocket of old growth reaching a good but waterless camp (elev. 4725 ft) at 5.8 miles upon cresting Crescent Ridge. A few steps away is a big rock at the edge of the blast zone where the views will blow you away! Look out across the South Fork Toutle River canyon to Castle Ridge, Coldwater Lake and Coldwater Peak, and Mount Rainier in the distance.

Now start descending along Crescent Ridge above the South Fork Toutle River trench that was created by a lahar the morning of the eruption when glaciers and snows above rapidly melted. Traverse patches of huckleberries and toppled timber. The way loses elevation at a good clip. Reenter old growth that was spared from the blast. At 7.6 miles come to a junction with the Toutle Trail on a bluff (elev. 3250 ft) overlooking the South Fork Toutle River.

The Loowit Trail continues right for a very challenging crossing of the South Fork Toutle. You want to go left on a brushy slumping route above the river, rounding the base of Crescent Ridge. At 8 miles cross two unbridged creeks (elev. 3130 ft) where good campsites can be found among beautiful groves of ancient forest. Then begin climbing, switchbacking through some of the biggest and oldest noble firs in the state. Elk are prolific in this area, and you'll see plenty of elk sign.

At 9.2 miles, just after crossing Sheep Creek on a sturdy wooden bridge, come to a junction with the Sheep Canyon Trail coming from the old trailhead. Continue left, soon coming to a familiar junction. Head right here, retracing the first three miles of your hike back to the trailhead.

EXTENDING YOUR TRIP

Several alternative loops can be made. The Blue Horse Trail, which follows old roads and some new tread, can be hiked 3 miles back to the Toutle Trail, where it's a 0.3-mile hike west to the trailhead. You can also follow the Sheep Canyon Trail west from the creek bridge, passing a waterfall and monstrous noble fir and reaching the old trailhead (elev. 3375 ft) in 0.6 mile. From there (don't bother with the old viewpoint spur, which has long been grown over), you can walk 5.1 miles back to the trailhead on decommissioned FR 8123—although this route will be of more interest to mountain bikers. Another loop can be made via the Butte Camp Trail (see Hike 36).

36 Butte Camp

RATING/ DIFFICULTY	ROUNDTRIP	ELEV GAIN/ HIGH POINT	SEASON
****/3	7.6 miles	1650 feet/ 4750 feet	late June– Nov

Map: Green Trails Mt St. Helens 332S; **Contact:** Mount St. Helens National Volcanic Monument; **Notes:** Trail open to bicycles; **GPS:** N 46 08.613 W 122 14.105

Of all the feeder trails leading to the round-the-mountain Loowit Trail, the Butte Camp Trail is one of the nicest. The way winds through old lava flows, old-growth forest groves, and pumiced meadows bursting with wildflowers. Views are

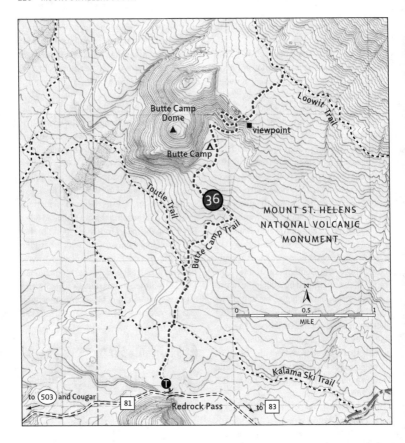

excellent and the trail isn't too crowded or too steep, and there's not too much elevation to gain along the way either.

GETTING THERE

From Woodland (exit 21 on I-5), follow State Route 503 east for 29 miles to Cougar. Continue east on SR 503 (which becomes Forest Road 90) for 7 miles, turning left onto FR 83. Follow this good paved road 3 miles, bearing left onto FR 81. Continue for another 2.9

miles (road becomes gravel at 1.7 miles) to the trailhead at Redrock Pass (elev. 3100 ft). Alternatively, the trail can be reached from FR 81 via Merrill Lake.

ON THE TRAIL

Starting on the Toutle Trail, head north, immediately coming to an old lava flow erupting with beargrass and a killer view of Mount St. Helens. Traverse the flow and enter an open forest of fir and pine. Bear right

Indian paintbrush adds color to St. Helens' gray slopes.

at an old ski trail and then shortly afterward come to a junction with the Kalama Ski Trail (Hike 92) at 0.6 mile.

Gently climbing, reach a junction (elev. 3400 ft) with the Butte Camp Trail at 1.1 miles. The Toutle Trail veers left, heading west 2.1 miles to FR 8123 before heading north to the Toutle River. You want to continue right, steadily ascending through pine groves and huckleberry patches.

At 2.4 miles reach Butte Camp (elev. 4000 ft) tucked in a flat alongside a good creek beneath Butte Camp Dome. The trail now starts climbing in earnest, switchbacking through a gorgeous old-growth grove

of noble firs. The way then breaks out of the forest to traverse open slopes granting excellent views south to Mount Hood, Indian Heaven Wilderness country, Trapper Creek Wilderness peaks, and Silver Star. Wildflowers paint these south-facing slopes in a wide array of colors throughout the summer.

Continue across open ledges, coming to a broad piney bench before hiking up an old lava flow erupting with flowers. Mount St. Helens looms above, creating a gorgeous and imposing backdrop. At 3.8 miles reach the Loowit Trail (elev. 4750 ft). Find yourself a nice rounded rock for sitting and staring at all of the beauty surrounding you. Before the 1980 eruption, this was a popular route for climbers seeking Mount St. Helens' summit. Return the way you came.

EXTENDING YOUR TRIP
Wander left or right as far as you'd like on the Loowit Trail across pumiced meadows rife with flowers and views. Strong hikers can make a 14.7-mile loop by following the Loowit Trail left (north) 3.2 miles to the Sheep Canyon Trail (Hike 35). Then follow this trail 1.6 miles to the Toutle Trail. From there it's 6.1 miles back to your vehicle.

37 Trail of Two Forests

RATING/ DIFFICULTY	LOOP	ELEV GAIN/ HIGH POINT	SEASON
**/1	0.4 mile	50 feet/ 1900 feet	Mar–Dec

Map: Green Trails Mt St. Helens 332S; **Contact:** Mount St. Helens National Volcanic Monument; **Notes:** NW Forest Pass or interagency pass required. Wheelchair accessible. Dogs permitted on-leash; **GPS:** N 46 05.957 W 122 12.776

Cast of a tree from a forest long gone

It was the best of times, it was the worst of times for these two forests. One was engulfed in flames as a lava flow enveloped it, leaving behind empty casts where giants once stood; the other rose like a phoenix from the volcanic ashes to continue the circle of life. Walk across this land of contrasts admiring the volcanic forces that continue to shape this landscape.

GETTING THERE

From Woodland (exit 21 on I-5), follow State Route 503 east for 29 miles to Cougar. Continue east on SR 503 (which becomes Forest Road 90) for 7 miles. Turn left onto FR 83 and follow this good paved road 1.7 miles, turning left again onto paved FR 8303. Continue 0.2 mile to the trailhead (elev. 1900 ft). Privy available.

ON THE TRAIL

Constructed by a consortium of groups, including inmates from the Larch Mountain Corrections Center, this beautifully built trail consists primarily of boardwalks. Hikers and naturalists of all ages will enjoy this interpretive site. And adventurous children and nonclaustrophobic hikers may want to check out The Crawl.

The trail starts out paved before soon coming to a junction. Now, head right on boardwalk across an old lava flow. The way weaves through what are in essence two forests separated by a span of 2000 years. Here old-growth firs and cedars grow among the lava casts (cavities in the ground) of trees incinerated during the ancient lava flow. It's a fascinating landscape of greenery growing among a heavily pockmarked forest floor.

Along the way, the trail reaches The Crawl, where you'll have the option to crawl through casts left by downed trees. Otherwise continue above ground to eventually loop back to your start. It's a short hike, but plan on spending quality time reading the numerous interpretive panels.

38 Ape Cave

RATING/ DIFFICULTY	ROUNDTRIP	ELEV GAIN/ HIGH POINT	SEASON
*****/3	1.5 miles (lower tube) / 2.5 miles (upper tube)	360 feet/ 2450 feet	May–Nov

Maps: Green Trails Mt St. Helens 364S; **Contact:** Gifford Pinchot National Forest, Cowlitz Valley Ranger District; **Notes:** NW Forest Pass or interagency pass required; **GPS:** N 46 06.503 W 122 12.691

Get a spelunker's-eye view of the southern Washington Cascades' volcanic history in the longest continuous lava tube in the United States.

GETTING THERE

From Woodland (exit 21 on I-5), follow State Route 503 east for 29 miles to Cougar. Continue east on SR 503 (which becomes Forest Road 90) for 7 miles, turning left onto FR 83. Follow this good paved road 1.7 miles, turning left onto paved FR 8303. Continue 0.9 mile, turning right into the Ape Cave Interpretive Site and proceeding 0.1 mile to a large parking area and trailhead (elev. 2100 ft). Privy available.

ON THE TRAIL

Not for the claustrophobic, Ape Cave comprises the longest continuous lava tube in North America—almost 2.5 miles. The cave got its name from the Mount St. Helens Apes, a local Boy Scout troop that made frequent explorations in the tube shortly after its discovery around 1947. Of about sixty known lava tubes in the basalt flow south of Mount St. Helens, Ape Cave is the only one that is open to visitors.

Two tubes, lower and upper, form the cave. The upper cave encompasses the upper two-thirds of Ape Cave and is the more difficult of the two. Expect to spend time on hands and knees negotiating chunks of fallen basalt, including several drop-offs up to eight feet high that must be scaled sans rope. Except for the skylight three-quarters of the way in, you'll do it all in the dark. From the skylight exit at the upper end, follow the beargrass-bordered trail 1.25 miles back to the parking lot.

With its sandy floor and shorter length, the lower tube is the better bet for parties

Ape Cave by headlamp

with children or those with mobility issues. No matter which tube you choose, bring a light source for each hiker—back-up batteries wouldn't be a bad idea either. And because the cave stays a consistent, cool, and moist 42 degrees Fahrenheit, stuff a hat and jacket in your pack before you head inside. Finally, bring a sense of respect for

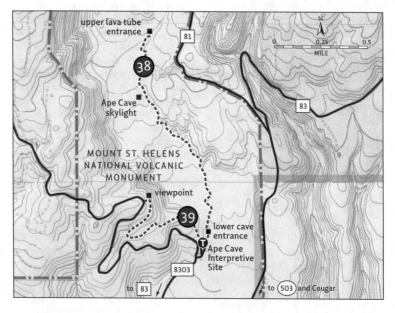

this awe-inspiring place: because of its popularity, Ape Cave welcomes tourists not well-versed in Leave No Trace ethics, and careless visitors have left candy wrappers and cigarette butts on the cave floor. Try to leave the cave in better shape than when you, or the Apes, found it.

39 Volcano Viewpoint Trail

RATING/ DIFFICULTY	ROUNDTRIP	ELEV GAIN/ HIGH POINT	SEASON
**/2	1.6 miles	400 feet/ 2500 feet	May–Nov

Map: Green Trails Mt St. Helens 332S; **Contact:** Mount St. Helens National Volcanic Monument; **Notes:** NW Forest Pass or interagency pass required; **GPS:** N 46 06.498 W 122 12.704

Don't go bananas over the crowds at Ape Cave. Instead, leave them behind by following this new trail through cool forest to a nice little view of Mount St. Helens. Survey Ptarmigan Ridge and the lava flows forming the Ape Cave while enjoying the peace and quiet away from those busy destinations.

GETTING THERE

From Woodland (exit 21 on I-5), follow State Route 503 east for 29 miles to Cougar. Continue east on SR 503 (which becomes FR 90) for 7 miles, turning left onto FR 83. Follow this good paved road 1.7 miles, turning left onto paved FR 8303. Continue 0.9 mile, turning right into the Ape Cave Interpretive Site and proceeding 0.1 mile to large parking area and trailhead (elev. 2100 ft). Privy available.

ON THE TRAIL

Constructed by the Forest Service with the help of volunteers with the Washington Trails Association and the Mount St. Helens Institute, the Volcano Viewpoint Trail was opened to the public in 2014. Locate this new trail to the left of the Ape Cave Visitor Station.

Volcano Viewpoint Trail offers good south slope views of Mount St. Helens.

The way enters thick, cool, second growth and immediately climbs on old skid roads and new tread. The grade is easy enough, and the trail nicely designed, with curves and twists through the old roadbeds. After about a half-mile, the path emerges from dark conifer forest to switchback through a grove of alders and mossy boulders.

Next skirt an old quarry before reaching, at 0.8 mile, a viewpoint at the edge of a hillside. Enjoy the good view of Mount St. Helens' south face, with its old lava flows making up the Worm Flows and the Ape Cave below. Beyond, the trail continues a short distance, ending at FR 8303 (elev. 2500 ft).

The Forest Service hopes in the near future to construct an ADA-accessible path here to the viewpoint. Return the way you came and check out the lava tube cave (Hike 38) if it's not too crowded.

40 June Lake

RATING/ DIFFICULTY	ROUNDTRIP	ELEV GAIN/ HIGH POINT	SEASON
**/1	2.6 miles	415 feet/ 3140 feet	late May– Nov

Map: Green Trails Mt St. Helens 332S; **Contact:** Mount St. Helens National Volcanic Monument; **GPS:** N 46 08.236 W 122 09.411

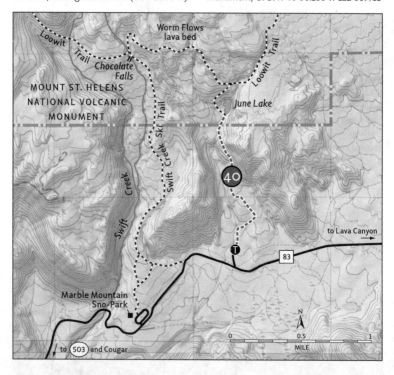

![icons] An easy and pop-
ular hike perfect
*for family picnicking, the lake isn't much,
but the setting is peaceful and geologically
intriguing. Formed by an old mudflow, June
Lake is fed by a 70-foot waterfall tumbling off
basalt cliffs from an old lava flow.*

GETTING THERE
From Woodland (exit 21 on I-5), follow
State Route 503 east for 29 miles to Cougar.
Continue east on SR 503 (which becomes
Forest Road 90) for 7 miles, turning left onto
FR 83. Follow this good paved road 7 miles
to the trailhead turnoff (the first turnoff past
the Marble Mountain Sno-Park). Proceed
0.2 mile to the trailhead (elev. 2725 ft).

ON THE TRAIL
The trail to June Lake is the shortest access
to the Loowit Trail, making it popular with
snowshoers and backpackers. Add scads
of families and hikers from all walks of
life—and you have one popular trail. Follow
the wide and well-groomed trail through
second-growth forest along and above a
cascading creek.

At about 1 mile, Mount St. Helens comes
into view, hovering over a large lava flow.
Soon afterward enter old-growth forest and
cross the now familiar creek on a bridge. A
few steps farther, at 1.3 miles, reach June
Lake (elev. 3140 ft), set in a small bowl at the
toe of an old lava flow. A feeding waterfall
among reflecting snags and old-growth
trees adds charm to the scene. Picnic on the
sandy shore or consider hiking some more.

EXTENDING YOUR TRIP
Follow the trail beyond the lake, steeply
climbing through a grove of big old firs and
hemlocks and reaching the Loowit Trail

A small waterfall feeds June Lake.

(elev. 3410 ft) in 0.3 mile. You can hike right
on the Loowit Trail to the Ape Canyon Trail
for five stunningly scenic miles. Or hike left
on the Loowit Trail across the Worm Flows,
a centuries old large lava flow. The going is
rough over basalt talus and routefinding can
be tough—look for metal poles marking the
way. At 1.3 miles from the junction reach
the Swift Creek Ski Trail (elev. 3680 ft) at a
gully where Swift Creek's silty brown waters
plunge over a ledge forming Chocolate
Falls. Return the way you came or follow the
hikable Swift Creek Ski Trail (see Hike 93)
for 2.6 miles to the Marble Mountain Sno-
Park. Then walk 1 mile on FR 83 back to your
vehicle for a loop.

41 Pine Creek

RATING/ DIFFICULTY	ROUNDTRIP	ELEV GAIN/ HIGH POINT	SEASON
**/1	2.2 miles	200 feet/ 3125 feet	May–Nov

Map: Green Trails Mt St. Helens 332S; **Contact:** Mount St. Helens National Volcanic Monument; **GPS:** N 46 09.285 W 122 06.182

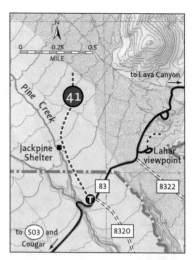

A short and easy hike to a historic shelter, the Pine Creek Trail makes for a nice, quick, quiet getaway. While you won't see much of Pine Creek, you will see plenty of pines—and firs and hemlocks too—in pretty forest at the edge of the Muddy River lahar.

Jackpine Shelter was built during the 1920s.

GETTING THERE

From Woodland (exit 21 on I-5), follow State Route 503 east for 29 miles to Cougar. Continue east on SR 503 (which becomes Forest Road 90) for 7 miles, turning left onto FR 83. Follow this good paved road 10.3 miles to the trailhead (elev. 2925 ft), located on left. No parking at trailhead; it's best to park along dirt FR 8320, located across FR 83 from trailhead.

ON THE TRAIL

Start in old-growth timber following a wide and gentle trail to the east of Pine Creek. Shortly after passing through an old cut, reach the 1920s-built Adirondack-style shelter (elev. 3020 ft) near a dry streambed at 0.4 mile. The historical shelter is in great shape thanks to a group of volunteers who restored it in 1991. It makes a good place to get out of the rain for a lunch break.

While some maps, including this one, label this structure as the Jackpine Shelter, you won't find jack pines growing anywhere near here. Jack pines can be found in the Canadian Shield and a few places in the US upper Midwest and Northeast. The pines growing near the shelter are lodgepole and western white pines, although hemlocks and firs are more prevalent in the surrounding forest.

The trail continues beyond the shelter, but it's not maintained. It can still be followed, though, if you don't mind stepping over a few downed trees. Follow discernible tread through pocket meadows and open forest to where it finally peters out at the edge of the Muddy River lahar (elev. 3125 ft) at 1.1 miles. Catch some limited views of Mount St. Helens and explore around if you care to. Then return the way you came.

EXTENDING YOUR TRIP

There's a short nature trail at the Lahar Viewpoint located off FR 83 (at FR 8322) 0.5 mile east of the trailhead. The shelter also makes a nice winter destination from the June Lake trailhead.

42 Ape Canyon

RATING/ DIFFICULTY	ROUNDTRIP	ELEV GAIN/ HIGH POINT	SEASON
****/3	9.4 miles	1550 feet/ 4175 feet	June–Nov

Map: Green Trails Mt St. Helens 332S; **Contact:** Mount St. Helens National Volcanic Monument; **Notes:** NW Forest Pass or interagency pass required. Trail open to bicycles; **GPS:** N 46 09.924 W 122 05.537

Hike along a ridge cloaked in old-growth timber above the nearly mile-wide Muddy River lahar. Take in excellent views of the south flank of Mount St. Helens, as well as Mount Adams in the distance. And marvel at the stark, tightly notched walls of Ape Canyon.

GETTING THERE

From Woodland (exit 21 on I-5) follow State Route 503 east for 29 miles to Cougar. Continue east on SR 503 (which becomes Forest Road 90) for 7 miles, turning left onto FR 83. Follow this good paved road 11.3 miles, bearing left to the trailhead before the end of the road (and the Lava Canyon trailhead) (elev. 2875 ft). Privy available at nearby Lava Canyon trailhead.

ON THE TRAIL

The way starts in an easy traverse through patches of old forest interspersed with

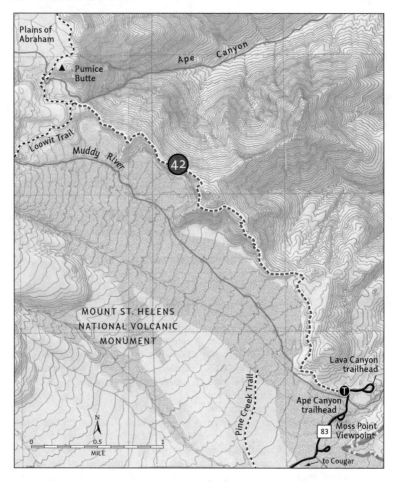

tracts cut pre-eruption. The trail is well groomed and well traveled, particularly by mountain bikers. It's one of their favorite routes in the national volcanic monument, so be aware—and perhaps plan to hike here on a weekday when the traffic is lighter.

The way follows along the edge of a huge lahar (giant mudslide) caused by rapid melting of snow and ice on St. Helens' upper reaches and Shoestring Glacier during the 1980 eruption. A thick slurry of mud and debris rushed down the mountain, scouring a path nearly a mile wide. Today the Muddy River channels through the gray rubble as colonizing plants slowly bring life back to the swath.

Approaching Ape Canyon rim near Loowit Trail junction

After passing several excellent views of the lahar, the trail begins to climb more earnestly, switchbacking up the ridge through a gorgeous old-growth forest of Douglas-fir, silver fir, noble fir, and western hemlock. Enjoy limited views east through a patch of alder before cutting through a swath of maple and reaching a viewpoint (elev. 4050 ft) west of Mount St. Helens at about 3 miles.

The way then descends through a tunnel of ancient trees to a small saddle (elev. 3900 ft), before resuming to climb. After climbing 150 feet, drop 100 feet, and then resume climbing once again. Big trees slowly give way to snags and downed wood as the trail transitions into a landscape altered by the 1980 eruption. Now on a narrower and more open ridge, enjoy excellent views north to Rainier, east to Adams, and St. Helens before you.

Ape Canyon too comes into better view. After rounding a knoll housing seismic measuring equipment, the trail skirts the canyon's rim, coming to a junction (elev. 4175 ft) with the Loowit Trail at 4.7 miles. Here at the scoured canyon's upper reaches, the walls are a mere eight feet apart. It's quite dramatic, especially framing Mount Adams in the distance. The only apes you'll see, however, are your fellow hikers. Supposedly the canyon received its name after a group of apemen threw rocks at a miners' cabin in the canyon back in 1924. The apes were actually young outdoorsmen who were probably unaware of the cabin.

EXTENDING YOUR TRIP

Head right on the Loowit Trail, crossing a couple of gullies to reach a campsite (elev. 4325 ft) at a spring and small waterfall at 0.8 mile. Then continue past Pumice Butte through a spectacular carpet of lupine across the Plains of Abraham for a near-level mile to the Abraham Trail (see Hike 56). Thousands of grasshoppers will accompany you as you enjoy sweeping views of this once lush meadow turned desolate flat and now once again a flowering paradise.

You can also head left on the Loowit Trail for a rougher but less traveled side trip across pumiced slopes offering excellent views south to Mount Hood rising over waves of emerald ridges. Reach a bluff (elev. 4425 ft) above the eroded gully housing Shoestring Creek in 1.4 miles—a good spot to turn around.

43 Lava Canyon

RATING/ DIFFICULTY	ROUNDTRIP	ELEV GAIN/ HIGH POINT	SEASON
****/3	3.9 miles	1085 feet/ 2840 feet	mid-Apr– Nov

Map: Green Trails Mt St. Helens 332S; **Contact:** Mount St. Helens National Volcanic Monument; **Notes:** NW Forest Pass or interagency pass required. Dogs prohibited. Lower section of trail is exposed and uses a ladder: not recommended for children or hikers scared of heights. Trail slippery and potentially dangerous when wet. The upper overlooks are wheelchair accessible; **GPS:** N 46 09.944 W 122 05.294

Hike into a dramatic chasm formed by an ancient lava flow and scoured clean of vegetation by a massive mudflow during the 1980 eruption. Pass by a half dozen waterfalls. Cross a high suspension bridge. Teeter along the edge of steep cliffs and descend into the heart of the chasm on a 30-foot steel ladder. While much of this hike is for the sure-footed only, the upper reaches can be enjoyed by all.

GETTING THERE

From Woodland (exit 21 on I-5), follow State Route 503 east for 29 miles to Cougar. Continue east on SR 503 (which becomes Forest Road 90) for 7 miles, turning left onto FR 83. Follow this good paved road 11.4 miles to its end at the trailhead (elev. 2840 ft). Privy available.

ON THE TRAIL

The trail begins paved, allowing wheelchair access to a couple of overlooks of the canyon. Stop at interpretive plaques along the way for a journey of discovery. Here about 2500 years ago a massive lava flow coursed down the Muddy River valley. The river eventually eroded sections of the flow, creating falls, cliffs, and interesting formations. Then the 1980 eruption triggered a huge lahar that scoured away cloaking vegetation to reveal and further define Lava Canyon.

At 0.4 mile, the pavement ends at a junction near a steel bridge. You'll be returning on the bridge to the right—so continue straight, immediately coming to an overlook of a thundering waterfall. Now hike along the edge of the canyon, admiring roiling waters through polished rock flanked by cliffs of columnar andesite and basalt. Do heed all of the warning signs along the way about staying on the trail. Several hikers have perished here, swept away by the river.

At 0.6 mile, come to another junction (elev. 2600 ft). The way right across an airy suspension bridge is your return route now if you opt to skip the lower reaches of the canyon—or your return route later upon returning to this point from the canyon's lower depths.

A hiker carefully descends on a fixed ladder in the Lava Canyon.

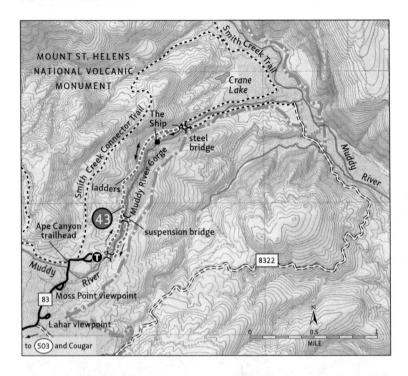

To continue down the canyon, stay left on an exposed path along the canyon wall above a crashing waterfall. A fixed cable provides some stability, but use extreme caution. Quickly reach a ledge above a magnificent 200-foot waterfall. Then continue along exposed cliffs, crossing side creeks before switchbacking through big trees that survived the lahar.

The trail here is blasted into the ledge above more cascades and churning pools. After passing beneath an overhanging ledge, reach the top of a 30-foot steel ladder. Carefully clutch its rungs and work your way down into the belly of the canyon. Pass through a gap and come to a junction (elev.

2050 ft) at 1.4 miles. A must-hike, 0.2-mile side trip leads rightward up steep tread with the help of a small ladder, taking you to the top of The Ship (elev. 2170 ft). From this massive lava outcrop (be careful), gaze upcanyon to waterfalls and columnar cliffs. Then retrace your steps back to the junction and continue right 0.3 mile to a junction on a broad alluvial fan.

The Smith Creek Trail (Hike 44) heads left for its long journey up the lonely Smith Creek valley. Turn right and walk a short distance to a big steel bridge spanning the Muddy River (elev. 1875 ft). The trail continues 1.2 miles to the Smith Creek trailhead, an alternative starting point. This is a good place to turn around and start your return journey back up the canyon (but see Extending Your Trip).

Carefully retrace your way 1.1 miles to the loop junction at the suspension bridge. Now go left, crossing the impressive 125-foot-long bridge high above the churning river. Follow the river along its south bank, traveling on polished ledges and beneath andesite ledges. After climbing a stairway, recross the river on a sturdy steel bridge, coming to a familiar junction at 3.5 miles. Head left on the paved path, returning to the trailhead at 3.9 miles.

EXTENDING YOUR TRIP

Continue 1.2 miles to the Smith Creek trailhead. Or stop at the Lahar Viewpoint (just west of the trailhead) and walk its short 0.2-mile trail for good views of Mount St. Helens, Moss Spring, and the path of the lahar that sculpted Lava Canyon.

44 Smith Creek

RATING/ DIFFICULTY	ROUNDTRIP	ELEV GAIN/ HIGH POINT	SEASON
***/4	13.6 miles	850 feet/ 2000 feet	June–Nov

Map: Green Trails Mt St. Helens 332S; **Contact:** Mount St. Helens National Volcanic Monument; **Notes:** Trail open to bicycles and popular with hunters. Creek fords can be dangerous in high water; **GPS:** N 46 10.871 W 122 03.261

Remnants of an old logging road in the Smith Creek valley

Hikers will find much to their liking on this long valley trail that is also part of a popular mountain-biking circuit. Hike along rushing Smith Creek through a deep valley laid waste by the 1980 eruption, yet graced with old-growth groves that miraculously survived and a spectacular waterfall created by the infamous eruption.

GETTING THERE

From Woodland (exit 21 on I-5), follow State Route 503 east for 29 miles to Cougar. Continue east on SR 503 (which becomes Forest Road 90) for 7 miles, turning left onto FR 83. Follow this good paved road 10.6 miles, turning right (easy to miss) onto gravel FR 8322. Continue 4.8 miles (being sure to bear left at 0.4 mile) to the trailhead (elev. 1700 ft) at road's end.

ON THE TRAIL

The trail used to start by crossing the Muddy River on a bridge, but the river had other plans. The steel supports of the washed-out bridge are still there. You can ford the river if you dare—but not unless you're experienced with river crossings and the river is running low.

Instead, start on the Lava Canyon Trail and head west along bluffs above the Muddy River to another bridge. Enjoy good views across the wide and rocky alluvial plain to Mount St. Helens and Smith Creek Butte. Enter the national volcanic monument and a patch of old growth before dropping down to the river and crossing it on the sturdy steel bridge at about 1.2 miles. Shortly afterward, come to a junction (elev. 1875 ft).

The Lava Canyon Trail continues left up Lava Canyon (see Hike 43). Go right on the Smith Creek Trail, now on the north bank of the Muddy River. At 2.2 miles, come to the old trail access at the former bridge (elev. 1700 ft). Turn left and begin your way through grassy flats and young forest up the Smith Creek valley. At 2.5 miles, come to a junction with an old road-turned-trail, primarily used by mountain bikers, leading 3.3 miles to the Ape Canyon trailhead.

Cross a creek on a big log and continue upstream. At 3.9 miles, reach a beautiful patch of old-growth forest that was shielded from St. Helens' recent blast. The way then follows an old road atop a bluff with good valley views. After a short climb come to a nice campsite (elev. 1900 ft); then leave the road for real trail.

At 4.7 miles, ford Ape Canyon Creek (elev. 1800 ft) which offers glimpses of Mount St. Helens and minimal crossing problems during normal flows. The way then weaves through a jungle of new growth cloaking big, old, toppled trees. At 5.7 miles come to a major tributary of Smith Creek (elev. 1850 ft) that must be forded. It can be tricky and should not be attempted in high water. Look for a spot where it has fanned out and channeled for a shallower ford.

Once across, resume hiking the trail, which now follows an old mudflow dividing Smith Creek and the large tributary. The sides of the flow are steep and eroded, so watch your step. Continue along this narrow divide, eventually coming to an open grassy area (elev. 2000 ft) at 6.8 miles providing a breathtaking view of an amazing waterfall tumbling over 200 feet down steep cliffs on the valley's east wall. Stay awhile before making the long return back.

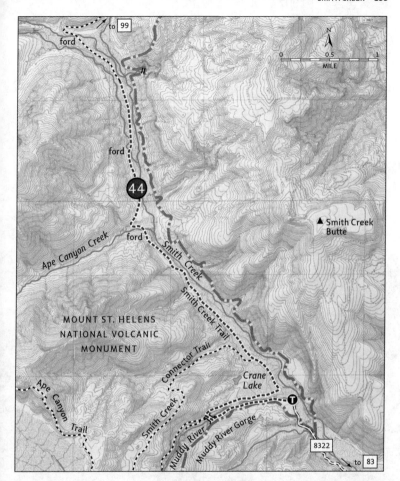

EXTENDING YOUR TRIP

The trail continues upriver, reaching two tricky creek fords and good camps at 7.6 miles before climbing steadily and steeply out of the valley. Views are excellent downvalley and of Mount St. Helens and surrounding mountains as you crest the high ridge (elev. 4300 ft) where the trail at 11.2 miles terminates on FR 99 (trailhead located 14.9 miles from FR 25 junction). If transportation can be arranged, consider doing the entire trail as a downhill one-way.

45 Smith Creek Butte

RATING/ DIFFICULTY	ROUNDTRIP	ELEV GAIN/ HIGH POINT	SEASON
***/5	11.6 miles	2520 feet/ 3800 feet	late July– Oct

Map: Green Trails Mt St. Helens 332S; **Contact:** Mount St. Helens National Volcanic Monument; **Notes:** Hike requires a ford of the Muddy River, which can be dangerous and should only be attempted by experienced hikers and never during periods of high water flow. Trail is popular with hunters in hunting season; **GPS:** N 46 10.718 W 122 03.072

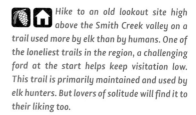 *Hike to an old lookout site high above the Smith Creek valley on a trail used more by elk than by humans. One of the loneliest trails in the region, a challenging ford at the start helps keep visitation low. This trail is primarily maintained and used by elk hunters. But lovers of solitude will find it to their liking too.*

GETTING THERE

From Woodland (exit 21 on I-5), follow State Route 503 east for 29 miles to Cougar. Continue east on SR 503 (which becomes Forest Road 90) for 7 miles, turning left onto FR 83. Follow this good paved road 10.6 miles, turning right (easy to miss) onto gravel

Co-author Craig Romano carefully fords the Muddy River at hike's start. (Photo by Jay Thompson)

FR 8322. Continue 4.5 miles (being sure to bear left at 0.4 mile), turning right on a spur road (just after a small bridge and 0.3 mile before Smith Creek trailhead). Drive a few hundred yards and park—this is the trailhead (elev. 1600 ft).

ON THE TRAIL

Walk out onto the Muddy River's wide gravelly alluvial fan. Then walk downriver for about 0.6 mile looking for a safe place to ford the river (preferably where the river has fanned and channeled). You are aiming for a grassy open area south of the steep bluffs cradling a cascade. If the river looks intimidating or you can't find a safe area to ford—turn around and hike the nearby Smith Creek Trail (Hike 44) instead.

Once across, locate an old road track (elev. 1550 ft) at 0.7 mile leaving the grassy area east for the forest. Your way climbs gently under an alder tunnel; look left for a bona fide trail (elev. 1650 ft) leading north at 1.1 miles. Take it and start climbing, traversing steep slopes above Clearwater Creek. The well-built trail crosses small creeks and winds through a deciduous forest with the feel of the Appalachians.

At 2.2 miles, come to an old logging road (elev. 2300 ft). Go right on it, enjoying pleasant walking through old growth and old cuts. At 3.6 miles, at the end of an old cut (elev. 2850 ft), locate light tread veering left into old forest. (If you miss this junction, continue on the old road another 0.7 mile to a junction with another old road. Turn left here and immediately pick up the trail again.)

Now, following this all but forgotten (but still decipherable) trail, hike through old forest and come to another old road (elev. 3150 ft) at 4.3 miles. Cross it and continue on light but good tread through attractive old

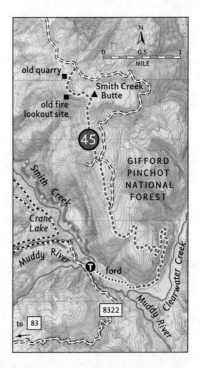

hemlock groves. Look for elk sign in the open forest. The way passes a seasonal creek before cresting wooded Smith Creek Butte (elev. 3790 ft) at 5.3 miles. The trail continues and so should you. Descend 100 feet to a small saddle and then climb again along a narrow ridge draped with old growth.

Pass an anvil-like rock offering a limited but excellent view of Mount St. Helens (use extreme caution here) before reaching the old fire lookout site (elev. 3800 ft) at 5.7 miles. Removed in 1968, the foundation is cloaked in jungle-like greenery. Continue another 0.1 mile on brushy trail, which emerges at the edge of a gravel quarry (elev. 3780 ft). It's anticlimactic, but the quarry does allow excellent views north of the Mount Margaret peaks.

The road leading to this gravel pit from the north is gated, so there is no need to worry about folks driving to this spot you worked hard to reach. Return the way you came, remembering the refreshing ford awaiting you at the end.

Opposite: Boot and Obscurity lakes from Mount Whittier

mount st. helens east

onsisting of lands within and along the periphery of the blast zone, the eastern reaches of the Mount St. Helens National Volcanic Monument contain some of the region's most dramatic scenery. Reached by winding paved (but deteriorating) Forest Service roads, this area is far from population centers and cannot be easily reached from the Monument's more popular southern and western regions. Some of the area's highest peaks and most challenging trails can be found here, offering hikers unsurpassed backcountry experiences. Still, novice hikers and those intent on gentler excursions will find plenty of nature trails and moderate backcountry routes here as well.

46 Strawberry Mountain

RATING/ DIFFICULTY	ROUNDTRIP	ELEV GAIN/ HIGH POINT	SEASON
*****/3	8.8 miles	1700 feet/ 5500 feet	July–Oct

Map: Green Trails Mt St. Helens 332S; **Contact:** Gifford Pinchot National Forest, Cowlitz Valley Ranger District; **Notes:** FR 2516 is brushy, rutted, and rough in spots—high clearance vehicle recommended. Berries in season; **GPS:** N 46 20.653 W 122 02.297

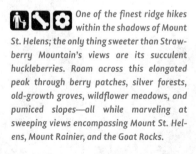 *One of the finest ridge hikes within the shadows of Mount St. Helens; the only thing sweeter than Strawberry Mountain's views are its succulent huckleberries. Roam across this elongated peak through berry patches, silver forests, old-growth groves, wildflower meadows, and pumiced slopes—all while marveling at sweeping views encompassing Mount St. Helens, Mount Rainier, and the Goat Rocks.*

GETTING THERE

From Randle, follow State Route 131 south for 2 miles to where it becomes Forest Road 25. Continue for 16 miles and turn right onto FR 2516. (From Woodland, exit 21 on I-5, follow SR 503 east for 29 miles to Cougar. Continue east on SR 503 [which becomes FR 90] for 18.5 miles, turning left onto FR 25. Continue 26.7 miles north to FR 2516 [near Milepost 17 just past the junction with FR 99].) Follow FR 2516 for 5.9 rough miles to the trailhead (elev. 4850 ft).

ON THE TRAIL

The Strawberry Mountain Trail runs 10 miles along the lofty elongated peak of the same name. FR 2516 bisects it, providing high elevation midtrail access. But despite this easy access to some of the most spectacular alpine terrain in the area, the trail is lightly used. A handful of hunters and commercial berry pickers use the trail in autumn. The latter, while permitted, are largely unsupervised and unversed in Leave No Trace ethics. Beware of the trash and human excrement they leave behind. That's the bad news. The good news is that they usually use only the first mile of trail, so you still should have most of this trail to yourself even during the harvest.

Follow the trail north and immediately climb a forested ridge (elev. 5100 ft). At 0.6 mile, reach the edge of an old clearcut sporting productive berry patches. The way gets a little confusing here due to intersections with old skid roads. Turn right at the first one you encounter—then soon afterward turn left onto another old road. Walk a short distance to a small saddle (elev. 5000 ft) and, at 0.8 mile, pick up the trail again leading right.

A hiker surveys Strawberry Mountain's long southern ridge from below the summit.

Now gently climbing, the trail traverses a slope (elev. 5100 ft) carpeted in berries and punctuated by silver snags and stumps. Enjoy expansive views westward to the Mount Margaret Backcountry, Green River valley, and Goat and Tumwater mountains. Drop 200 feet into a saddle (elev. 4900 ft), coming to a junction at 1.5 miles with the eastern terminus of the Green River Trail. Used primarily by horse packers, this trail descends open slopes and old cuts, reaching FR 26 in 3 miles. You want to continue straight.

The trail now climbs steeply through an open meadow of pumice and wildflowers beneath a big block of ledge. The scenery is stunning and the views breathtaking: east to Mount Adams, north to Mount Rainier, west to Mounts Whittier and Margaret, and south

to Mounts Hood and Jefferson. Eventually you will emerge upon the crest of this high divide between the Quartz and Iron Creek drainages, where you can soak up more scenery.

The way dips slightly before topping a 5170-foot knoll then dropping to a 5070-foot saddle shaded in old-growth greenery. Now start climbing again to round a small knoll before, at 3.1 miles, reaching the edge of a meadow (elev. 5300 ft). If you're intent on bagging the 5720-foot summit of Strawberry Mountain, leave the trail here and steeply climb 0.3 mile through meadows to the mostly forested summit block. Views are better along the ridge.

The trail continues, skirting below the summit before reaching a 5500-foot forested shoulder. From here your route follows

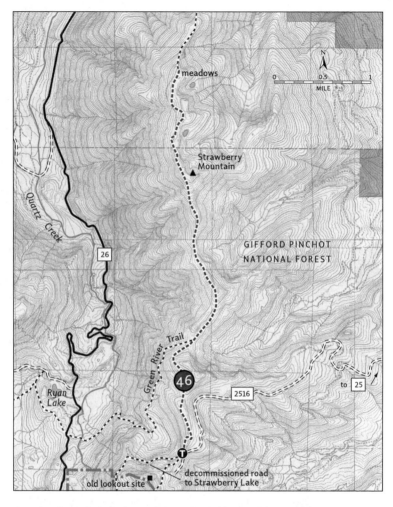

the ridge, descending 100 feet and passing high above a small pond cradled by towering timber. Keep hiking through meadows to a 5500-foot knoll before once again descending. At 4.4 miles reach a small stretch of open ridge (elev. 5350 ft) high above another hidden little lake. Beyond this spot the trail reenters forest and rapidly descends, making this grassy spot with good views over the Cowlitz Valley to Mount Rainier a fortuitous spot to turn around. Enjoy the great scenery again on your return.

EXTENDING YOUR TRIP

With a shuttle, you can continue north and downhill 2.6 miles to the trail's northern terminus on a private logging road. From here walk the road 1.9 miles to its junction with FR 26 (located 3.4 miles from the junction with FR 25).

From the trailhead on FR 2516, you can hike south 0.8 mile for a shorter route to the old Strawberry Mountain Lookout site (Hike 47). Or you can follow the decommissioned road west for about 2 miles to a broad flat frequented by elk near Strawberry Lake.

47 Strawberry Mountain Lookout Site

RATING/ DIFFICULTY	ROUNDTRIP	ELEV GAIN/ HIGH POINT	SEASON
****/3	4.8 miles	1400 feet/ 5464 feet	July–Oct

Map: Green Trails Mt St. Helens 332S; **Contact:** Mount St. Helens National Volcanic Monument; **Notes:** NW Forest Pass or interagency pass required; **GPS:** N 46 18.848 W 122 02.150

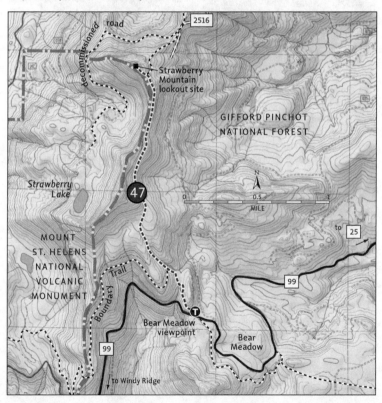

Excellent view of the Green River valley from the old Strawberry Mountain lookout site

🦴🍃🏠❌ Hike a little-used trail through primeval forest at the edge of the blast zone. Then emerge upon a narrow ridge and survey the cataclysmic forces of Mount St. Helens below you. The views of the Mount Margaret Backcountry and the Green River valley are grand from the old lookout site—so too, the views of Strawberry Lake twinkling below and usually hosting a herd of elk.

GETTING THERE

From Woodland (exit 21 on I-5), follow State Route 503 east for 29 miles to Cougar. Continue east on SR 503 (which becomes Forest Road 90) for 18.5 miles, turning left onto FR 25. Follow this good paved road 25 miles north to FR 99. (From Randle, follow SR 131 south for 2 miles to where it becomes FR 25, continuing for 17.7 miles and turning right onto FR 99.) Continue on paved FR 99 for 4.6 miles to the trailhead (elev. 4100 ft) at Bear Meadow viewpoint. Privy available.

ON THE TRAIL

Watching for traffic, carefully cross FR 99 and start hiking west on Boundary Trail No. 1. Climbing, soon come to a view of Mount St. Helens far better than the one from Bear Meadow, which is growing in. The trail steepens, heading up a dark draw in deep timber to reach a junction (elev. 4375 ft) at 0.5 mile. The Boundary Trail continues left. You want to head right on the lightly used Strawberry Mountain Trail.

The trail receives little maintenance and is in danger of being abandoned: expect to climb over a few blowdowns along the way. But while the trail is slumping and brushy in spots too, it is not difficult to follow. Paralleling a creek, the way climbs steeply through beautiful old-growth forest. A few windows in the woods provide good views out to Mounts Adams and Rainier.

The trail works its way up a long ridge—which acts as the Monument boundary and the demarcation between a blasted and devastated forest and a lush, primeval one. At 1.9 miles, crest the ridge (elev. 5100 ft) and teeter on the edge of the blast zone. The stumps below were left not from the eruption but the subsequent logging operation to salvage the merchantable downed timber. Just the same, the view is awesome—but it gets better.

Now hike along the ridge crest, marveling at views east and west. At 2.2 miles, just after reaching a small knoll (elev. 5325 ft), come to a junction in a small saddle (elev. 5295 ft). To the right, the Strawberry Mountain Trail descends into old-growth timber to reach FR 2516 (Hike 46) in 0.6 mile.

Head left instead, immediately coming to an old logging road and a couple of rusting fuel tanks. Cross the road and climb a steep, pumiced slope to arrive at the lookout site (elev. 5464 ft) at 2.4 miles. Not much remains of the tower that stood watch here from 1931 to 1967. But there is plenty to still watch over. Take in the 360-degree views: to the east, Mount Adams and the Goat Rocks; to the west, Goat and Tumwater mountains; to the north, the long lofty spine of Strawberry Mountain; and to the south, Mount St. Helens rising above a blasted and recovering landscape. Return the way you came after you have thoroughly examined the landscapes before you.

EXTENDING YOUR TRIP

Arrange a shuttle so you can hike the entire Strawberry Mountain Trail (Hike 46) one-way.

48 Meta Lake

RATING/ DIFFICULTY	ROUNDTRIP	ELEV GAIN/ HIGH POINT	SEASON
***/1	0.6 mile	minimal/ 3625 feet	mid-June–Nov

Map: Green Trails Mt St. Helens 332S; **Contact:** Mount St. Helens National Volcanic Monument; **Notes:** NW Forest Pass or interagency pass required. Wheelchair accessible; **GPS:** N 46 17.758 W 122 04.691

A platform allows visitors to look for aquatic life in Meta Lake.

Walk a paved path to an observation deck at the edge of little Meta Lake. Learn how certain life forms survived the 1980 eruption and how this small body of water helped the regeneration of life within the blast zone. Then walk another paved path to a different outcome—a demolished car belonging to three people who perished from the forces of Mount St. Helens.

GETTING THERE

From Randle, follow State Route 131 south for 2 miles to where it becomes Forest Road 25, continuing for 17.7 miles and turning right onto FR 99. (From Woodland, exit 21 on I-5, follow SR 503 east for 29 miles to Cougar.

Continue east on SR 503—which becomes FR 90—for 18.5 miles, turning left onto FR 25. Follow this good paved road 25 miles north to FR 99.) Now continue west on paved FR 99 for 9.2 miles (just past the junction with FR 26) to the Meta Lake Interpretive Site (elev. 3625 ft).

ON THE TRAIL

Two paved paths diverge from the parking lot. Take the left one, bur be careful not to step on the myriad newts and toads that often crawl and hop all over the trail. The toads are prolific—and they are a big part of the Meta Lake story. When Mount St. Helens erupted on May 18, 1980, the lake

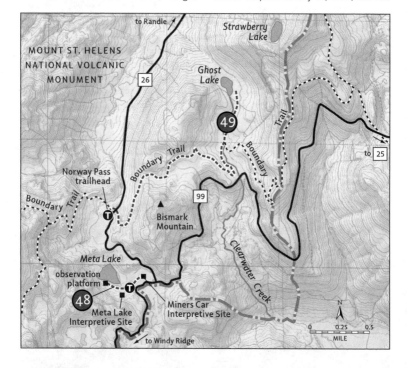

lay beneath eight feet of snow. The snow-pack protected small plants and hibernating animals from the lateral blast. Come summer, thanks to warming waters and an algae bloom, thousands of western toads emerged from the lake, providing food for predators and hastening the repopulation of wildlife within the blast zone.

At 0.15 mile reach a viewing platform over the lake. Stay for a while, seeing how many different critters you can identify. Then retrace your steps back to the parking lot and continue on the paved path heading east. Cross a creek and in 0.15 mile arrive at the Miners Car Interpretive Site. Here a mangled car stands testament to the forces of the eruption when a 300 mile-per-hour lateral blast of gas, ash, and rock demolished the surrounding forest. The car's original three occupants were at a nearby mining claim at the time of the eruption. They, along with fifty-four other folks (many believing they were a safe distance away from the volcano), perished during the powerful eruption. Return the way you came, reflecting upon nature's nurturing and destructive ways.

Wander along a rarely hiked section of the Boundary Trail to a small hidden lake within the blast zone. Meander through blown-down forest, regenerating forest, and patches of forest untouched by the blast thanks to shielding ridges. Birds, amphibians, and mammals small and large are prolific around the lake—and chances are good of seeing them too, as few people mosey this way.

GETTING THERE

From Randle and US Highway 12, follow State Route 131 south for 2 miles to where it becomes Forest Road 25, continuing 17.7 miles to turn right onto FR 99. (From Woodland, exit 21 on I-5, follow SR 503 east

49 Ghost Lake

RATING/ DIFFICULTY	ROUNDTRIP	ELEV GAIN/ HIGH POINT	SEASON
***/2	5.2 miles	640 feet/ 4000 feet	mid-June– Nov

Map: Green Trails Mt St. Helens 332S; **Contact:** Mount St. Helens National Volcanic Monument; **Notes:** NW Forest Pass or interagency pass required. Bikes and horses also allowed; **GPS:** N 46 18.308 W 122 04.956

New forest adds life to Ghost Lake.

for 29 miles to Cougar. Continue east on SR 503—which becomes FR 90—for 18.5 miles, turning left onto FR 25. Follow this good paved road 25 miles north to FR 99.) Now continue west on paved FR 99 for 9 miles, turning right onto FR 26. Reach the trailhead (elev. 3680 ft) on the left after 1 mile. Privy available.

ON THE TRAIL

From the large parking area, follow a well-beaten trail and immediately come to a junction with the Boundary Trail. Left leads to Norway Pass and Mount Margaret (Hike 50), and that's where almost everyone starting from this trailhead will be going. You want to go right on the Boundary Trail on the path less taken, soon coming to FR 26.

Carefully cross the road and resume hiking on Boundary Trail No. 1 through the blast zone. What boundary, you may be thinking. It was the boundary between the Mount Rainier and Columbia National Forests of the time, and this trail ran along it. In 1933, the Rainier National Forest was dissolved, its lands administered by the Columbia and two other national forests. In 1949 the Columbia was named the Gifford Pinchot National Forest in honor of the first chief of the US Forest Service.

Hike through shoulder-high fireweed and huckleberry bushes. Flowers brighten the surrounding slopes throughout the summer. Views are good north to Goat Mountain. At 0.9 mile, pass through a gap (elev. 4000 ft) between Bismarck Mountain and an unnamed peak to the north. Catch a glimpse of Mount St. Helens and Mount Adams before descending to a broad bench frequented by elk.

Continue gently descending, entering a pocket of old-growth forest protected from

the winds and gasses of Mount St. Helens' 1980 eruption by surrounding ridges. At 1.9 miles, come to a collapsed bridge over Clearwater Creek (and a potentially feet-wetting crossing) just before a junction (elev. 3730 ft).

Now, turn left to follow the gently flowing creek, passing beaver dams and grassy wetland meadows. At 2.6 miles, after crossing a pumice patch and crashing through an alder thicket, reach little Ghost Lake (elev. 3780 ft). Despite its name, this little body of water is quite lively. Sit for a while, watching for wildlife. Return the way you came when ready to head back.

EXTENDING YOUR TRIP

If you can arrange a shuttle, continue hiking from the lake spur junction left (east) on the Boundary Trail. You'll pass a short-cut spur to FR 99 before traversing open slopes that grant excellent views. After climbing 700 feet, enter deep old-growth forest harboring a couple of pretty cascades before reaching the Bear Meadow trailhead at 3.6 miles.

50 Norway Pass— Mount Margaret

RATING/ DIFFICULTY	ROUNDTRIP	ELEV GAIN/ HIGH POINT	SEASON
*****/4	11.4 miles	2375 feet/ 5858 feet	mid-July– Oct

Map: Green Trails Mt St. Helens 332S; **Contact:** Mount St. Helens National Volcanic Monument; **Notes:** NW Forest Pass or interagency pass required. Dogs prohibited. Water scarce after snowmelt. Camping allowed only at designated sites and by permit (see Introduction); **GPS:** N 46 18.308 W 122 04.956

⚙ *Hike to a high summit in the heart of the blast zone. Marvel at horizon-sweeping views and slopes flush with dazzling wildflowers. From Norway Pass cherish a classic view of Spirit Lake sparkling below the mountain— St. Helens—that greatly altered it. And from Mount Margaret, savor monumental views of the volcanic monument and of other volcanoes north, south, and east.*

GETTING THERE

From Randle, follow State Route 131 south for 2 miles to where it becomes Forest Road 25, continuing for 17.7 miles and turning right onto FR 99. (From Woodland, exit 21 on I-5, follow SR 503 east for 29 miles to Cougar. Continue east on SR 503—which becomes FR 90—for 18.5 miles, turning left onto FR 25. Follow this good paved road 25 miles north to FR 99.) Now continue west on paved FR 99 for 9 miles, turning right onto FR 26. Reach trailhead (elev. 3680 ft) on left after 1 mile. Privy and water available.

ON THE TRAIL

Your route starts on the Boundary Trail, which marks the old boundary between what were once the Columbia and Rainier National Forests, since amalgamated into the Gifford Pinchot National Forest. Hike west up slopes laid waste on May 18, 1980. Nature has been doing a pretty good job re-greening and repopulating the area since. Mountain ashes, huckleberry bushes, and firs carpet the formerly ravaged landscape. And throughout the summer scores of wildflower species paint the pumiced slopes in an array of dazzling colors. These hills are alive with critters too—from colonies of ground squirrels to herds of elk.

The trail gently climbs—views growing with every step. Watch for Meta Lake spar-

kling below and Mount Adams shining on the eastern horizon. At 1.2 miles, reach a junction (elev. 4300 ft) with the Independence Ridge Trail (Hike 53). Bend right to round Independence Ridge and take in views north to Goat and Strawberry mountains. Descend slightly into a gully, and then resume gentle climbing. At 2.2 miles reach the Independence Pass Trail (Hike 53) at Norway Pass (elev. 4500 ft). Get your camera out. The view here across waterlogged (literally) Spirit Lake to Mount St. Helens is a classic and one of the most photographed scenes within the national volcanic monument.

The hike to this point has been fairly easy and good for kids. Things radically change beyond. Continue on the Boundary Trail, crossing a section blasted into ledge then make a long sweeping traverse up open slopes. The views are breathtaking and the wildflowers copious. Switch back and reach a junction (elev. 4875 ft) with the Lakes Trail (see Hike 51) at 3.1 miles.

Continue straight ahead, soon cresting a high ridge with glorious views down to Grizzly Lake and out to volcano-blasted Mount Whittier, emerald-cloaked Tumwater Mountain, and glacier-capped Mount Rainier. At 3.7 miles, the way traverses steep slopes that can be dangerous when covered in snow. The way then crests another ridge, granting views across a verdant basin to Mount Margaret.

Now enjoy easy walking across slopes once gray and barren, now sporting resplendent wildflower meadows. At 4.4 miles reach the Mount Margaret Backcountry camp (elev. 5435 ft), where a creek usually runs year-round for water replenishment.

Continue across open slopes, rounding a high basin. Views are breathtaking, including down to Boot and Obscurity lakes. After

Mount Rainier seen from Mount Margaret

reaching an elevation of 5675 feet, the way slopes downward, coming to a junction (elev. 5575 ft) with the Mount Whittier Trail (Hike 52) in a broad gap at 4.9 miles. From here, follow the trail across lingering (and potentially dangerous) snowfields beneath a high rocky pinnacle. Scan the basin below for elk. Look back through the gap at intimidating Mount Whittier.

Climb 75 feet—then lose them again dropping to a small saddle. Climb once more, reaching a junction (elev. 5690 ft) on Mount Margaret's shoulder at 5.6 miles. Head right, up meadow and pumice, on the short 0.1-mile spur trail to Mount Margaret's 5858-foot summit. Now take a break and enjoy the views. They're varied and extensive, from Rainier to Jefferson and the Dark Divide to the Willapa Hills. The view of Spirit Lake below St. Helens is simply sublime.

EXTENDING YOUR TRIP

Sure-footed hikers can make a challenging and exhilarating loop via the Lakes and Mount Whittier Trails (see Hikes 51 and 52).

51 Mount Margaret Backcountry Lakes

RATING/ DIFFICULTY	ROUNDTRIP	ELEV GAIN/ HIGH POINT	SEASON
****/5	15 miles	3350 feet/ 5150 feet	mid-July– Oct

Map: Green Trails Mt St. Helens 332S; **Contact:** Mount St. Helens National Volcanic Monument; **Notes:** NW Forest Pass or interagency pass required. Dogs prohibited. Camping allowed only at designated sites and by permit (see Introduction); **GPS:** N 46 18.308 W 122 04.956

Travel through the 1980 blast zone to a series of alpine lakes tucked within rugged ridges. Despite taking a full hit from Mount St. Helens' famous eruption that leveled ancient forests and blanketed the region in pumice, the Mount Margaret Backcountry is no barren wasteland. Nature has been busy recolonizing the area. Wildlife and wildflowers are prolific. The topography is harsh and the trail is tough, with tread that frequently washes out. But this rugged landscape is also simply awe-inspiring.

GETTING THERE

From Randle, follow State Route 131 south for 2 miles to where it becomes Forest Road 25, continuing for 17.7 miles and turning right onto FR 99. (From Woodland, exit 21 on I-5, follow SR 503 east for 29 miles to Cougar. Continue east on SR 503—which becomes FR 90—for 18.5 miles, turning left onto FR 25. Follow this good paved road 25 miles north to FR 99.) Now continue west on paved FR 99 for 9 miles, turning right onto FR 26. Reach trailhead (elev. 3680 ft) on left after 1 mile. Privy and water available.

ON THE TRAIL

Follow the Boundary Trail west up slopes laid waste on May 18, 1980. Nature has been doing a good job regreening and repopulating the area since. Wildflowers paint the pumiced slopes in an array of dazzling colors, and colonies of ground squirrels and herds of elk browse among the blossoms.

The trail climbs gently—views growing with every step. At 1.2 miles reach a junction (elev. 4300 ft) with the Independence Ridge Trail (Hike 53). Bend right to round Independence Ridge and then descend slightly into a gully. Resume gentle climbing, coming to the

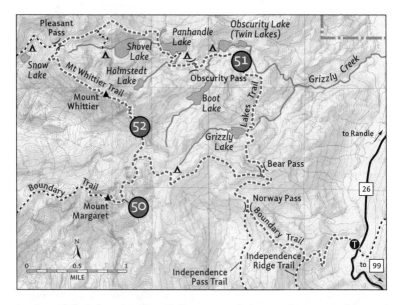

junction with the Independence Pass Trail at Norway Pass (elev. 4500 ft) at 2.2 miles.

Continue on the Boundary Trail, making a long, sweeping traverse up open slopes. The views are breathtaking and the wildflowers copious. Switch back and reach a junction (elev. 4875 ft) at 3.1 miles. Straight goes to Mount Margaret (Hike 50). You want to go right on the Lakes Trail, your portal into the Mount Margaret Backcountry. Now climb 0.1 mile to Bear Pass (elev. 4950 ft), where stunning views of Mounts Adams, Rainier, and St. Helens await you.

Begin a steep (and if snow is present, potentially treacherous) descent, losing 650 feet in less than 1 mile to arrive at Grizzly Lake (elev. 4300 ft). No grizzlies, but the surroundings are *bare*. Rock hop across Grizzly Creek and follow the trail through a tight draw and across slopes prone to washing out. Drop another 100 feet before beginning

a gradual ascent into a waterfall-graced basin. At 5.4 miles, reach Obscurity Lake (also known as Twin Lakes, elev. 4350 ft), with its campsite and composting toilet.

Cross a trout-filled creek on a log bridge and, after passing a waterfall emanating from hidden Boot Lake, climb to 4675-foot Obscurity Pass. Now descend, arriving at a junction (elev. 4550 ft) on a bench above beautiful Panhandle Lake at 6.3 miles. To reach the lake (elev. 4500 ft), head right 0.2 mile to its attractive lakeside campsite. For most day hikers, this is a good spot to turn around.

Strong hikers can continue on the Lakes Trail, skirting a cliff above Panhandle Lake where you can see the panhandle. Now, cross a creek and steeply ascend an open ridge granting superb views of the Green River valley, Goat Mountain, and Mount Rainier in the distance. Emerge on a rocky crest high above Shovel Lake, where you can dig into some awesome views of that lake twinkling beneath austere Mount Whittier. The way continues climbing, traversing steep slopes that often harbor dangerous snowfields well into summer. At 7.5 miles, reach a junction with the Shovel Lake Trail (elev. 5150 ft). This is a great spot to call it a hike. Have your lunch and enjoy the views!

EXTENDING YOUR TRIP

Very strong day hikers and backpackers can contemplate other options. If the Shovel Lake campsite is your objective, follow the recently rebuilt Shovel Lake Trail. The 0.5-mile trail loses 350 feet to land you at a secluded site on a bench high above the lake. Or, you can continue west on the Lakes Trail 0.4 mile to 5200-foot Pleasant Pass,

Panhandle Lake

and from here proceed another 0.5 mile to Snow Lake with its backcountry campsite. If transportation can be arranged, lengthen your trip another 8 miles, hiking to the Coldwater Lake trailhead (see Hike 86).

You can also follow the Mount Whittier Trail back to the Boundary Trail for a challenging and heart pounding 14.9-mile loop recommended only to the most sure-footed hikers comfortable with extreme exposure (Hike 52).

52 Mount Whittier

RATING/DIFFICULTY	LOOP	ELEV GAIN/HIGH POINT	SEASON
*****/5	14.9 miles	3450 feet/5883 feet	late July–Oct

Map: Green Trails Mt St. Helens 332S; **Contact:** Mount St. Helens National Volcanic Monument; **Notes:** NW Forest Pass or interagency pass required. Dogs prohibited; **Warning:** The 2.3-mile Mount Whittier Trail is one of the most difficult, potentially dangerous trails in the Cascade Mountains. Much of the way is more of a route than a trail, traversing a knife-edge ridge with extreme exposure to sheer drop-offs of several hundred feet. This trail should only be attempted by confident scramblers who are comfortable with exposure. The trail should be avoided when snow covered and in inclement weather. Heavy or large backpacks should be avoided too while hiking this trail, so that hikers can better maintain their balance and keep their footing; **GPS:** N 46 18.308 W 122 04.956

One of the most challenging, invigorating, and exciting trails in the Pacific Northwest, Mount Whittier is not for the faint of heart. Walk along knife-edges and narrow ledges teetering high above narrow valleys. Negotiate narrow passages blasted into sheer cliffs while ducking below towering rock faces. Go where only mountain goats (and intrepid hikers) dare go. And marvel at sparkling lakes below and craggy-volcano-blasted peaks all around you.

GETTING THERE
From Randle, follow State Route 131 south for 2 miles to where it becomes Forest Road 25, continuing for 17.7 miles and turning right onto FR 99. (From Woodland, exit 21 on I-5, follow SR 503 east for 29 miles to Cougar. Continue east on SR 503—which becomes FR 90—for 18.5 miles, turning left onto FR 25. Follow this good paved road 25 miles north to FR 99.) Now continue west on paved FR 99 for 9 miles, turning right onto FR 26. Reach trailhead (elev. 3680 ft) on left after 1 mile. Privy and water available.

ON THE TRAIL
The Mount Whittier Trail is best done as a loop using the Lakes and Boundary Trails. It's also best done counter-clockwise so that upon reaching the summit, you've got generally a downhill route back to the trailhead. Strong day hikers should have little trouble completing the route. If you want to do this hike as a backpacking loop, note that a large backpack may be cumbersome along this ridge, as you must use your hands in many spots. Also note that camping is only allowed in designated sites and with reserved permits.

Start your hike by following the description in Hike 51 (Mount Margaret Backcountry Lakes) to the Shovel Lake Trail junction. Then continue an easy 0.4 mile on the Lakes Trail, reaching Pleasant Pass (elev. 5200 ft)

A hiker carefully negotiates a knife-edge section of trail.

and the junction with the Mount Whittier Trail at 7.9 miles.

Now prepare for one of the most spectacular and stimulating, and perhaps the most intimidating, 2 miles of trail anywhere. Count on taking a couple of hours to complete it.

Heading south from the pass, the trail immediately climbs, cutting through a grove of firs. Bypassing a steep slope, the way then follows a recent reroute up a somewhat-less-but-still-steep slope which come August is awash in purple thanks to a profusion of lupine. Now on the bulky mass of Mount Whittier, several false summits await before you reach the high point.

The views are already spectacular. Gaze across the blast zone, a mixture of silver snags and fallen logs being rapidly overtaken by feisty new greenery. Coldwater Lake sparkles in the west, Shovel Lake twinkles in the east. Mount Rainier floats to the right of Mount Venus. At 8.5 miles, crest a 5775-foot false summit from which you can see Whittier's true summit straight ahead. Then begin gingerly negotiating a knife-edge. Slightly descending, follow the route along narrow, blasted exposed ledges. Take your time; be careful not to lose the trail. Watch for arrows painted on rocks pointing the way.

At 8.7 miles reach a saddle (elev. 5660 ft) above steep snowfields. Do not take the "obvious" trail left. It's a goat path (look for mountain goats—they're up here). Instead stay on the ridge, climbing on rock and ledge through a short and extremely exposed section (don't look down), soon reaching a small meadow and a reprieve from the intensity. Pause for the views of Mount St. Helens and the Mount Margaret Backcountry lakes and peaks. Then walk along a broad, flowered shoulder, coming to Mount Whittier's 5883-foot summit at 9.1 miles. The views here, like those along the entire trail, are simply mind-blowing!

Rest, gather your nerves, and then continue, slowly descending. Traverse a small meadow with excellent views of obscure Boot Lake below. The way then continues down another knife-edge before traversing steep and intimidating slopes beneath a huge rock face. After reaching a small saddle (elev. 5500 ft) the trail veers to the west side of the ridge and gently climbs. You made it! At 10 miles the trail ends, meeting up with the Boundary Trail at a junction in a broad gap (elev. 5575 ft). Turn around and admire Mount Whittier, reflecting on what an incredible traverse that was. Then turn left on the Boundary Trail to climb 100 feet before beginning a long descent (see trail details

in Hike 50 for Mount Margaret), returning to the trailhead at 14.9 miles.

53 Independence Ridge Loop

RATING/ DIFFICULTY	LOOP	ELEV GAIN/ HIGH POINT	SEASON
****/3	6.8 miles	1075 feet/ 4700 feet	July–Oct

Map: Green Trails Mt St. Helens 332S; **Contact:** Mount St. Helens National Volcanic Monument; **Notes:** NW Forest Pass or interagency pass required. Dogs prohibited. Berries in season. The Independence Pass Trail is subject to landslides and as of the summer of 2014 was closed by a slide: contact ranger station for trail status; **GPS:** N 46 16.923 W 122 05.803

Hike high above Spirit Lake, taking in stunning views of the mountain responsible for reshaping this body of water and filling it with thousands of downed ancient trees. Stare across the massive lake to the Pumice Plain and into St. Helens' active crater. And admire Tephras Pinnacle, a geological oddity sure to intrigue.

GETTING THERE
From Randle, follow State Route 131 south for 2 miles to where it becomes Forest Road 25, continuing for 17.7 miles and turning right onto FR 99. (From Woodland, exit 21 on I-5, follow SR 503 east for 29 miles to Cougar. Continue east on SR 503—which becomes FR 90—for 18.5 miles, turning left onto FR 25. Follow this good paved road 25 miles north to FR 99.) Now continue west on paved FR 99 for 12 miles to the trailhead at Independence Pass (elev. 4050 ft).

ON THE TRAIL

Begin climbing and immediately start enjoying views of Mounts Hood and Adams. Spirit Lake soon comes into view too. After rounding a knoll and traversing several ledges, reach a junction (elev. 4475 ft). You'll be returning on the trail to the right—so head left to continue on the Independence Pass Trail, dropping into a spring-fed basin frequented by elk.

Ignoring elk paths, follow the trail west to wrap around Independence Ridge. At 1.7 miles, reach an excellent overlook (elev. 4400 ft) above Spirit Lake. This is a good spot to turn around if hiking with children or if you're skittish of heights. Beyond, the

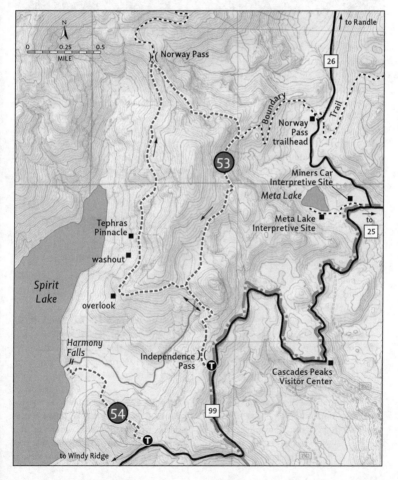

Independence Ridge offers excellent views of Spirit Lake and Mount St. Helens.

trail traverses steep and at times exposed slopes high above Spirit Lake. This section is prone to washouts (it was closed as of 2014) and crosses several gullies that may be unnerving.

Hiking below exposed columns of old basalt, look down for a new formation, Tephras Pinnacle. It's a 70-foot-tall narrow tower formed of fused ash from the 1980 eruption. The trail passes just above it then climbs into a small basin flush with berries in late summer. Continue climbing to round a shoulder (elev. 4700 ft) before descending and reaching a junction at Norway Pass (elev. 4500 ft) at 3.5 miles.

Savor the classic St. Helens–Spirit Lake view from this popular pass and then turn right, following the well-trodden Boundary Trail for 1 mile to a junction (elev. 4300 ft). The Boundary Trail continues left for 1.2 miles to the Norway Pass trailhead (an alternative start to this loop; see Hike 50). You want to go right on the Independence Ridge Trail, traversing brushy slopes to reach a 4650-foot shoulder with excellent

views of Strawberry Mountain and Mount Adams. From here descend through clusters of evergreens above a basin frequented by elk. At 5.8 miles, come to a familiar junction. Turn left and reach your starting point in one downhill mile.

54 Harmony Falls

RATING/ DIFFICULTY	ROUNDTRIP	ELEV GAIN/ HIGH POINT	SEASON
***/2	2.4 miles	650 feet/ 4060 feet	mid-June– Nov

Map: Green Trails Mt St. Helens 332S; **Contact:** Mount St. Helens National Volcanic Monument; **Notes:** NW Forest Pass or interagency pass required. Dogs prohibited; **GPS:** N 46 16.469 W 122 06.251

From a bluff overlooking Spirit Lake, follow a well-graded, well-trodden trail down to this famous body of water. This is the only trail granting access to Spirit's shoreline view of

Mount St. Helens from across the altered lake's log-jammed waters. And the falls? They're gone—submerged after the eruption that damned the lake's outlet, causing its water level to rise by over 250 feet. All that remains of Harmony Falls now is a small set of smaller, melodious cascades.

GETTING THERE

From Randle, follow State Route 131 south for 2 miles to where it becomes Forest Road 25, continuing for 17.7 miles and turning right onto FR 99. (From Woodland, exit 21 on I-5, follow SR 503 east for 29 miles to Cougar. Continue east on SR 503—which

Log-littered Spirit Lake shoreline

becomes FR 90—for 18.5 miles, turning left onto FR 25. Follow this good paved road 25 miles north to FR 99.) Now continue west on paved FR 99 for 13.1 miles to the trailhead (elev. 4060 ft).

ON THE TRAIL
Immediately descend as you hike through a tunnel of alders. As in other parts of the blast zone, the rate and amount of forest regeneration going on here is remarkable. Come back in a few years for a completely different experience. At about 0.4 mile, the way wiggles beneath some overhanging ledges dripping with moisture and creating a lush grotto.

The way bends right to eventually emerge upon an open plain plush with wildflowers. The path then bends left, traversing ledge striated by past glaciers and scoured clean of vegetation in 1980 by the massive eruption-caused landslide that plunged into the lake, creating a monstrous wave over 800 feet high. Forests hundreds of years old were immediately toppled—and thousands of fallen giants were swept to the lake, where they now float in massive logjams.

As it nears the lake, the trail winds down ledge, brushing against a small creek cascading over polished rock. This small chute is now referred to as Harmony Falls. The original Harmony Falls were impressively big and tumbled through big timber to the lake near a rustic lodge. Harmony Falls Lodge, along with the falls and several other lodges and camps, are all gone now, their original locations submerged under 250 feet of water.

At 1.2 miles, the trail ends at the log-lined lake (elev. 3410 ft). The logs shift with the winds and can be dangerous—use caution around them. Do enjoy the great views though across the lake to Mount St. Helens, the Pumice Plain, Harry's Ridge, and Cold-water Peak. Return the way you came, except now it's uphill.

55 Windy Ridge Lookout

RATING/ DIFFICULTY	ROUNDTRIP	ELEV GAIN/ HIGH POINT	SEASON
***/2	3 miles	600 feet/ 4475 feet	mid-June– Nov

Map: Green Trails Mt St. Helens 332S; **Contact:** Mount St. Helens National Volcanic Monument; **Notes:** NW Forest Pass or inter-agency pass required. Exposed trail section not advised for children or those afraid of heights. Dogs prohibited; **GPS:** N 46 15.021 W 122 08.223

Climb more than 400 steps to a spectacular viewpoint overlooking Spirit Lake, the Pumice Plain, and the north face of Mount St. Helens. Peer straight into St. Helens' crater, catching a glimpse of Loowit Falls. Then wander on a little-hiked section of the Truman Trail along steep ledges teetering high above Spirit Lake. And if the views don't blow you away, the breezes surely will on the appropriately named Windy Ridge.

GETTING THERE
From Randle, follow State Route 131 south for 2 miles to where it becomes Forest Road 25, continuing for 17.7 miles to turn right onto FR 99. (From Woodland, exit 21 on I-5, follow SR 503 east for 29 miles to Cougar. Continue east on SR 503—which becomes FR 90—for 18.4 miles, turning left onto FR 25. Follow this good paved road 25

Mount Margaret Backcountry peaks frame Spirit Lake.

miles north to FR 99.) Now continue west on paved FR 99 for 16.2 miles to its end at the trailhead (elev. 4050 ft). Privy available.

ON THE TRAIL

Windy Ridge is one of the busiest spots in the national volcanic monument, so try to plan your visit early or late in the day. Otherwise, prepare to share the viewpoint with busloads of tourists and the occasional ranger-led organized walk group (which is something you may well seek out). Take a few minutes to read the excellent interpretive displays. Then put your cardiovascular system to the test. The path heads straight up the northern extent of the open and pumiced Windy Ridge via a long procession of wooden steps—446 by my count.

Upon reaching the last step, heart rate now fully elevated, relax and stroll over to the viewpoint (elev. 4250 ft) and its excellent interpretive displays at 0.2 mile. The view too is excellent, and one of the best for fully capturing the magnitude of the changes wrought upon the surrounding landscape by the 1980 eruption.

After fully embracing the view, loosen your legs some more by continuing your hike to head north on a lightly traveled section of the Truman Trail. The way heads up the ridge before rounding a broad shoulder. Next the trail traverses steep slopes high above the sparkling lake. The views are superb over the massive lake and out to Mount Rainier. After reaching a 4475-foot-high point at about 1 mile, you may want to turn around if you're hiking with kids or uncomfortable with exposure. From here the trail descends across a steep, narrow, and exposed stretch (that occasionally washes out) beneath a band of cliffs. It may raise your heart rate like the steps. After this section, the trail barrels beneath a tunnel of alder to reach FR 99 just south of the Smith Creek trailhead (elev. 4300 ft) at 1.5 miles.

The Forest Service once planned to continue the trail north, connecting it to Independence Ridge and allowing hikers

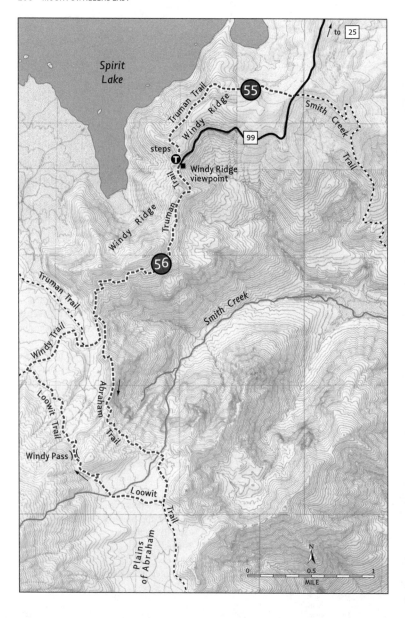

to trek around Spirit Lake completely on trail. But until (if) that happens, you'll need to walk on FR 99 to make the loop. This is not advisable: blind corners and encroaching vegetation narrow the right-of-way. For now, turn around and hike back the way you came.

56 Windy Ridge and the Plains of Abraham

RATING/ DIFFICULTY	LOOP	ELEV GAIN/ HIGH POINT	SEASON
*****/3	8.8 miles	1400 feet/ 4850 feet	July–Oct

Map: Green Trails Mt St. Helens 332S; **Contact:** Mount St. Helens National Volcanic Monument; **Notes:** NW Forest Pass or interagency pass required. Bikes allowed on Windy Ridge and Plains of Abraham. Dogs prohibited north of Windy Pass and west of the Truman and Abraham Trails junction. Water and shade are scarce, pack accordingly; **GPS:** N 46 14.935 W 122 08.169

Venture along barren, blasted ridges to a sprawling, near-level plain shrouded in pumice and pyroclastic debris. Carpets of wildflowers brighten the blighted landscape. And the views are explosive— from Mount St. Helens looming immediately above you to snowcapped Mount Adams floating over emerald ridges in the distance.

GETTING THERE
From Randle, follow State Route 131 south for 2 miles to where it becomes Forest Road 25, continuing for 17.7 miles to turn right onto FR 99. (From Woodland, exit 21 on I-5, follow

Mount St. Helens looms over the Plains of Abraham.

SR 503 east for 29 miles to Cougar. Continue east on SR 503—which becomes FR 90—for 18.4 miles, turning left onto FR 25. Follow this good paved road 25 miles north to FR 99.) Now continue west on paved FR 99 for 16.2 miles to its end at the trailhead (elev. 4050 ft). Privy available.

ON THE TRAIL

Locate a gated road heading south—that's the Truman Trail, your route. Here it starts off on an old roadbed, hugging Windy Ridge's eastern slopes high above the Smith Creek drainage. Thick rows of alder line the way, colonizing the landscape disturbed by the 1980 blast. Most of the trail, however, still remains fairly open, granting nearly continuous views from St. Helens to other Cascade volcanoes in the distance.

Pass some seismic measuring equipment and lots of dangling culverts. The way climbs about 200 feet before slowly descending. After 1.7 miles, reach a junction (elev. 4150

ft). You'll be returning from the right, so continue left on the Abraham Trail as it straddles a narrow ridge. After a slight descent, the way steeply climbs via a series of sand ladders. Question the decision to allow bikes on this section of trail as you assess the deeply eroded tracks parallel to the ladders.

At 2.2 miles, crest the ridge (elev. 4440 ft) and take a break enjoying sweeping eastward views out to Mount Rainier, the Mount Margaret Backcountry peaks, and the Dark Divide. Then continue along the narrow ridge, dropping 50 feet before climbing again to top out at around 4570 feet. The way then wraps around the ridge's grassy eastern slopes, dipping in and out of several gullies on a downward trajectory to the Plains of Abraham. Pass clusters of colonizing firs and mountain ash. In summer a myriad of wildflowers paints the slopes, while huckleberry bushes set it on fire in autumn.

After crossing Smith Creek (elev. 4350 ft) and the rocky outwash of the Nelson Glacier,

CLIMATE CHANGE: A GLACIER IS BORN

While almost all of the glaciers in the Cascades are currently receding because of climate change—with many in danger of completely vanishing—at Mount St. Helens a glacier grows. In fact this growing glacier lodged within the volcano's crater is North America's youngest glacier, born shortly after the 1980 eruption. Known officially as the Crater Glacier (although referred to by some folks as the Tulutson Glacier, from the Cowlitz language word for "ice"), this glacier continues to grow, encircling the lava domes within the crater.

Situated at an elevation of about 6700 feet, the glacier is fed by heavy snows, avalanches, and rockfalls that come crashing down from the summit rim. The steep northern walls of the crater keep much of the glacier shaded throughout the year, spurring the ice pack's growth. While this glacier is quite young, it is already over 600 feet thick in spots. Several smaller glaciers have also formed within the crater and they continue to grow as well, some now merging with the Crater Glacier.

The glacier's meltwaters feed Loowit Creek, which flows out of the crater in a series of beautiful waterfalls and cascades. The story of the Crater Glacier is yet just another chapter of destruction and rejuvenation in this fascinating landscape.

reach a junction (elev. 4475 ft) with the around-Mount St. Helens Loowit Trail at 3.9 miles. Here spread out before you is the Plains of Abraham, a near-level expanse named not for the father figure of biblical fame but after the famed battlefield in Quebec City. An early adventurer here saw some semblance, but certainly the plains in Quebec *sont plus vertes!* In early summer, the pumiced plains are painted purple thanks to a proliferation of lupine.

You can saunter out across the plain if you'd like (see Extending Your Trip below) before continuing on your way. Head right on the Loowit Trail, to skirt the edge of the plains. Recross Smith Creek and a series of outwashes, some of them resembling arroyos. Admire St. Helens before you with the Dogs Head in clear view. Before the 1980 eruption, the Dogs Head route was the standard way to climb St. Helens.

Begin climbing now across patches of pumice and scree, which will tax your stride. The trail traverses ledges prone to slides too, so use caution. At 4.8 miles, reach Windy Pass (elev. 4850 ft) with its great view north of the Pumice Plain, Spirit Lake, and the Mount Margaret Backcountry. Now, using caution, begin descending on a narrow path traversing steep slopes and ledges.

Cross several rocky gullies before reaching a junction (elev. 4300 ft) at 6 miles. Turn right on the Windy Trail and, paralleling a creek, descend to reach the Truman Trail (elev. 4050 ft) at 6.8 miles. Turn right to return to the trailhead, passing the Abraham Trail in 0.3 mile before reaching your start at 8.8 miles.

EXTENDING YOUR TRIP

Venture across the Plains of Abraham by following the Loowit Trail south from the Abraham Trail junction. At 0.8 mile, reach a campsite (elev. 4300 ft) and creek. Beyond this point, the trail descends the plains reaching the Ape Canyon Trail (Hike 42) in another mile.

57 Loowit Falls

RATING/ DIFFICULTY	ROUNDTRIP	ELEV GAIN/ HIGH POINT	SEASON
****/3	8.8 miles	1250 feet/ 4575 feet	July–Oct

Map: Green Trails Mt St. Helens 332S; **Contact:** Mount St. Helens National Volcanic Monument; **Notes:** NW Forest Pass or interagency pass required. Dogs and bikes prohibited west of the Truman and Abraham Trails junction; **GPS:** N 46 14.935 W 122 08.169

Hike across the blast zone to the mouth of Mount St. Helens' massive crater. Then stand mesmerized, gazing at a glacier-born waterfall crashing into a tight barren chasm. It's an awesome scene in a dynamic landscape still in flux. And despite the terrain's harsh facade, this hike harbors few, if any, hardships.

GETTING THERE

From Randle, follow State Route 131 south for 2 miles to where it becomes Forest Road 25, continuing for 17.7 miles to turn right onto FR 99. (From Woodland, exit 21 on I-5, follow SR 503 east for 29 miles to Cougar. Continue east on SR 503—which becomes FR 90—for 18.4 miles, turning left onto FR 25. Follow this good paved road 25 miles north to FR 99.) Now continue west on paved FR 99 for 16.2 miles to its end at the trailhead (elev. 4050 ft). Privy available.

Loowit Falls thunders from St. Helens' crater.

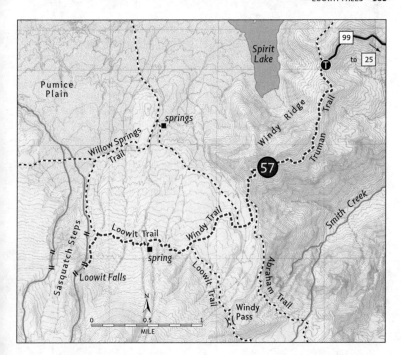

ON THE TRAIL

Locate a gated road heading south—that's the Truman Trail, your start. Follow this road-turned-trail to hug Windy Ridge's eastern slopes high above the Smith Creek drainage. The way climbs about 200 feet before slowly descending. After 1.7 miles, reach a junction (elev. 4150 ft). The Abraham Trail parts left (Hike 56). You want to head right, continuing on the Truman Trail and reaching another junction (elev. 4050 ft) in 0.3 mile, where this time you head left, leaving the old roadbed for the Windy Trail. Now following this bona fide trail, begin climbing. Spirit Lake soon comes into view. The way bends left and parallels a creek, reaching the Loowit Trail (elev. 4300 ft) at

2.8 miles. Here beneath a knoll on St. Helens known as the Dogs Head, turn right on the famous round-the-mountain Loowit Trail.

Immediately cross a creek and traverse grassy tundra-like terrain. Views are excellent of Spirit Lake, Coldwater Peak, The Dome, and Mount Margaret. At 3.1 miles in a jungle of willows, cross a spring-fed cascading creek flanked with monkey flowers. The going then gets rough in spots, climbing and dipping a couple of times. Cross another creek and a rocky gully and reach the Loowit Falls Trail junction (elev. 4300 ft) at 3.8 miles.

Bear left then round a ridge and hike up a rocky rib, reaching, at 4.4 miles, an excellent and fairly close viewpoint (elev.

4575 ft) of the crater-emanating falls. It's an awesome sight and an incredibly volatile and evolving landscape. Needless to say, don't go beyond this spot. The falls' source is the Crater Glacier, which is one of the few in the continental United States not receding but growing, and its snout is now less than a mile from Loowit Falls. Landslides, rockfalls, and snowmelt continue to gouge and carve the canyon housing the 180-foot falls. Though the terrain before you is more barren than other parts of the blast-zone, colonizing nitrogen-fixing plants like lupines are making some progress in this blast zone ground-zero locale. Eventually the surrounding gray will yield to green. In the meanwhile, enjoy the hydro show!

EXTENDING YOUR TRIP

From the Loowit Falls Trail junction, you can vary your return by hiking north on the Loowit Trail 0.8 mile to reach the Willow Springs Trail. Then take that trail 0.9 mile back around to the Truman Trail (elev. 3700 ft). Turn right and follow the Truman Trail 3.4 miles back to your vehicle.

Opposite: Goat Mountain Trail

mount st. helens north

The least visited area of the Mount St. Helens National Volcanic Monument, the north consists of large tracts of old-growth forest, lofty ridges, and deep valleys. Access is via a private logging road (subject to closures) and a crumbling Forest Service road in desperate need of maintenance. Within Mount St. Helens north, you can hike for miles and see nary a human soul. Despite the light usage, the trails in this region are in decent shape, offering long day hikes and excellent backpacking opportunities. A couple of short nature trails can be found here too—and unlike the busy nature trails in other areas of the Monument, they are places where you can enjoy some quiet contemplation.

58 Ryan Lake

RATING/ DIFFICULTY	LOOP	ELEV GAIN/ HIGH POINT	SEASON
**/1	0.7 mile	165 feet/ 3465 feet	June–Oct

Map: Green Trails Mt St. Helens 332S; **Contact:** Mount St. Helens National Volcanic Monument; **Notes:** NW Forest Pass or interagency pass required. FR 26 is in dire need of maintenance and should be driven with caution. Be alert for road hazards, including sinkholes, slumping, uneven pavement, and encroaching vegetation; **GPS:** N 46 21.106 W 122 03.822

Ryan Lake is surrounded by new growth planted after the 1980 eruption.

👥🐕🚶❌ *Walk through a recovering forest near a small lake that hosts a myriad of winged and furry critters. Learn about the salvage logging that took place after the 1980 blast and witness a landscape rapidly recovering after both nature and man left a large imprint upon it. A delightful, family-friendly interpretive loop, unfortunately this trail hasn't seen any maintenance since the 1990s.*

GETTING THERE

From Randle on US 12, follow State Route 131 south for 2 miles to where it becomes Forest Road 25 and continue for 6.7 miles. Just after the bridge over the Cispus River, turn right onto paved but rough FR 26. Drive for 12.4 miles, turning right (shortly after the FR 2612 junction) into the Ryan Lake Interpretive Site and trailhead (elev. 3300 ft). Privy available.

ON THE TRAIL

The parking lot and trail are being reclaimed by vegetation, and the interpretive signs are showing three decades of weathering. Like the deteriorating Forest Road you drove on to get here, this site and so many others in our national parks and forests need adequate funding and regular maintenance. Consider sending off a letter addressing this to your elected representatives upon returning home.

For now, however, follow the loop (starting on the west end of the parking lot) up a small hillside above pretty little Ryan Lake. A couple of spots along the way grant excellent viewing over the lake and out to nearby Goat and Strawberry mountains. You're 12 miles north of Mount St. Helens here, yet the old growth surrounding you was toppled by the 1980 eruption's 300-mph winds, volcanic gasses, and debris flows. Three people camping here perished.

The Gifford Pinchot National Forest implemented a massive operation to salvage merchantable downed timber. In all, over 1.6 billion board feet of timber were damaged in the Gifford Pinchot National Forest from the eruption. Over 340 million board feet were salvaged—wood enough to build 35,000 homes. Forest Service practices at that time put a large emphasis on recovering merchantable timber. Forest ecologists would have liked to have seen more downed timber left on the ground for habitat for recovering wildlife species.

The interpretive displays along the way focus on this salvage operation and the replanting of the surrounding forest. After climbing to about 3465 feet, the trail winds back down through a thick tunnel of regenerating trees to the parking lot, closing the loop at 0.7 mile.

59 Green River

RATING/ DIFFICULTY	ROUNDTRIP	ELEV GAIN/ HIGH POINT	SEASON
***/2	10 miles	425 feet/ 2800 feet	June–Nov

Map: Green Trails Mt St. Helens 332S; **Contact:** Mount St. Helens National Volcanic Monument, Cowlitz Valley Ranger District; **Notes:** Trail open to horses and bicycles. FR 26 is in dire need of maintenance and should be driven with caution. Be alert for road hazards, including sinkholes, slumping, uneven pavement, and encroaching vegetation; **GPS:** N46 21.007 W122 06.585

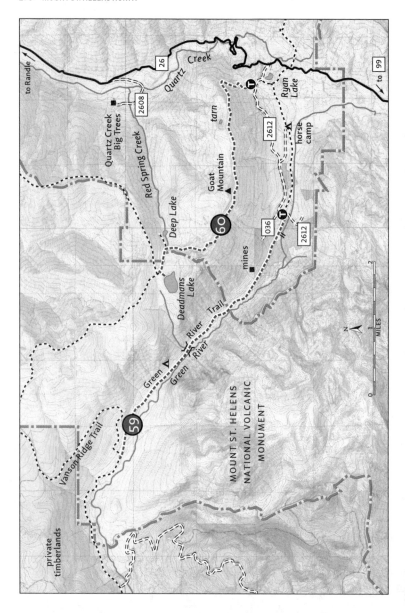

to Randle

26

Quartz Creek

99

to 99

2608

Quartz Creek
Big Trees

Red Spring Creek

tarn

Ryan Lake

2612

horse camp

Goat
Mountain

Deep Lake

60

036

2612

mines

Deadmans
Lake

River Trail

Green River

Green River

Vanson Ridge Trail

59

MOUNT ST. HELENS
NATIONAL VOLCANIC
MONUMENT

private
timberlands

N

0   1   2

MILES

A trail runner pauses to admire some big, old trees.

Hike along a delightful waterway through a deep, glacier-carved valley shrouded in spectacular old-growth forest. Some of the biggest and oldest trees in the area can be found along this trail, one of the quietest within the Monument. There are no alpine views, so save this hike for an overcast day. And have camera in hand, as elk and black bear sightings are frequent in this valley.

GETTING THERE

From Randle on US Highway 12, follow State Route 131 south for 2 miles to where it becomes Forest Road 25 and continue for 6.7 miles. Just after the bridge over the Cispus River, turn right onto paved but rough FR 26. Drive for 12.3 miles, turning right onto FR 2612. Continue for 2.6 miles (just past the junction with spur 036) to the trailhead (elev. 2800 ft).

ON THE TRAIL

Starting in an area that was salvaged logged after the 1980 blast, follow the Green River Trail west downriver. Look up at the heavily logged slopes to feisty new greenery. High above in hidden basins and hanging valleys alpine lakes give birth to the silver strands of cascading creeks that help feed the Green River.

The Green River, too, cascades, and you'll soon come to a nice waterfall. The way next passes a couple of historic mines and traverses an active mining claim. Conservationists and recreationists have grown concerned over the prospect of a large open-pit copper mine that the current claim holder is considering. Market forces, environmental laws, and citizen involvement will determine the outcome.

Continue through old cuts on brushy-at-times tread, reaching the national volcanic monument boundary and old-growth forest at about 2 miles. Now enjoy hiking through luxuriant primeval forest untouched by volcano and chainsaws. The way continues downriver, weaving through groves of behemoth Douglas-firs, western hemlocks, and western red cedars. After a bridged crossing of a side creek, come to good riverside camps which double as good lunch spots for day hikers. Continue down the glacially carved U-shaped valley through magnificent ancient forest groves and across sparkling creeks. If Sasquatch exists, this is prime habitat for him.

At 5 miles, reach a junction (elev. 2375 ft) with the Vanson Ridge Trail (see Hike 88), a good spot to turn around. Mosey back to the trailhead the way you came, savoring the beauty of this magnificent forest.

EXTENDING YOUR TRIP

The Green River Trail continues downriver through more spectacular groves of ancient trees for another 3 miles, terminating at a private road (elev. 1850 ft) on Weyerhaeuser land. Access from this side is complicated and limited, but occasionally horse parties begin their trip here. Trail is brushy in spots with a few blowdowns but is generally in decent shape. Solitude is guaranteed.

60 Goat Mountain and Deadmans Lake

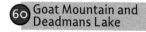

RATING/ DIFFICULTY	ROUNDTRIP	ELEV GAIN/ HIGH POINT	SEASON
*****/4	11.2 miles	2400 feet/ 5025 feet	July–Oct

Map: Green Trails Mt St. Helens 332S; **Contact:** Gifford Pinchot National Forest, Cowlitz Valley Ranger District; Mount St.

Helens National Volcanic Monument; **Notes:** Trail open to horses and bicycles. FR 26 is in dire need of maintenance and should be driven with caution. Be alert for road hazards, which include sinkholes, slumping uneven pavement, and encroaching vegetation; **GPS:** N46 21.380 W122 04.202

Hike along a lofty ridge at the demarcation of the blast zone. Look south at blown-down and toppled forests and a series of sparkling alpine lakes surrounded by silver snags. Look north at alpine meadows flush with wildflowers and hillsides cloaked in verdant old-growth canopies. One of the best trails for comparing before and after the eruption landscapes, Goat Mountain is also one of the best for views.

GETTING THERE

From Randle on US Highway 12, follow State Route 131 south for 2 miles to where it becomes Forest Route 25 and continue for 6.7 miles. Just after the bridge over the Cispus River, turn right onto paved but rough FR 26. Drive for 12.3 miles, turning right onto FR 2612. Continue for 0.3 mile to the trailhead (elev. 3300 ft).

ON THE TRAIL

Starting in an old clear-cut, waste no time climbing. Using old skid roads and short switchbacks, the way steeply climbs, attacking Goat Mountain's south slope. As the trail leaves young regenerating forest to enter handsome old growth, you will immediately notice the temperature difference (especially on a sunny summer day).

The way makes a sweeping switchback to crest Goat's ridgeline. Then it turns westward to begin a long and scenic journey

A high basin beneath Goat Mountain often harbors a herd of elk.

across the mountain just below its ridge crest. At 1.9 miles, skirt a small open basin (elev. 4750 ft) housing a pretty little tarn and a killer view of Mount Rainier. The way then continues to climb, entering subalpine meadows that explode with wildflower blossoms in summer. Reach a 5025-foot high point just beneath a knoll and briefly descend about 150 feet before traversing across the mountain's open south face.

The trail continues now along the demarcation of the 1980 blast zone. Wildflowers and hummingbirds proliferate here. Woodpeckers too, take to the silver

snags left standing on this high ridge. Take your time—the views are breathtaking. The Green River valley spreads out below. Mount St. Helens rises above the Mount Margaret Backcountry. Mounts Adams and Hood stand tall in the distance. The way scoots below Goat Mountain's 5400-foot summit (an easy scramble) before reaching a 4930-foot saddle at about 3.9 miles.

The way then hugs the north side of the ridge, providing exceptional views to Mount Rainier and a basin below oft-frequented by elk. Continuing, the trail steeply descends into gorgeous old-growth forest and enters the Monument. After crossing a small creek in a boggy area, the way reaches a junction at 5.3 miles with an unmarked, brushy, and obscure path leading right 0.4 mile to tiny Deep Lake (elev. 4000 ft).

Continue a short distance to another junction (elev. 4375 ft), this one heading left. Take it and within minutes arrive at Deadmans Lake (elev. 4350 ft), 5.6 miles from the trailhead. Despite the name, the lake is a lively place, particularly active with amphibians and mosquitoes. But if the bugs aren't bad, stay awhile. The lake's pumiced bottom and sandy shore make it an attractive swim hole. There are good camps here too if you're inclined to spend the night.

61 Quartz Creek Big Trees

RATING/ DIFFICULTY	LOOP	ELEV GAIN/ HIGH POINT	SEASON
***/1	0.4 mile	minimal/ 2000 feet	Apr–Nov

Map: Green Trails Mt St. Helens 332S; **Contact:** Gifford Pinchot National Forest, Cowlitz Valley Ranger District; **Notes:** FR 26 is in dire need of maintenance and should be driven with caution. Be alert for road hazards, including sinkholes, slumping, uneven pavement, and encroaching vegetation; **GPS:** N 46 23.511 W 122 04.410

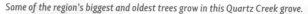 *The trail is short, but the trees are long on grandeur! Wander beside some of the biggest, tallest, and oldest western red cedars, western hemlocks, and Douglas-firs within the Gifford Pinchot National Forest. Neither chainsaws nor Mount St. Helens' fury ever reached this magnificent primeval stand of trees growing along the lush bottomlands of Quartz Creek.*

GETTING THERE
From Randle on US Highway 12, follow State Route 131 south for 2 miles to where it becomes Forest Road 25 and continue

Some of the region's biggest and oldest trees grow in this Quartz Creek grove.

for 6.7 miles. Just after the bridge over the Cispus River, turn right onto paved but rough FR 26. Drive for 8.1 miles, turning right onto unsigned FR 2608. Continue on this good dirt road for 1.4 miles to the trailhead (elev. 2000 ft). Privy available.

ON THE TRAIL

It's a short loop, but plan on spending time here admiring some monstrous trees. The well-built path (originally designed for wheelchairs, but difficult for them now) winds through a dank mossy grove of behemoth trees along Quartz Creek. You'll pass by several Douglas-firs 6 to 10 feet in diameter and over 600 years old. There are quite a few impressive western red cedars and western hemlocks in this lush stand too. Hike the loop in either direction. The way is pretty level, with a nice stretch of boardwalk about midsection.

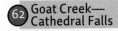

62 Goat Creek— Cathedral Falls

RATING/ DIFFICULTY	ROUNDTRIP	ELEV GAIN/ HIGH POINT	SEASON
***/2	5.6 miles	400 feet/ 2750 feet	May–Nov

Map: Green Trails Mt St. Helens 332S; **Contact:** Mount St. Helens National Volcanic Monument; **Notes:** Access is via a gated private timber road that is periodically subject to closing (usually during high fire danger). Trail is also open to horses and bicycles; **GPS:** N 46 25.763 W 122 09.289

Hike through deep old-growth forest high above cascading Goat Creek to beautiful Cathedral Falls plunging from an overhanging ledge. Follow the trail behind the falls, in Columbia River Gorge fashion, through a massive mossy alcove. Then continue along the trail, eventually becoming acquainted with Goat Creek.

GETTING THERE

From Morton, travel east on US Highway 12 for 5.3 miles, turning right at Milepost 103 onto Kosmos Road. (If coming from Randle, follow US 12 west for 12 miles to the same turnoff.) After 0.1 mile turn left onto Champion Haul Road and continue 4.3 miles (passing Taidnapum Park) to the bridge over the Cowlitz River. Turn right onto a graveled forest road, and after 0.8 mile bear left at a Y-junction onto Forest Road 2750. Follow this road 4 miles to its end at the trailhead (elev. 2400 ft).

ON THE TRAIL

Goat Creek drains a large forested and fairly undisturbed section of the Mount St. Helens National Volcanic Monument. Handfuls of families and Riffe Lake campers regularly wander to Cathedral Falls. But beyond, the Goat Creek and its connector trails remain fairly deserted, offering nice opportunities for solitude.

The trail starts on old road, quickly transitioning to single track. Traversing steep forested slopes, Goat Creek tumbles far below in a tight valley. Cross a couple of creeks that may, in early season, leave your feet wet before arriving at Cathedral Falls (elev. 2550 ft) at 1.1 miles. Also known as Leona Falls, it is formed by an unnamed Goat Creek tributary plunging 248 feet before you.

The trail darts behind the falls, crossing beneath the massive overhanging ledge. Two large cedars give the illusion of acting as support beams for the overhang. The falls

A hiker pauses to photograph Cathedral Falls.

may be a mere trickle in autumn—but they can be quite impressive in late spring. Most folks call it quits here.

The trail continues on a gentle ascent, crossing another potentially foot-soaking creek before descending a bit to eventually parallel pretty cascading Goat Creek. At 2.2 miles reach a junction (elev. 2550 ft) with the Tumwater Trail. Here the Goat Creek Trail continues right to Vanson Lake and Peak (Hike 63). For this Goat Creek hike, instead stay straight ahead to continue up the Tumwater Trail through lush ancient forest. You will cross another creek and pass a couple of pretty waterfalls, compliments of Goat Creek. At 2.8 miles, come to Goat Creek (elev. 2750 ft), which must be forded to continue. This is a good spot to turn around unless you're intent on hiking all the way to Tumwater Mountain (Hike 64).

63 Vanson Peak

RATING/ DIFFICULTY	ROUNDTRIP	ELEV GAIN/ HIGH POINT	SEASON
****/4	13.2 miles	2600 feet/ 4948 feet	July–Nov

Map: Green Trails Mt St. Helens 332S; **Contact:** Mount St. Helens National Volcanic Monument; **Notes:** Access is via a gated private timber road that is periodically subject to closing (usually during high fire danger). Trail is also open to horses and bicycles; **GPS:** N 46 25.763 W 122 09.289

It's a long hike to the former lookout site on Vanson Peak (and its tranquil lake tucked below in deep old timber). But it's a pretty hike along a cascading creek through primeval forest rife with wildlife and short on people. En route, pass through pocket meadows and by waterfalls and wetland pools. Enjoy sweeping views of the Cowlitz Valley, Tumwater Mountain, and a couple of Cascades volcanoes from the summit.

GETTING THERE
From Morton, travel east on US Highway 12 for 5.3 miles, turning right at Milepost 103 onto Kosmos Road. (If coming from Randle,

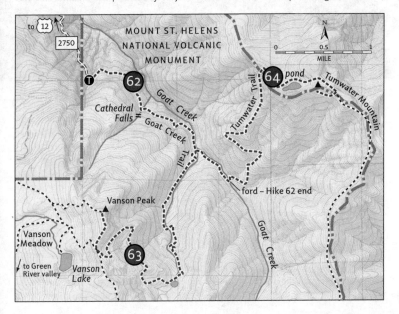

A hiker admires, from Vanson Peak, the unbroken forests of Tumwater Mountain.

follow US 12 west for 12 miles to the same turnoff.) After 0.1 mile turn left onto the Champion Haul Road and continue 4.3 miles (passing Taidnapum Park) to the bridge over the Cowlitz River. Turn right onto a graveled forest road, and after 0.8 mile bear left at a Y-junction onto Forest Road 2750. Follow this road 4 miles to its end at the trailhead (elev. 2400 ft).

ON THE TRAIL

Follow the Goat Creek Trail, crossing a couple of potentially boot-soaking creeks before coming to Cathedral Falls at 1.1 miles. Then hike behind the falls beneath a massive overhanging ledge and continue on a gentle ascent. The way then descends a little to meet up with cascading Goat Creek. At 2.2 miles reach a junction (elev. 2550 ft) with the Tumwater Trail. The way straight ahead leads to Tumwater Mountain (Hike 64). You want to go right, continuing on the Goat Creek Trail.

Now, paralleling a main tributary to Goat Creek, climb in earnest, crossing numerous creeks that in early season and during rainy periods may leave your boots wet. The surrounding forest is gorgeous, with many monstrous old Douglas-firs causing you to stop, cock your head back, and let out sighs of amazement. Climbing higher, admire the rushing waterway by your side as it cuts through a tight ravine.

At 3.3 miles, you'll need to ford the tributary or use a fallen log spanning it. The way then follows another creek, ascending through a spectacular primeval forest of hemlocks and firs. At 4.4 miles, skirt an alder-lined, wildlife rich pond (elev. 3750 ft). Then commence climbing, traversing thinning forest, grassy wetlands, and pocket meadows that flourish with flowers, amphibians, and insects. The trail bends beneath Vanson's summit, working its way up to a 4700-foot saddle coming to a four-way junction at 6.1 miles.

Left heads to Deadmans Lake and Goat Mountain (Hike 60). Straight ahead is the way for Vanson Lake. For Vanson Peak, go right, climbing along a narrow ridge. At 6.5 miles, come to a junction (elev. 4900 ft). Continue straight 0.1 mile through alders and beargrass to reach the 4948-foot summit of Vanson Peak, which housed a fire lookout until the 1960s. The views are good, especially west of the Cowlitz Valley and its patchwork of forested hills and manmade lakes. The view is good too of the Goat Creek drainage and Tumwater Mountain with its virgin forest undisturbed by chainsaws or volcanic eruptions. Rainier and Adams are visible too, but not St. Helens. After soaking up the views either return the way you came—or, if you have extra energy, consider a side trip to Vanson Lake (see below).

EXTENDING YOUR TRIP

Retrace your steps 0.1 mile from the summit to a junction. Turn right and steeply descend, reaching another junction (elev.

4100 ft) in 0.7 mile. Right leads to private timberlands and once allowed for a much shorter hike from the west to Vanson Lake and Peak. Today this trail is frequently used by renegade motorcyclists and ATVers illegally riding to the lake, which is closed to motor vehicles.

Turn left, and in 0.3 mile come to a junction with the Vanson Ridge Trail coming up from the Green River valley (Hike 88) and a spur heading 0.1 mile straight to Vanson Meadow. Continue left, and after 0.2 mile come to a junction with the Vanson Lake Trail. Take this good trail right to placid, forest-flanked Vanson Lake (elev. 4150 ft) in 0.3 mile.

To return, retrace your steps back to the previous junction and turn right. Climb 0.7 mile back to the four-way junction at the saddle and continue straight on the Goat Creek Trail back to your vehicle. The lake loop adds 2.5 miles and 600 feet of elevation to your hike.

64 Tumwater Mountain

RATING/ DIFFICULTY	ROUNDTRIP	ELEV GAIN/ HIGH POINT	SEASON
***/5	14.4 miles	2900 feet/ 5245 feet	July–Oct

Map: Green Trails Mt St. Helens 332S; **Contact:** Mount St. Helens National Volcanic Monument; **Notes:** Access is via a gated, private timber road that is periodically subject to closing (usually during high fire danger). Trail is also open to horses and bicycles; **GPS:** N 46 25.763 W 122 09.289

 *Tumwater is one of the loneliest trails in all of the Mount St. Helens National Volcanic*

Monument; chances are good you'll encounter more four-legged hikers than two-legged ones. Hike through miles of deep virgin forest to a subalpine meadow cradling a small pond. Then head to an isolated and seldom visited summit for sweeping views of the northern, little explored region of the Monument.

GETTING THERE

From Morton, travel east on US Highway 12 for 5.3 miles turning right at milepost 103 onto Kosmos Road. (If coming from Randle, follow US 12 west for 12 miles to the same turnoff.) After 0.1 mile, turn left onto Champion Haul Road and continue 4.3 miles (passing Taidnapum Park) to the bridge over the Cowlitz River. Turn right onto a graveled forest road, and after 0.8 mile bear left at a Y-junction onto Forest Road 2750. Follow this road 4 miles to its end at the trailhead (elev. 2400 ft).

ON THE TRAIL

Follow the Goat Creek Trail (Hike 62), crossing a couple of potentially boot-soaking creeks before coming to Cathedral Falls at 1.1 miles. Then hike behind the falls under a massive overhanging ledge and continue on a gentle ascent. The way then descends a little to meet up with cascading Goat Creek. At 2.2 miles reach a junction (elev. 2550 ft) with the Tumwater Trail. The way right leads to Vanson Peak (Hike 63). You want to continue straight on the Tumwater Trail.

Although *tumwater* is Chinook language jargon for "strong water," there's not much water along the Tumwater Trail come late summer. Be sure to keep your water bottles filled. Hiking through lush ancient forest, cross a creek and pass a couple of pretty waterfalls on Goat Creek. Then, at 2.8 miles,

you'll need to ford Goat Creek (elev. 2750 ft), which can be tricky at higher water levels early in the season.

Once across, the way steadily climbs, traversing steep slopes carpeted in wood sorrels and shrouded in beautiful old-growth forest. After crossing a small creek, soon come to a manzanita-lined viewpoint overlooking the Goat Creek valley. Then continue climbing through open, uniform forest. Skirt some ledges displaying showy sedums and granting window views of the lands around you.

Upon cresting a ridge, the trail bends south and the climbing subsides. Pass some shallow wetland pools before reaching a meadow bursting with wildflowers and often harboring large-hoofed mammals. At 6 miles, reach a small pond (elev. 4840 ft) surrounded by meadows beneath Tumwater Mountain's craggy summit. This is a good spot to call it a hike. Set yourself down, have lunch, and watch for wildlife.

However, if the peak above the pond has you intrigued, continue hiking along the trail. Shortly after reaching a small saddle come to an easy-to-miss junction (elev. 5075 ft) at 6.7 miles. Here the abandoned but still somewhat decipherable spur to Tumwater's summit veers sharply right. Follow it through blowdowns, passing the remains of an old cabin. The path eventually peters out at 0.5 mile on some ledges just below the 5245-foot summit.

Being careful not to disturb fragile plants, explore the ledges, where excellent views can be had of the little pond below, and of much of the lonely surrounding forested ridges, peaks, and valleys. Out of the blast zone and never logged, the Goat Creek drainage contains some of the largest tracts

A small pond below Tumwater Mountain

of old growth in the Monument. Views are good too of familiar peaks in the distance. And take time to admire some of the flowers growing atop this peak—particularly the cat's-eared lilies growing here at the northern extent of their range.

EXTENDING YOUR TRIP

A great loop can be made by continuing south on the Tumwater Trail to the Goat Mountain Trail and returning to the trailhead via the Goat Creek Trail. See Hike 89 in the Backpacking Trips section.

Opposite: Upper Lewis Falls

lewis river valley

A major tributary of the mighty Columbia, the Lewis River starts high on Mount Adams before flowing west below the south flank of Mount St. Helens. The river carves its way through narrow basalt canyons, throws itself from thunderous waterfalls, and wends its way through the largest tract of intact old-growth forest in southern Washington. Although it is not named for the famed Meriwether who passed this way—that distinction goes to A. Lee Lewis, an early homesteader who settled near the mouth of the river—this Wild and Scenic River candidate still harbors plenty of primeval country for modern-day explorers.

65 Yale Reservoir Logging Road Trail

RATING/ DIFFICULTY	ROUNDTRIP	ELEV GAIN/ HIGH POINT	SEASON
**/2	7.5 miles	310 feet/ 650 feet	Year-round

Tree-lined Yale Logging Road

Map: USGS Cougar; **Contact:** PacifiCorp; **Notes:** Trail open to horses and bicycles. Dogs permitted on-leash; **GPS:** N 46 03.332 W 122 15.298

On this haul-road-turned-hiking-path, enjoy unobstructed views of Yale Reservoir, a lake along the Lewis River, and several waterfalls that flow next to—and sometimes over—the pleasantly motor-free road.

GETTING THERE

From Woodland (exit 21 on I-5), follow State Route 503 east for 29 miles to Cougar. Continue east on SR 503 for 3.1 miles and, immediately after the road changes to Forest Road 90 (look for the power substation on the right), take a sharp right onto an unmarked gravel road. Immediately bear right and follow this rough road over a bridge crossing the Lewis River. At the Y-intersection, continue straight to a gate and the trailhead (elev. 600 ft).

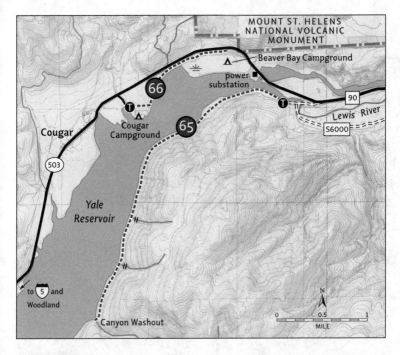

ON THE TRAIL

Known locally as the "International Paper" or "IP" Road, the road tracing the southeast shore of Yale Lake, a reservoir along the Lewis River created by the Yale dam, hasn't seen a log truck rumble across its surface in a decade. As part of its licensing renewal agreement for its North Fork Lewis River dams, PacifiCorp plans to convert the road-bed into proper paved trail. In the meantime, users who can negotiate a few walk-around washouts will find easy walking on the only public foot access to the east side of the reservoir.

Beginning near Beaver Bay, the route descends through dense forest to lake level and the only significant rock slide at 0.6 mile. Climb over the rock pile and continue on surprisingly intact asphalt. Peer out over the quiet east shore, with only the occasional boater for company. Save for a few willows and the pervasive—and invasive—Scotch broom, little obstructs the view of the nearly four-thousand-acre lake. Cross small debris slides at 2.2 miles and again at 3.1 miles; at the latter, check out the pavement cascades caused by the outlet of a waterfall flowing across the road. Admire, too, the heavily forested flank of the hillside, a surprise in a sea of clear-cuts. The official trail will end at an area known informally as Canyon Washout, at 3.75 miles, where a 2009 slide washed away several hundred feet of roadbed.

Sunset over Yale Reservoir

EXTENDING YOUR TRIP
Past Canyon Washout, hikers and bikers will be able to continue on another mile of undeveloped road to the end of PacifiCorp property.

66 Cougar—Beaver Bay

RATING/ DIFFICULTY	ROUNDTRIP	ELEV GAIN/ HIGH POINT	SEASON
**/1	2 miles	70 feet/ 590 feet	May–Oct

Map: USGS Cougar; **Contact:** PacifiCorp; **Notes:** Dogs permitted on-leash; **GPS:** N 46 03.543 W 122 17.208

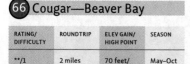 *Get a bird's-eye view of Yale Reservoir on this wooded 1-mile walk connecting two popular Pacifi-Corp campgrounds. And get eye-to-eye with birds, too, at Beaver Bay's bountiful wetlands.*

GETTING THERE
From Woodland (exit 21 on I-5), follow State Route 503 east for 29 miles to Cougar. Continue east on SR 503, 0.2 mile to Cougar Park. Turn right into the park and drive to the campground area and trailhead (elev. 590 ft).

ON THE TRAIL
As part of its relicensing agreement for the North Fork Lewis River dams (see Hike 65), PacifiCorp has implemented an ambitious trail plan for its properties on Yale Reservoir, including this route connecting popular Cougar and Beaver Bay campgrounds (due to be completed in 2015). Although it's a worthwhile walk for water-skiing weary campers, the views of Beaver Bay's wetlands framed by the forest of the North Fork Lewis River are worth a stop for day-trippers too.

From the old roadbed near the entrance to the campground, the trail traverses a steep sidehill before attaining a broad, flat bench shaded by western hemlock. Underfoot is forest cover typical of the area: sword fern, vanilla leaf, salal, and Oregon-grape. The highway encroaches from the left, but Beaver Bay beckons below. At 0.6 mile, descend off the bench, bird song replacing road noise. From here, according to plans, the trail will eventually wrap around the broad swath of Beaver Bay, connecting to the Beaver Bay Campground at 1 mile.

EXTENDING YOUR TRIP
At trail's end, a short boardwalk over Beaver Bay offers up-close exploration of the wetland.

67 Cedar Flats Research Natural Area

RATING/ DIFFICULTY	LOOP	ELEV GAIN/ HIGH POINT	SEASON
***/1	1 mile	minimal/ 1360 feet	Apr–Dec

Map: Green Trails Mt St. Helens 332S; **Contact:** Gifford Pinchot National Forest, Mount St. Helens Ranger District; **Notes:** Research natural area—stay on trail; **GPS:** N 46 06.716 W 122 01.108

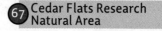 *Stroll through a dark flat above the Muddy River that harbors some of the tallest, oldest, and grandest trees in the state. The trail is short and nearly level, making it easy on the legs. You may strain your eyes and neck however, from constantly cocking your head back to admire the magnitude of so many gigantic trees.*

Massive ancient cedars

GETTING THERE

From Woodland (exit 21 on I-5), follow State Route 503 east for 29 miles to Cougar. Continue east on SR 503 (which becomes Forest Road 90) for 18.5 miles, turning left onto FR 25. Continue for 3.6 miles to the trailhead (elev. 1360 ft) on your right.

ON THE TRAIL

Pass through a cedar split-rail fence and come to an interpretive sign. This trail makes a short loop through the 680-acre Cedar Flat Research Natural Area. Occupying deep alluvial soils from past mudflows, the research area was established in 1946 to study a forest community undisturbed by human activity. Conditions here have been favorable for growing some colossal trees. One of the largest Douglas-firs in the state once grew here. It must have made one heck

of a sound (whether anyone heard it or not) when it fell to the ground in 2002.

Start hiking in dark forest thanks to a thick canopy provided predominantly by towering Douglas-firs, western red cedars,

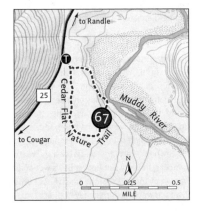

and western hemlocks. Clusters of vine maple flourish where gaps in the canopy have allowed sunlight to filter to the forest floor. After about 0.1 mile reach a junction. Now go left or right on an 0.8-mile loop, wandering through an impressive forest containing massive trees exceeding 200 feet tall and with trunks up to 10 feet wide. Many of the cedars here are well over 500 years old.

While the old trees are the attraction, the trail swings by a couple of spots on the edge of a flat, offering good window views of the Muddy River below. Elk sightings are always a possibility too out on the flat. Take your time hiking through this special forest.

A curiously misspelled sign at Curly Creek Falls

68 Curly Creek Falls

RATING/ DIFFICULTY	ROUNDTRIP	ELEV GAIN/ HIGH POINT	SEASON
**/1	0.4 mile	minimal/ 1285 feet	Apr–Nov

Map: Green Trails Lone Butte 365; **Contact:** Gifford Pinchot National Forest, Mount St. Helens National Volcanic Monument and Surrounding Area Headquarters; **Notes:** NW Forest Pass or interagency pass required. Wheelchair accessible; **GPS:** N 46 03.635 W 121 58.366

Views of two tantalizing torrents on the Lewis River will whet the appetites of waterfall lovers on this easy hike.

GETTING THERE
From Woodland (exit 21 on I-5), follow State Route 503 east for 29 miles to Cougar. Continue east on SR 503 (which becomes Forest Road 90) for 18.5 miles. At the junction with FR 25, immediately past the Pine Creek Information Center, bear right onto the Lewis River Road (FR 90), which immediately crosses the Lewis River. Proceed 5.1 miles and turn left onto FR 9039. Drive 1 mile to the trailhead on the left (elev. 1260 ft). Privy available.

ON THE TRAIL
On wide, well-groomed tread, walk through a verdant western hemlock forest. The trail soon encounters an unmarked junction with the Lewis River Trail. Bear right to check out the viewing platform for Curly Creek Falls. Although the US Geological Survey denotes it as "Curly Creek," some old maps and guidebooks use the name "Curley Creek." To confuse matters more, the knucklehead who carved the wooden sign here spelled it "Curely Creek Falls"!

The same geologic process that has scooped out the waterfalls on the Lewis River has shaped a natural basalt bridge that frames the falls. Look closely: erosion has begun a second arch above the first. Continue down the trail a few hundred feet for a second viewing platform, this one with a vantage of Miller Falls, which pours into a small cove on the far side of the Lewis River.

Enjoy the cascades, then head back the way you came. You may now find yourself tempted to hike the Lewis River Trail for reach-out-and-touch-it access to the emerald waters below.

69 Lower Lewis River

RATING/ DIFFICULTY	ROUNDTRIP	ELEV GAIN/ HIGH POINT	SEASON
***/3	5.6 miles	425 feet/ 1300 feet	Mar–Nov

Map: Green Trails Lone Butte 365; **Contact:** Gifford Pinchot National Forest, Mount St. Helens National Volcanic Monument and Surrounding Area Headquarters; **Notes:** NW Forest Pass or interagency pass required. Trail open to bicycles. Fishing options; **GPS:** N 46 03.635 W 121 58.366

Wander a wide and wild stretch of the Lewis River to explore a recently restored cedar-shingle camp. Although it lacks awesome cataracts, the Lower Lewis River makes up for it with foot-soaking river access.

GETTING THERE

From Woodland (exit 21 on I-5), follow State Route 503 east for 29 miles to Cougar. Continue east on SR 503 (which becomes Forest Road 90) for 18.5 miles. At the junction with FR 25, immediately past the Pine Creek Information Center, bear right onto the Lewis River Road (FR 90), which immediately crosses the Lewis River. Proceed 5.1 miles and turn left onto FR 9039. Drive 1 mile to the trailhead on the left (elev. 1260 ft). Privy available.

ON THE TRAIL

On wide, well-groomed tread, walk through a verdant western hemlock forest. The trail soon encounters an unmarked junction. To

Western flowering dogwood

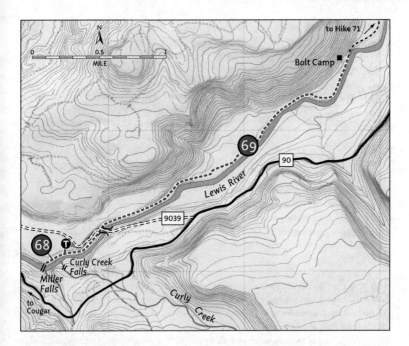

the right is Curly Creek Falls (Hike 68). Bear left onto the Lewis River Trail, which gradually descends as it parallels the Lewis River upstream, with the deep green of the water some fifty feet below.

The trail crosses FR 9039 near the bridge over the Lewis River—watch for mountain bikes—and unspools through a cool bottomland of centuries-old Douglas-firs. Note the river, much wider here than the narrow gorge near Curly Creek Falls.

Cross three creeks in quick succession before the trail gradually angles away from the river. Birdsong briefly replaces river chatter before the river draws near again. At 2 miles, cross a small depression and ascend a small rise; the open forest canopy offers

a fine view of the river from this vantage. Odds are good of spotting elk here too. At 2.3 miles, find a wide spot on a small cove; this makes a good picnic spot—or swimming spot late in the summer—with an excellent downriver vista.

Continue, flanked by the spider-legged limbs of vine maples and a carpet of vanilla-leaf, to Bolt Camp at 2.8 miles. Built in 1921 as a processing site for western red cedar bolts—the small blocks from which shingles are cut—the shelter at Bolt Camp had fallen into disrepair until a dedicated group of retired Forest Service employees restored the building in 2012. Today, the shelter offers a rainy-day reprieve with cedar-shingle siding and roof.

EXTENDING YOUR TRIP
Consider arranging a shuttle to hike 10 more miles through an increasingly narrow Lewis River canyon to its intersection with FR 90.

70 Middle Lewis Falls

RATING/ DIFFICULTY	ROUNDTRIP	ELEV GAIN/ HIGH POINT	SEASON
**/2	1 mile	200 feet/ 1800 feet	Mar–Nov

Map: Green Trails Lone Butte 365; **Contact:** Gifford Pinchot National Forest, Cowlitz Valley Ranger District; **Notes:** NW Forest Pass or interagency pass required. Trail open to bicycles. Fishing options; **GPS:** N 46 09.953 W 121 52.096

Used by anglers for access to the Lewis River, this trail offers a quick fix for waterfall-watchers too. Descend to Middle Lewis Falls and its emerald pools, then get a fish-eye view of tiny Copper Creek Falls.

GETTING THERE
From Woodland (exit 21 on I-5), follow State Route 503 east for 29 miles to Cougar. Continue east on SR 503 (which becomes Forest Road 90) for 18.5 miles. At the junction with FR 25 immediately past the Pine Creek Information Center, bear right onto the Lewis River Road (FR 90), which immediately crosses the Lewis River. Proceed 15.1 miles to the Middle Falls trailhead on the right (elev. 1780 ft).

ON THE TRAIL
From the trailhead, descend a scree slope sidelined by mossy boulders onto a broad flat. Widely spaced western hemlocks tower above; sword fern, salal, Oregon-grape and bunchberry crowd the forest floor.

At 0.1 mile, with the Lewis River ringing in your ears, begin a gentle descent and at 0.2 mile intersect the Lewis River Trail. Bear left. The trail undulates among hanging gardens of green moss and reaching ferns.

At 0.5 mile, cross a sturdy footbridge

Douglas squirrel on a young hemlock

over Copper Creek, which pours over a slick rock face into the Lewis River. Just beyond, Middle Lewis Falls sprays in broad fans over basalt. A well-worn angler's perch below the falls is a great place to enjoy lunch, whether you brought it or caught it.

Continuing on the trail, climb several eroding switchbacks and at 0.6 mile, turn left on Copper Creek Falls Trail. Ascend along the crumbling basalt of Copper Creek gorge. At 0.9 mile, Copper Creek Falls comes into view, spilling out of a narrow creek bed onto a stone basin 15 feet below. Marvel from afar, then cross a bridge directly over the falls. Now through boulder-strewn

forest, leisurely make your way back to the trailhead to complete the loop.

71 Upper Lewis River

RATING/ DIFFICULTY	ROUNDTRIP	ELEV GAIN/ HIGH POINT	SEASON
****/2	5 miles	680 feet/ 1700 feet	Apr–Nov

Map: Green Trails Lone Butte 365; **Contact:** Gifford Pinchot National Forest, Cowlitz Valley Ranger District; **Notes:** NW Forest Pass or interagency pass required. Trail open to bicycles; **GPS:** N 46 09.296 W 121 52.754

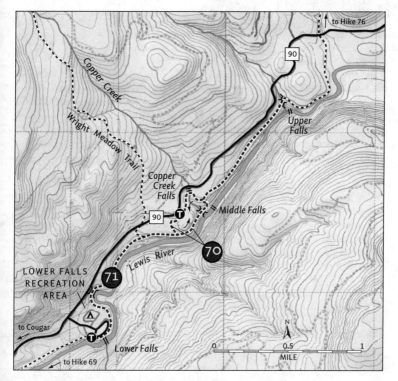

Lower Lewis Falls

Construction of the Lewis River Road carved up the once-wild Lewis River Trail. But several of its chunks still make for compelling hikes, none more so than this one, which boasts three great cascades—and more if you're willing to go the extra mile. Amble three virtually flat miles along the lush Lewis River through hemlocks and a smattering of old-growth Douglas-firs. Its low elevation allows the Lewis River trail to be enjoyed year-round—spring for peak waterfalls, summer for shade and foot-soaking, and autumn for golden alder leaves reflected in the river.

GETTING THERE

From Woodland (exit 21 on I-5), follow State Route 503 east for 29 miles to Cougar. Continue east on SR 503 (which becomes Forest Road 90) for 18.5 miles. At the junction with FR 25, immediately past the Pine Creek Informa-

tion Center, bear right onto the Lewis River Road (FR 90), which immediately crosses the Lewis River. Proceed 14.1 miles to the Lower Falls Recreation Area on the right and follow signs for the day-use parking loop and trailhead (elev. 1520 ft). Privy available.

ON THE TRAIL

The Lewis River Trail never strays far from the Lewis River Road—in fact, many stretches of the pavement were constructed on the original tread. But the steady churn of the river on one side and thick forest of hemlocks and Douglas-firs on the other do a good job masking traffic.

From the day-use parking area, find the trailhead and descend toward the river. This is a dessert-first hike, with the biggest and most visually arresting falls at the beginning. Lower Lewis Falls plunges more than 40 feet across a 200-foot wide fan into a large plunge pool. High spring snowmelt tends to blow out the falls; come when flows have slowed in early summer to appreciate the contours of the cascades.

From Lower Lewis Falls, continue on the wide path on the periphery of the campground. Immediately after leaving the campground behind, cross a rivulet on a small bridge at 0.6 mile and enter an attractive forest of western hemlock and Douglas-fir. The walking is easy, the scenery sublime.

Scan the river for an old bridge foundation in the river, which used to cross over to the now-defunct Lewis River campground. At 1 mile, cross a bridge that's in much better repair. The path then passes through an alder forest pungent with the scent of decaying leaves.

At 1.2 miles pass the junction with the Wright Meadow Trail, and at 1.3 miles the junction with the Middle Falls Trail (Hike 70). Continue straight, descending toward the river on tread framed by ferns.

At 1.5 miles, cross a bridge over Copper Creek to reach Middle Lewis Falls. More modest than its neighbors up- and downstream, Middle Falls is nonetheless a pleasing sight, the Lewis River cascading in broad fans around a basalt knuckle. This well-used spot on the river is a great perch from which to drop a line or dip a toe.

From Middle Falls, continue on the trail as it ascends switchbacks and passes the junction with Copper Creek Falls Trail. From here the tread narrows, now on crumbling basalt some fifty feet above the river; step carefully. More lightly traveled than the lower section of the trail, this stretch has a more wilderness-like character than the tourist- and angler-traveled sections downstream,

with green gardens of mosses and ferns clinging to steep basalt cliffs. Undammed from its source on Mount Adams to Eagle Cliff Park, the Lewis River has been designated by the Forest Service as a Wild and Scenic candidate.

Descend once again into woods, past deeply furrowed Douglas-firs. At 2.5 miles cross a footbridge. Immediately beyond is Upper Lewis Falls, which pours into a broad plunge pool. Large rocks on the edge of the pool invite shoreline scrambling. Or, continue another 0.3 mile to a viewpoint above the falls.

EXTENDING YOUR TRIP
To bag a fourth waterfall, continue 0.5 mile past Upper Falls to Taitnapum Falls. From here it's an easy amble in drier forest to the Upper Falls trailhead on FR 90, 1 mile distant.

72 Spencer Butte

RATING/ DIFFICULTY	ROUNDTRIP	ELEV GAIN/ HIGH POINT	SEASON
***/3	4.8 miles	2240 feet/ 4325 feet	June–Oct

Map: Green Trails Lone Butte 365; **Contact:** Gifford Pinchot National Forest; **Notes:** Trail open to motorcycles and bicycles; **GPS:** N 46 10.352 W 121 55.832

The Spencer Butte lookout is long gone, and so are the views, but at trail's end Breezy Point boasts a beaut. And be on the lookout for grouse, owls, mule deer, and elk, which—outside of hunting season—outnumber humans along this out-of-the-way trek.

GETTING THERE

From Woodland (exit 21 on I-5), follow State Route 503 east for 29 miles to Cougar. Continue east on SR 503 (which becomes Forest Road 90) for 18.5 miles. At the junction with FR 25, immediately past the Pine Creek Information Center, bear left and continue on FR 25, crossing the Muddy River, 5.5 miles before turning right on FR 93. Proceed on FR 93, a paved one-lane road with pull-outs, for 10.8 miles to an unmarked dirt road on the left. Drive this often-muddy road 0.5 mile, passing several dispersed campsites, to its end and the trailhead (elev. 3410 ft).

ON THE TRAIL

Spencer Butte Trail has two trailheads, but there's nothing to be gained from a one-way shuttle: your best option is to make this an out-and-back from the scenic Spencer Meadow end of the route. Begin in a uniform forest of western hemlock with a maple and fern understory. The trail is ATV-wide—perhaps a vestige of the lookout supply route—but open only to motorcycles.

After a brief climb, the trail levels out in open forest of beargrass, pipsissewa, and western white pine. Scan the ground for signs of deer and elk. Quiet hikers are likely to catch a glimpse of the latter, especially during autumn. The trail steepens; log step-ups provide some erosion control, but the route is still heavily rutted. The deep ruts will test your magnanimity toward motorbikes, or at least toward Forest Service multiple-use policy.

Keep climbing, with few views for company, until the trail levels at about 1 mile on broad Spencer Butte. (Some maps show a spur trail here to "Spencer Arch," but as of this writing the trail no longer exists.) Aside from the concrete footings, the former fire

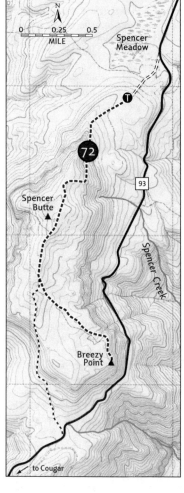

lookout is gone. Fire suppression was clearly a success, because second-growth forest blocks any views, but a pleasant plain of flowers remains. And there's a better view beyond.

The trail descends Spencer Butte through

Mount Adams from the old Breezy Point lookout site

doghair hemlock. At 1.4 miles, turn left at the signed junction for Breezy Point 30A. Beargrass borders the trail as it dips in and out of seasonal creek beds.

At 2 miles, the trail peters out briefly in a small clearing; bear left and pick it up, and at 2.2 miles reach the edge of the bluff. Once again, the trail grows faint; tack left to find traces of tread on the bluff edge.

At 2.4 miles, the trail dead-ends on a small knoll. Built in the 1930s, Breezy Point lookout, like its kin on Spencer Butte, is gone; a tangle of wires and wood is all that marks the spot. Marvel at Mount Adams in the distance. Marvel, too, that a fire lookout was once perched here on a rock barely big enough to hold an outhouse. Once you've finished marveling, retrace your steps to your Spencer Meadow start.

EXTENDING YOUR TRIP

Spencer Meadow is a popular elk hangout. Spend some time on the edge of the broad, wet meadow, especially first thing in the morning, and chances are good you'll spot a small herd.

VANISHING INTO THIN AIR AND THICK FOREST: D. B. COOPER

On Thanksgiving Eve 1971, a man identifying himself as Dan Cooper stepped up to the Northwest Orient ticket counter at Portland International Airport and paid $20 cash for a one-way ticket to Seattle-Tacoma Airport. Once seated, Cooper hijacked and threatened to blow up the airliner. He extorted $200,000 from the airline then leaped from the airborne 727 with twenty-one pounds of $20 bills strapped to his torso in a daring nighttime dive above the Lewis River.

He left behind few clues but one of the most famous criminal aliases—the "D. B." added erroneously by excited reporters—and most recognizable police sketches in modern history. Authorities launched an extensive and expensive manhunt, but weeks of searching by air and on foot turned up nothing.

In February 1980, an eight-year-old boy digging in a sandy bank of the Columbia River unearthed three bundles of deteriorating currency—$5800 in all, all in $20 bills. The serial numbers matched Cooper's cash. Before investigators could unearth any other clues from the river, Mount St. Helens erupted and buried any more evidence under a river of ash and mud. Since then, the FBI has investigated thousands of persons of interest, but the case remains unsolved—and technically open—nearly half a century later.

Cooper has become the Bigfoot of crime. And today there's something altogether quaint about his heist, perhaps because no one got hurt, perhaps because air travel—and air security—are so different now than when Cooper hijacked the flight. And in an era of air piracy, Cooper didn't fit the profile of previous pirates: his clean-cut look—hat, coat, dress shoes—suggested not a political dissident or Castro collaborator but a Madison Avenue ad-man boarding the subway. Cooper's caper seems more like the type to be immortalized in an outlaw-country ballad than debated on cable-news shows. More importantly, like the enduring legend of Bigfoot, the D. B. Cooper case suggests that the landscape is still wild enough that such disappearing acts are not outside the realm of possibility.

Opposite: The long ridge of Council Bluff

dark divide roadless area

Named for the nineteenth-century miner and settler John Dark, the Dark Divide Roadless Area encompasses the latticework of ridges that separates the Lewis and Cispus River drainages and connects Mount St. Helens with Mount Adams to the east. The southern part of Dark Divide drains into the Lewis River and is defined by heavily forested volcanic ridges and some of the largest remaining, unprotected old-growth stands in Washington's southern Cascades. Though spared St. Helens' wrath and the saw, most trails have fallen victim to neglect and Forest Service management that allows—actually, actively promotes—motorized use despite the fragile volcanic soils. But a few great trails still beckon hikers. And steep trails and challenging access keep uses of all kinds light, rewarding hikers willing to work for big trees and big volcano views.

73 Wright Meadow

RATING/ DIFFICULTY	ROUNDTRIP	ELEV GAIN/ HIGH POINT	SEASON
**/2	3 miles	380 feet/ 3730 feet	June–Oct

Map: Green Trails Lone Butte 365; **Contact:** Gifford Pinchot National Forest; **Notes:** Trail open to motorcycles, horses, and bicycles; **GPS:** N 46 12.523 W 121 54.111

Wildlife watchers can't go wrong with a visit to Wright Meadow. Berry pickers, too, will do all right. And even if one's inclination is to never leave the straight-and-narrow tread, this is one of the easiest-to-reach old-growth walks in the Dark Divide Roadless Area.

GETTING THERE

From Woodland (exit 21 on I-5), follow State Route 503 east for 29 miles to Cougar. Continue east on SR 503 (which becomes Forest Road 90), bearing left onto FR 25 at 18.5 miles. Continue on FR 25, crossing the Muddy River, 5.5 miles before turning right on FR 93. Proceed on FR 93, a one-lane road with pull-outs, for 14.1 miles to the trailhead on the left (elev. 3720 ft).

ON THE TRAIL

Wright Meadow Trail reaches from the Lewis River all the way up to the steep drainages of the Dark Divide. Trenches cut

A ruddy and ripe blueberry

by off-road vehicle traffic and old clear-cuts mar the beauty of most of the route, but this pleasant upper portion—and the spectacular meadow it skirts—is too good to abandon to the bray of motors.

Once on the trail, immediately enter cool forest—on a warm summer day a welcome respite from the surrounding clear-cuts. Motorcycles and horses frequent this trail, particularly during hunting season, but the tread here remains pleasantly rut-free. Admire the old-growth Douglas-fir and western hemlock; nurse logs nurture a healthy population of blueberries.

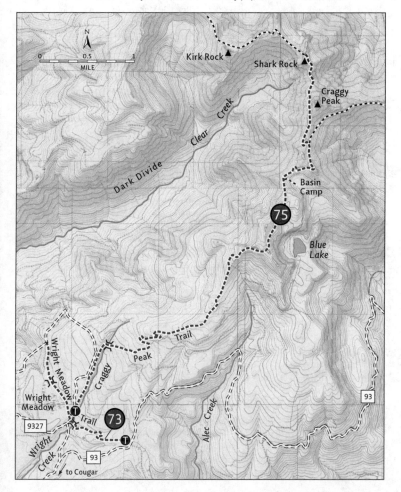

At 0.3 mile, enter a clear-cut, the sun-bleached stumps a legacy of logging practices past. Now, fireweed, beargrass, and blueberries take advantage of the sunlight. After a couple hundred yards, regain shade, and at 0.6 mile cross a wooden bridge over quiet Wright Creek. Cross Craggy Peak Trail (Hike 75) at 0.7 mile and a gravel road shortly after. After a few hundred yards, you'll be able to glimpse Wright Meadow through the trees to the left. The open understory invites an off-trail excursion to explore the edge of this impressive mid-elevation meadow the size of three football fields. Scope the expanse for birds, black bear, deer, and elk—and scan the ground for scat.

Continuing on the trail, cross a wooden bridge at 1.2 miles, and at 1.5 miles meet an old decommissioned road. The tread continues from here, but best to turn around and spend more time scanning the meadow for wildlife.

74 Badger Peak

RATING/ DIFFICULTY	ROUNDTRIP	ELEV GAIN/ HIGH POINT	SEASON
****/4	10.4 miles	2390 feet/ 5664 feet	July– mid-Oct

Map: Green Trails McCoy Peak 333;
Contact: Gifford Pinchot National Forest;
Notes: NW Forest Pass or interagency pass required. Trail open to motorcycles, horses, and bicycles; **GPS:** N 46 17.344 W 121 58.002

Scramble to round-the-compass views of new volcanoes—Mount St. Helens and her kin—and old—Pinto Rock—from the site of a former lookout. Afterward, soak pumice-scrubbed feet on the grassy lawn of shallow Badger Lake. This is without a doubt the southern Dark Divide's premier ridgeline hike.

GETTING THERE
From Woodland (exit 21 on I-5), follow State Route 503 east for 29 miles to Cougar. Continue east on SR 503 (which becomes Forest Road 90) for 18.5 miles. At the junction with FR 25 immediately past the Pine Creek Information Center, bear left and continue on FR 25, 22 miles to Elk Pass and the trailhead parking lot on the left (elev. 4080 ft). (From Randle, drive south 1 mile on SR 131 to a junction with FR 23. Bear right—south—to continue on SR 131, which becomes FR 25, and proceed 23 miles to Elk Pass.)

ON THE TRAIL
From the Elk Pass parking lot, cross FR 25 and walk along the shoulder 50 yards to the signed Boundary Trail trailhead. Hemmed in by western hemlock, blueberry, and huckleberry, the route is well insulated from traffic noise from FR 25 and nearby ATV routes.

After a brief, stiff climb, the trail levels out at 0.3 mile in open forest of old-growth hemlock—perhaps the finest high-elevation forest walking on the Dark Divide.

Two more switchback-scarce and pumice-slick climbs follow, each time alleviated by the pleasant forest setting. Mycologists will marvel at the variety of mushrooms crowding the forest floor, king boletes and more thriving in the rich volcanic humus.

At 2.4 miles, come to an opening. Mosquito Meadows Trail enters from the left. To the right, huckleberries and firs screen clear-cuts. Continue straight, ascending the only significantly motorcycle-rutted section of the hike. Views of Mount St. Helens to the southwest should assuage any frustration at poor trail management.

Mount Adams and the drainages of the Dark Divide

Cross a small bridge at 2.7 miles to continue ascending through doghair forest of Pacific silver fir, with Mount Rainier barely visible to the north. At 4.2 miles, climb one more, steep, straight trail stretch followed by several switchbacks through seasonal creek beds and the junction with Badger Peak Trail.

Turn left and climb, bearing right at a signed junction. The way left descends 1.25 miles to the Badger Peak 257A trailhead. It's a much quicker hike to the summit, but the

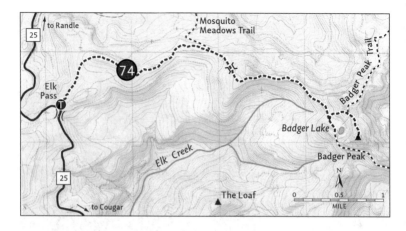

drive to the trailhead is not recommended for any but high-clearance rigs. Traverse an open sidehill; below, screened by trees, is the steep, shallow basin of Badger Lake. Heather and wildflowers flank the narrow tread.

Round one final switchback and scramble the last 30 yards to the summit at 4.9 miles. Fused glass and scraps of metal are all that remain of the former lookout, burnt down by the Forest Service during its mid-century zeal to scrap lookout sites. But the views remain. And what views! Due north is Mount Rainier, followed in clockwise succession by Mounts Adams, Hood, and St. Helens. Just east of Badger Peak lies volcanic ancestor Pinto Rock, its blown-out cinder cone a millennia-old predecessor to Mount St. Helens.

Descend from the lookout, and at the Boundary Trail junction bear left. Cross a grassy meadow to cycle-chewed campsites on the shore of Badger Lake. Looking more like a beaver pond than an alpine lake, Badger is not a bad place to shake the pumice out of your boots and while away an hour or two.

EXTENDING YOUR TRIP
From Badger Lake, climb east on the Boundary Trail (Hike 86) to access the rocky interior of the Dark Divide Roadless Area.

75 Craggy Peak

RATING/ DIFFICULTY	ROUNDTRIP	ELEV GAIN/ HIGH POINT	SEASON
****/4	14.6 miles	3070 feet/ 5260 feet	July–Oct

Maps: Green Trails Lone Butte 365, McCoy Peak 333; **Contact:** Gifford Pinchot National Forest, Mount St. Helens National Volcanic Monument and Surrounding Area Headquarters; **Notes:** Trail open to motorcycles, horses, and bicycles; **GPS:** N 46 12.741 W 121 54.994

Mountain goats roam this pencil-shaped pinnacle, the roof of an ancient volcano, in the heart of the Dark Divide. So do motorcycles, thanks to Forest Service management. But although tire tracks have trashed the thin pumice tread, motorcycles are few, especially midweek. Come for sprawling subalpine meadows and glorious old-growth forest—and perhaps a glimpse of those shaggy scrambling beasts.

GETTING THERE

From Woodland (exit 21 on I-5), follow State Route 503 east for 29 miles to Cougar. Continue east on SR 503 (which becomes Forest Road 90) for 18.5 miles. At the junction with FR 25 immediately past the Pine Creek Information Center, bear left and continue on FR 25, crossing the Muddy River, 5.5 miles before turning right on FR 93. Proceed on FR 93, a paved one-lane road with pull-outs, for 12.9 miles, then turn left on FR 9327 and travel 0.5 mile to the trailhead, in a well-used outfitter's camp, on the right (elev. 3520 ft).

ON THE TRAIL

From the trailhead, ascend an old clear-cut encompassing Wright Creek on dusty, deeply rutted track. In the summer, the sun bears down here, but beargrass blooms provide a distraction.

At 1 mile (elev. 3880 ft), cross Wright Creek on a wooden walkway and enter an intact forest of Douglas-firs spared the saws. Pocket meadows of lupine and false hellebore punctuate the forest. At 1.5 miles, the trail ascends another old clear-cut before the climb eases, at 2.3 miles, in the last of the logged areas. Enter forest. Motorcycle ruts, at times waist deep, will test your balance and patience. But the flowers lining the trail should improve your mood.

At 2.75 miles reach a broad intersection

Dusty summer dusk over Mount St. Helens

IN SEARCH OF BIGFOOT

Although the particulars differ, "wildman" stories feature heavily in the lore of the various indigenous populations of the Pacific Northwest. Canadian newspaperman J. W. Burns—collecting the various myths for a series of newspaper articles in the early 1920s—coined the term "Sasquatch," which derived from the Halkomelem people's language *sςsq'ets*. He applied it to the general classification of a large, hairy, semi-human creature that stalked the cedar and hemlock forests of the Northwest. Since then, Sasquatch, like D. B. Cooper, has become a celebrity in *absentia*. The heavily timbered, nigh-impenetrable drainages between Mount St. Helens and Mount Adams seem to be a hotbed for sightings of these hairy creatures.

Artist Paul Kane, in his classic 1847 treatise on the Coastal Indians, described his hosts' fear of *skoocums*, a race of human-like cannibals, or "mountain devils," who inhabited Mount St. Helens. In 1924, local newspapers reporting a supposed encounter between a group of miners and a pack of these mountain devils referred to them as "mountain apes"—and the name stuck.

Were these the same creatures as Sasquatch? More than likely the *skoocums* embodied the restless spirit that seemed to inhabit constantly smoking Mount St. Helens. And more than likely, Sasquatch is the product of myth. But as acclaimed lepidopterist Robert Michael Pyle notes in *Where Bigfoot Walks: Crossing the Dark Divide*, documenting his month-long trek across the Dark Divide Roadless Area in search of the West's most famous recluse, Sasquatch is an invisible indicator species for our physical and psychological landscape. As long as our natural areas remain wild enough to entertain the possibility of such atavistic creatures, he says, our wild imaginations remain healthy.

where the Stabler Camp Trail joins up with the Craggy Peak Trail (elev. 4960 ft). Continue straight. The next mile is pure hiking delight as the trail steadily switchbacks through lupine and false azalea, firs towering above. Cross a sun-baked scree slope at 3.8 miles, which offers the hike's first views, those of the fir-cloaked slopes of the Indian Heaven Wilderness to the south.

The trail re-enters forest. At 4.2 miles (elev. 5200 ft), ignore an abandoned trail—helpfully signed "abandoned trail"—and bear left across a broad subalpine meadow. Barely glimpsed Blue Lake—the one-time destination of that abandoned trail—twinkles to your right.

The trail crosses sunny subalpine meadows moistened by a tiny creek—your last reliable source of water for a while. Ascend a shaded draw, where snow may linger as late as July, before dropping to a trail junction at 5.2 miles (elev. 5100 ft). To the right, Basin Camp provides backpackers a rare flat spot to set up camp, provided mosquitoes haven't claimed all the sites.

Continue straight, past a shallow pond, before cresting the ridge. Pause for views of Juniper Ridge and Mount Adams beyond. Cross another steep meadow, and at 6 miles (elev. 5180 ft), intersect the Boundary Trail (Hike 86) on the southeast flank of Craggy Peak.

Turn left, and at 6.2 miles gain the spine of Craggy Peak (elev. 5260 ft), its summit spire still hidden. This is a great turnaround point, but to continue, descend into open forest. Mount St. Helens looms in the distance. In the foreground drains Clear Creek, its 500-year-old Douglas-firs part of the largest intact old-growth forest in southern Washington.

Traverse wooded side slopes, enjoying peek-a-boo views of jagged Shark and Kirk Rocks. At 7 miles, switchback up the east side of Shark Rock, which so inspired Mountaineers author E. M. Sterling that he first proposed a Shark Rock Wilderness in 1975. Its steep spires and luxurious meadows still inspire.

At 7.3 miles, gain the spine of Shark Rock (elev. 5260 ft). No summit trails here; the route is far too steep. Best leave it to the mountain goats, which can often be seen playing here. Return the way you came.

EXTENDING YOUR TRIP

From the junction with the Boundary Trail (Hike 86) on the southeast flank of Craggy Peak, continue east or west as far as your feet will take you. Yellowjacket Pass, 2 miles east of Craggy Peak, makes a nice overnighter destination.

76 Quartz Creek

RATING/ DIFFICULTY	ROUNDTRIP	ELEV GAIN/ HIGH POINT	SEASON
****/3	8.2 miles	2000 feet/ 2365 feet	June–Nov

Maps: Green Trails Lone Butte 365, McCoy Peak 333; **Contact:** Gifford Pinchot National Forest, Mount St. Helens National Volcanic Monument and Surrounding Area Headquarters; **Notes:** NW Forest Pass or

interagency pass required. Trail open to horses and bicycles. Fishing options; **GPS:** N 46 10.961 W 121 50.944

Quartz Creek Trail is one of the most spectacular old-growth valley treks in southwest Washington. And after years of neglect, it's getting some love, thanks to the Washington Trails Association. With the exception of a few big blow-downs at the end, the first 4 miles to Snag-tooth Creek are free and clear. This is a great hike to escape the heat or rain—or any time you want to marvel at old-growth trees and rushing creeks.

GETTING THERE

From Woodland (exit 21 on I-5), follow State Route 503 east for 29 miles to Cougar. Continue east on SR 503 (which becomes Forest Road 90) for 18.5 miles. At the junction with FR 25 immediately past the Pine Creek Information Center, bear right onto the Lewis River Road (FR 90), immediately crossing the Lewis River. Proceed 17.2 miles to the Upper Falls trailhead on the right (elev. 1790 ft).

ON THE TRAIL

Cross FR 90 and join the trail. Once a part of the Lewis River Trail, construction of the Lewis River Road (FR 90) separated Quartz Creek, and years of neglect kept it off the radar of many hikers. We say it's the better trail, far from roads and close to old-growth forest. And it's a rarity in the Dark Divide area: a completely motor-free route. Kudos to Washington Trails Association for reviving it.

Pass the trail junction from the Lewis River Horse Camp, paralleling Quartz Creek's riffles and eddies. Once past several prime creekside fishing spots, quickly climb away from the creek through two washouts. Descend back to creek level at 0.5 mile and cross Platinum Creek on a sturdy bridge at 0.6 mile. Trailside geologists note the names: Quartz Creek and its tributaries are known as some of the best rockhounding spots in southwest Washington.

After Platinum Creek, your work begins. The trail quickly dispenses with switchbacks and climbs 500 feet in 0.5 mile. The silver (or platinum) lining: these steep slopes prohibited logging and preserved the magnificent old growth all around you—the largest block of old-growth forest remaining in the Gifford Pinchot National Forest.

At 1.2 miles, the grade eases, allowing for pleasant ambling, with Quartz Creek barely audible far below. Switchback downhill to

Straight Creek at 1.9 miles. Cautiously cross slick basalt. On the far side are the hike's best campsites.

Ascend again, this time through a woodland of hemlock, alder, and vine maple reminiscent of East Coast hardwood forest. Underfoot is a tangle of pipsissewa, huckle-berry, and Oregon-grape.

At 2.6 miles, the trail levels within an airy cathedral of old-growth Douglas-fir wreathed in vine maple. Cross a mossy bridge and enter a dimmer, closed-canopy forest. Angle across a steep hillside and into a small ravine—a choke point for blowdowns. At just over 4 miles, Snagtooth Creek's boulder-strewn creek bed beckons. Quiet, if close-in, campsites dot the far side: it's a good place to stay or to turn around

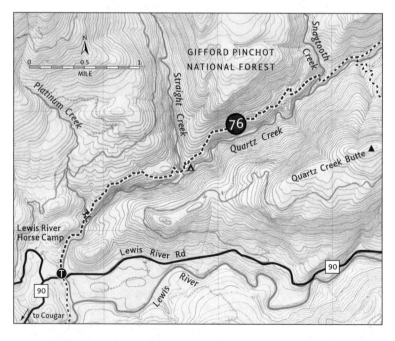

A small cascade on Snagtooth Creek

and return the way you came. From here, Quartz Creek continues 7 miles to the Boundary Trail (Hike 86), but the section has received little maintenance. Content yourself here with Quartz Creek's offerings, and contemplate a future trip—this time with crosscut saw in hand to continue the WTA's work.

DARK DIVISION: MOTORIZED WRECK-REATION

Left out of the 1984 Washington Wilderness Act because of the valuable ancient timber it harbors, the Dark Divide Roadless Area has seen saws steadily chew at its borders. But it's the management of motorized use that has doomed many of the Dark Divide's once-wilderness-worthy trails, such as Table Mountain, Cussed Hollow, and Summit Prairie.

We have nothing against motorcyclists: the few we've encountered on the trail were incredibly courteous in addition to being aware that a few bad apples in their midst mar them all. Many of the trails in the region would likely not be open without their maintenance efforts. Furthermore, riders have a legal right to these trails, the Forest Service having opened—in fact, actively promoted—many trails, including the Boundary Trail, to motorized use, despite the fact that these trails were neither engineered nor built with bikes in mind. The combination of soft pumice and straight-up, lookout-servicing routes have resulted in many trails that, in addition to being frustrating to hike, are virtually unrideable by all but the most skilled motorcyclists. Many cyclists would say as much.

Unfortunately, efforts to protect the Dark Divide and designate it as wilderness have for three decades failed to gain traction. Other solutions, such as seasonal closures for motorized vehicles when the trails are at their most vulnerable, or trail reconstruction and re-routing, will require crossing the rocky divide of hiker and biker relations. The alternative is the loss of these trails for everyone. And that would truly be the darkest outcome of all.

EXTENDING YOUR TRIP

Just past Snagtooth Creek, Quartz Creek Butte Trail picks up—and up and up—to the east of the creek drainage. WTA has helped clear this nigh-abandoned trail too.

Boulder Trail— Table Mountain

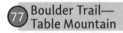

RATING/ DIFFICULTY	ROUNDTRIP	ELEV GAIN/ HIGH POINT	SEASON
**/2	2.6 miles	590 feet/ 4760 feet	late June– Oct

Map: Green Trails Blue Lake 334; **Contact:** Gifford Pinchot National Forest, Cowlitz Valley Ranger District; **Notes:** Trail open to motorcycles, horses, and bicycles; **GPS:** N 46 16.306 W 121 40.067

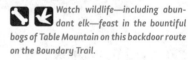

Watch wildlife—including abundant elk—feast in the bountiful bogs of Table Mountain on this backdoor route on the Boundary Trail.

GETTING THERE

From Randle, drive south 1 mile on State Route 131. At the junction, bear left (east) on Forest Road 23 and proceed for 31.8 miles (pavement ends at 23.5 miles), turning right on FR 2334, signed for Council Bluff. Follow FR 2334 for 3.4 miles to the signed spur for Boulder Trail 1C. Turn right and then immediately left onto an unmarked jeep track, proceeding 0.6 mile to its end and the trailhead (elev. 3940 ft). (Note: hikers driving low-clearance vehicles, particularly in wet conditions, may prefer to park at the beginning of the unmarked jeep track and walk to the trailhead.)

Bunchberry

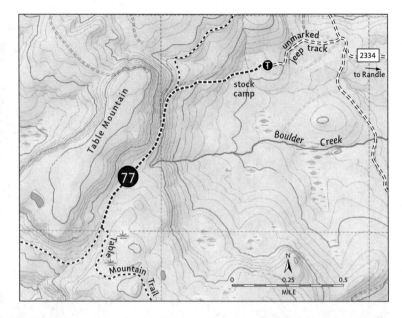

ON THE TRAIL

Sure, there's an actual Table Mountain Trail that's easily accessed from the Lewis River Road, but it's a steep motorcycle expressway—one of the most tire-beaten trails in the Dark Divide. Try this backdoor Boundary Trail approach instead. The destination is worthy, particularly for wildlife watchers. We saw a large herd of elk, including a trophy bull, during the height of hunting season in the expansive wetlands ringing Table Mountain.

Beginning at an old stock camp, rock-hop a small stream and climb little-used tread flanked by huckleberries and stately western hemlocks. Just after negotiating a short but steep, heavily rutted pitch, join the Boundary Trail at 0.6 mile and leave the ruts behind. Turn left and on soft level tread sketch the outline of heavily forested Table Mountain.

Perhaps owing to its level pitch or relative lack of use, this eastern trail section shows some of the least damage by motorcycles on the eastern Boundary Trail.

At 1.1 miles, follow the edge of a lush wetland bisected by a sluggish stream. Walk slowly and quietly and look for elk: they tend to bed down in the open undergrowth flanking the trail. Sated with wildlife viewing, continue to the Table Mountain Trail at 1.3 miles. The distressed tread at the junction is but an appetizer to the destruction on Table Mountain Trail. Give thanks that some of the Dark Divide hasn't yet been chewed up.

EXTENDING YOUR TRIP

Continue west on the Boundary Trail (Hike 86) for another mile of wetlands wandering. Past the last wetland, however, the tread gets increasingly distressed.

Dawn over Mount Rainier

78 Council Bluff

RATING/ DIFFICULTY	ROUNDTRIP	ELEV GAIN/ HIGH POINT	SEASON
****/2	3 miles	950 feet/ 5180 feet	late June– Oct

Map: Green Trails Blue Lake 334; **Contact:** Gifford Pinchot National Forest, Cowlitz Valley Ranger District; **Notes:** Trail open to motorcycles, horses, and bicycles; **GPS:** N 46 15.777 W 121 37.973

There's no debating it: this spectacular anyone-can-do-it trail rewards hikers with one of the region's best views of Mount Adams. The former site of a fire lookout and, before that, a Native American meeting place, Council Bluff will leave you at a loss for words, if not for breath.

GETTING THERE

From Randle, drive south 1 mile on State Route 131. At the junction, bear left (east) on Forest Road 23 and proceed 31.8 miles

(pavement ends at 23.5 miles), turning right on FR 2334, signed for Council Bluff. Continue 1.2 miles, bearing right onto the spur into Council Lake Campground. Find the trailhead (elev. 4239 ft) at the west end of the campground. Privy available.

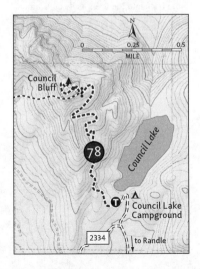

ON THE TRAIL

Beginning from the popular Council Bluff Campground, ascend the Boundary Trail—here an old, deeply gullied road. The way climbs purposefully, flanked by woodland flowers—foamflower, lupine, bunchberry, and vanilla leaf. A thick canopy of fir and hemlock mostly screens the slump-shouldered west face of Mount Adams from view. Don't fret; the bluff summit is attained soon enough.

At 0.8 mile, the road-trail relaxes, angling into subalpine forest. The way makes one more climb, this one capped by the best-yet glimpse of Mount Adams. Then, at 1.2 miles, the road-trail levels in a wide clearing on the shoulder of Council Bluff (elev. 4974 ft). The Boundary Trail continues straight; instead, look for the trail that ascends to the right (north) behind a wooden gate.

Now a true single track, the route climbs stiffly through a rock garden of juniper, huckleberry, mariposa and tiger lilies, and sulphur buckwheat. The way ducks once more back into the trees as its curls around the west face of the bluff before attaining the summit at 1.5 miles.

Behold Mount Adams, which seems close enough to touch. If you can take your eyes off Adams, admire its volcanic cousins: Mount Rainier to the north, Mount Hood to the south, and Mount St. Helens behind you. Closer at hand, Council Lake lies below.

With this area falling within the fluid boundary between the traditional range of the Upper Cowlitz (Taidnapam), a Yakama affiliate, and the lower Cowlitz, Council Bluff likely hosted many a parley between the two groups. Palaver with hiking partners or *patoo*—"Mount Adams" in the Taidnapum tongue—himself before returning the way you came.

EXTENDING YOUR TRIP

Add a little more than two miles of alpine rock gardens and thumbnail-sized huckleberries by descending the Boundary Trail (Hike 86), now on true single track, to its junction with FR 2334.

Opposite: Hemlock-clad Horseshoe Ridge

siouxon roadless area

South of Mount St. Helens, the Siouxon Roadless Area encompasses approximately 26,000 acres of pristine forestland amid a sea of clear-cuts. The Yacolt Burn of 1902 devastated the old-growth forest, but in the subsequent century a verdant and vigorous second-growth forest has grown in its stead. Nearly fifty miles of trails, most of them constructed by the Civilian Conservation Corp in the 1930s to patrol the forest for future conflagrations, allow for hikes of varying lengths among lush creek bottoms and lonely ridgelines. But the main attractions here are the waterfalls, beautiful and various—some of the best in Washington's south Cascades. If you're looking for the top waterfall hikes in the Mount St. Helens region, the Siouxon is a shoo-in!

79 North Siouxon Creek

RATING/ DIFFICULTY	ROUNDTRIP	ELEV GAIN/ HIGH POINT	SEASON
****/4	9.2 miles	2200 feet/ 1532 feet	May–Nov

Maps: Green Trails Lookout Mountain 396, Mt St. Helens 364; **Contact:** Washington Department of Natural Resources; **Notes:** Discover Pass required. Trail open to bicycles; **GPS:** N 45 58.749 W 122 15.292

Follow North Siouxon Creek as it sluices through rocky chutes to the vast bowl of Black Hole Falls, which just might be the best waterfall in southwest Washington you've never heard of. Along the

Black Hole Falls

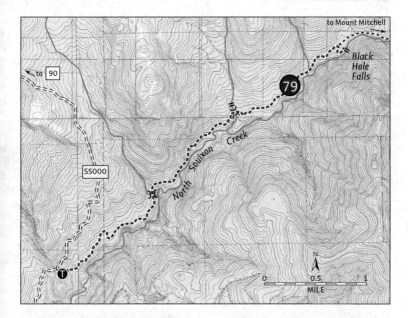

way, cross dozens of seeps, streams, creeks, and tiny trailside cascades in wilderness-quality woodland.

GETTING THERE

Drivers can access the North Siouxon Creek trailhead from Chelatchie Prairie near Amboy, but the roads here are exceedingly confusing and often unmarked. The following approach from Cougar is longer but easier to navigate. From Cougar, drive east on State Route 503. At 3.1 miles, immediately after the road changes to Forest Road 90 (look for the power substation on the right), take a sharp right. Immediately turn right again and follow this rough road over a bridge over the Lewis River. Drive 0.3 mile over a bridge on the Lewis River and turn left at a Y-junction.

Continue 0.4 mile and turn right onto Road S6000. Drive 3.8 steep, harrowing miles (which could be slippery when wet) to Road S5000. Bear left and continue another 1 mile to a four-way junction at a crest. Keep straight and head downhill for 3.5 steep, harrowing miles to a log-bordered gravel pullout and trailhead on the left (elev. 1290 ft).

ON THE TRAIL

From the parking area, your route descends steeply through hemlock forest. Skirt an old cut and enter an airy maple forest braided with small streams—you'll hop a half dozen in the first mile. The trail settles into a routine, dipping into shallow draws and then snaking back out. And speaking of snakes, they seem to find this trail particularly appealing.

BURNING DOWN THE FOREST

On September 11, 1902, the second-largest forest fire in Washington's history broke out. The cause of the Yacolt Burn was never determined but has been attributed to loggers burning slash in the Wind River valley. Fanned by unusually dry winds, the fire quickly spread, darkening the skies and dropping over a half an inch of ash on the city of Portland. Smoke reached Seattle, and many folks thought that Mount St. Helens or Mount Rainier had erupted. In three days' time, the fire scorched more than 238,000 acres and killed thirty-eight people in Clark, Cowlitz, and Skamania Counties. Rains eventually put out the blaze.

But the fire triggered action: The following year, the Washington State Legislature established a state fire warden. Then in 1910, after what's been termed the Great Fire (see author Timothy Egan's book *The Big Burn*) scorched three million acres of inland Northwest and Northern Rockies forest, President Taft's administration transformed the US Forest Service into a much larger agency with active and organized fire suppression programs. Almost all of the Siouxon Roadless Area and lands east toward the Wind River valley were touched by the Yacolt Burn of 1902 and today still show signs of that epic fire.

At 1.5 miles, spot for the first time through the trees the narrow ribbon of North Siouxon Creek. Views of the boulder-lined gorge are scant, but take heart: there's a first-rate, front-row view of the water at trail's end. Immediately afterward, cross the mouth of a large creek on a well-established log bridge and then climb, first above that creek and then curving around high above North Siouxon Creek.

Skip across four more trickles of water and continue under massive firs and hemlocks to another large, maple-shaded cascade at 2.9 miles. Cross the creek on a log bridge. Four more small creek crossings follow before the trail reaches the signed junction for Black Hole Falls at 4.5 miles. Turn right and descend 0.1 mile to your destination. Here, North Siouxon Creek pitches some fifty feet through a pinched canyon into Black Hole Falls below. Despite the forbidding name, swimmers and anglers will find welcoming water here.

EXTENDING YOUR TRIP

Continue 5.5 miles on progressively deteriorating tread to Mount Mitchell. Because a dispute with a private landowner has blocked the Department of Natural Resources access road to the Mount Mitchell trailhead, the North Siouxon is currently the only access to the once-popular summit.

80 Siouxon Creek

RATING/ DIFFICULTY	ROUNDTRIP	ELEV GAIN/ HIGH POINT	SEASON
****/3	13.8 miles	2360 feet/ 1840 feet	Mar–Nov

Map: Green Trails Lookout Mountain 396; **Contact:** Gifford Pinchot National Forest, Mount St. Helens National Volcanic Monument and Surrounding Area Headquarters; **Notes:** NW Forest Pass or interagency pass required. Trail open to bicycles. Fishing options; **GPS:** N 45 56.439 W 122 13.766

![family, dog, and binoculars icons] This popular and nearly level creekside cruise boasts a solid half-dozen of the best cataracts in the southern Washington Cascades—made all the more impressive by a wilderness-worthy forest setting. Save this shoulder-season hike for a rainy day, which are in abundant supply here, to see this creek at its peak.

GETTING THERE

From the Chelatchie Prairie General Store in Amboy, drive east on NE Healy Road, which eventually turns into Forest Road 54. (Note: FR 54 is heavily buckled and prone to washouts; it's best to check road conditions at Forest Service headquarters in Amboy first.) At 9.1 miles, bear left on FR 57. Drive 2.1 miles and, immediately after a small quarry, turn left on FR 5701. Follow this at-times potholed pavement 1 mile to the pullout and trailhead on the left (elev. 1840 ft).

ON THE TRAIL

The Siouxon Creek Trail spans the spectrum of waterfall flavors: punchbowl plunge pools; narrow, canyon-squeezed cataracts; and dramatic horsetail and bridal veil displays. The forested backdrop isn't too shabby, either—some of the best intact—and unprotected—lowland forest in the southern Washington Cascades.

From the unmarked trail terminus—you'll pass the main trailhead shortly—Siouxon Creek Trail dips in and out of clover-choked creek gullies. Although the Yacolt Burn scoured the slopes above Siouxon Creek, scattered old growth survived in the creek bottoms. Pass historic Hickman's Cabin, a storage site for the Forest Service firefighters tasked with protecting that remaining timber.

At 3 miles, pass the main trailhead and descend to a wooden bridge over West

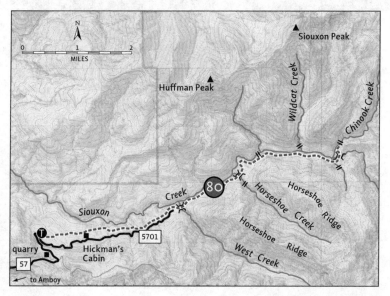

Siouxon Falls

Creek. The large dispersed campsites here and elsewhere along the creek testify to this trail's popularity. Pass the junction with Horseshoe Ridge Trail, and at just under 5 miles cross Horseshoe Creek. Horseshoe Falls calls: grab a good view of the nearly 50-foot double-horsetail cascade on a short spur trail 0.1 mile after crossing the creek.

Otherwise, amble through forest, hop over a tiny brook, and at 5 miles reach a viewpoint of Siouxon Falls, which plunges nearly thirty feet into a broad, oval-shaped punchbowl pool. Stop for a snack and photo op on a tiny bench, or continue on the trail as it curves around the falls in a narrowing gorge. The trail passes smaller cataracts above Siouxon Falls before it climbs away from the creek, drops down into broad

bottomland, and then climbs high above the creek.

At 6.8 miles, cross modest 14-Mile Falls at its slickrock base. In late summer the falls can be crossed with minimal foot-soaking; in high water, scout up the creek for a log bridge. Immediately afterward, reach a signed junction. Lunch here next to Siouxon Creek's narrow chasm, or cross the sturdy footbridge for a short trek to Chinook Falls (see Hike 83), before returning the way you came.

EXTENDING YOUR TRIP

Siouxon Creek Trail continues another 3.5 miles to its eastern trailhead, although it's primarily the province of mountain bikes past Chinook crossing.

81 Horseshoe Ridge

RATING/ DIFFICULTY	LOOP	ELEV GAIN/ HIGH POINT	SEASON
****/5	11.9 miles	3300 feet/ 3475 feet	May–Nov

Map: Green Trails Lookout Mountain 396; **Contact:** Gifford Pinchot National Forest, Mount St. Helens National Volcanic Monument and Surrounding Area Headquarters; **Notes:** NW Forest Pass or interagency pass required. Trail open to bicycles. Fishing options; **GPS:** N 45 56.790 W 122 10.671

Looking for a long shoulder-season hike that samples the breadth of *Siouxon Creek Roadless Area? You're in luck. Not for novices or the knock-kneed, Horseshoe Ridge rewards high-grade climbing with* subalpine rock gardens and sweeping views of Siouxon Creek's deep drainages.

GETTING THERE

From the Chelatchie Prairie General Store in Amboy, drive east on NE Healy Road, which eventually turns into Forest Road 54. (Note: FR 54 is heavily buckled and prone to washouts; it's best to check road conditions at the Forest Service headquarters in Amboy first.) At 9.1 miles, bear left on FR 57. Drive 2.1 miles and, immediately after a small quarry, turn left on FR 5701. Follow this at-times potholed pavement 3.7 miles to the road's end, parking, and trailhead (elev. 1260 ft).

ON THE TRAIL

Warm up on the Siouxon Creek Trail (Hike 80). At 1 mile, turn right on signed Horseshoe Ridge Trail. Steel yourself for a steep

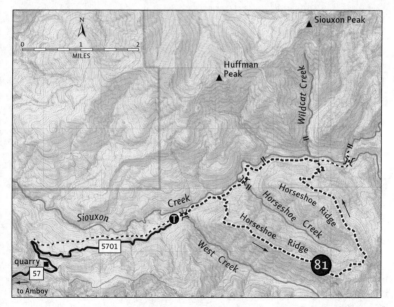

The foggy forested ridges of Siouxon Creek Roadless Area

ascent—you gain 1800 feet over the next 1.5 miles! The path is little more than a scratch in the earth in places, occasionally requires nearly hands-and-knees scrambling. Focus your climbing attention on the often-fog-enshrouded Huffman Peak behind a screen of pencil-straight Pacific silver fir. At 2.8 miles, take a photo break on a small rocky knoll. Beargrass, coral bells, lomatium, and creeping Oregon-grape drape the nearby rocks. Keep climbing: the rocky spine of the ridge becomes more visible even as the infrequently maintained tread threatens to disappear.

Cross a small bald at 3 miles, and attain the visual high point of the trail at 3.7 miles. From the open slope, peer down into the steep forested drainages that were spared both wildfire and the saw. Subalpine flowers—heather, phlox, lomatium—hug the rocks. Where the tread is faint, follow the elk pellets.

The trail returns to the trees and at 4.7 miles begins descending through a beautiful subalpine forest of huckleberry and old-growth hemlock. At 5 miles, cross through a dispersed campsite on the side of an old dirt road. At 5.2 miles, cross the road and pick up the trail (signed) on the other side. The narrow, rocky tread now traverses the northwest lobe of Horseshoe Ridge. At 7.2 miles, the going gets steep—you will lose the hard-won elevation earned on the other arm of the ridge on tread more elk trace than true trail. Spy Siouxon Peak through the trees, cross two creeks, and reach the Siouxon Creek Trail and level ground at 8.7 miles. Follow the trail downstream another 3.2 miles to the trailhead—and consider a soak of sore knees in Siouxon Creek.

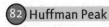 **Huffman Peak**

RATING/ DIFFICULTY	LOOP	ELEV GAIN/ HIGH POINT	SEASON
***/4	13.6 miles	3990 feet/ 3830 feet	July–Oct

Map: Green Trails Lookout Mountain 396;
Contact: Gifford Pinchot National Forest,
Mount St. Helens National Volcanic Monument and Surrounding Area Headquarters;
Notes: NW Forest Pass or interagency pass
required. Trail open to bicycles. Fishing
options; **GPS:** N 45 56.790 W 122 10.671

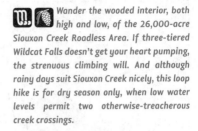 Wander the wooded interior, both
high and low, of the 26,000-acre
*Siouxon Creek Roadless Area. If three-tiered
Wildcat Falls doesn't get your heart pumping,
the strenuous climbing will. And although
rainy days suit Siouxon Creek nicely, this loop
hike is for dry season only, when low water
levels permit two otherwise-treacherous
creek crossings.*

GETTING THERE

From the Chelatchie Prairie General Store in
Amboy, drive east on NE Healy Road, which
eventually turns into Forest Road 54. (Note:

Calamity Peak from Huffman Ridge

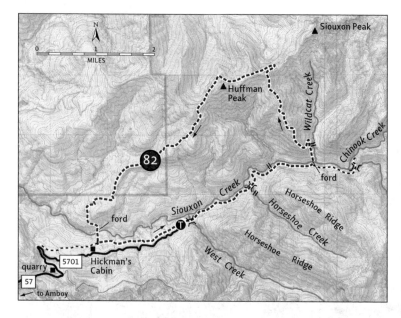

FR 54 is heavily buckled and prone to wash-outs; it's best to check road conditions at the Forest Service headquarters in Amboy first.) At 9.1 miles, bear left on FR 57. Drive 2.1 miles and, immediately after a small quarry, turn left on FR 5701. Follow this at-times potholed pavement 3.7 miles to the road's end, parking, and trailhead (elev. 1260 ft).

ON THE TRAIL

From the parking lot, follow the trail downhill to Siouxon Creek trail. Turn right and follow this nearly level trail 3.2 miles (see Hike 80 description) to the Wildcat Trail junction. Descend, passing a well-used campsite, to the shore of Siouxon Creek.

Contemplate your crossing: even at low flow, typically July through September, cross-ing Siouxon Creek requires a knee-deep ford through an insistent creek. If it's early in the

season or immediately after a rainstorm, choose the Siouxon Creek or Horseshoe Ridge routes instead (Hikes 80 and 81). Otherwise, unbuckle your backpack straps, get a firm grip on your trekking poles, and forge ahead.

Pick up the trail on the far side of the creek and proceed climbing. Shortly, you'll hear the roar of Wildcat Falls and, soon after, at a switchback in the trail you'll see the source. Plunging 225 feet in three tiers, Wildcat Falls is the most impressive set of cascades in the Siouxon Creek area. From this vantage only the lowest tier and partial drop is visible but, at 125 feet, it alone dwarfs its neighbors. A steep, slippery side trail descends to the base of the falls: most hikers will be content to enjoy the view from the main trail.

With your waterfall craving sated, con-tinue climbing. A salal-covered knob at 4.2

miles offers an aerial view of upper Wildcat Falls and the interior of Siouxon Creek Roadless Area. After this, the trail enters the trees and climbs with little reprieve—nearly 2000 feet in 2 miles. If you're not still wet from the Wildcat crossing, you'll soon be soaked in sweat. Take time to admire the scattered old-growth sentinels of western hemlock and Pacific silver fir, many bearing basal inverted-V scars, "cat faces," from the Yacolt Burn. The trail grows indistinct in places; when in doubt, follow the fall line.

Finally, at 5.5 miles, crest the rocky spine of Huffman Ridge and descend 0.25 mile to the junction with Siouxon Peak Trail. Turn left and catch your breath: it's all downhill from here.

At 6.8 miles, traverse a talus slope. Peak baggers: this is your best bet for claiming Huffman Peak. The lookout structure is gone, along with any access trail, so a summit attempt requires a talus scramble or a blowdown-choked bushwhack. Otherwise, settle in for a steady descent, first through beargrass and huckleberry, then, as the forest cover thins, vine maple. At just under 9 miles, at a break in the trees, peer across the pristine Siouxon Creek drainage. Look south to Horseshoe Ridge and, behind it, Calamity Peak. Keep descending, and at 11.5 miles, reach Siouxon Creek and the second ford. Fortunately, although this ford is farther across, the water is slower flowing, helping ease your crossing.

Climb the far side of the creek bank, and at 11.8 miles, rejoin the Siouxon Creek Trail. Turn left and follow the trail into and out of several small, clover-choked creek gully crossings—which should be no sweat after Siouxon Creek—returning back to the trailhead and your hike's start at 13.8 miles. You packed dry shoes in the car, right?

83 Siouxon Peak

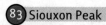

RATING/ DIFFICULTY	ROUNDTRIP	ELEV GAIN/ HIGH POINT	SEASON
****/5	15.3 miles	5120 feet/ 4169 feet	July–Oct

Map: Green Trails Lookout Mountain 396; **Contact:** Gifford Pinchot National Forest, Mount St. Helens National Volcanic Monument and Surrounding Area Headquarters; **Notes:** NW Forest Pass or interagency pass required. Trail open to bicycles. Fishing options; **GPS:** N 45 56.790 W 122 10.671

Want to experience the best of southwest Washington's Siouxon Creek Roadless Area? This strenuous trek from Siouxon Creek to Siouxon Peak and back again offers up-close views of several impressive waterfalls and far-off views of Mount St. Helens and her volcanic neighbors. The cost? Buckets of sweat, and a couple creek crossings that can be downright dicey during part of the year. If you have the energy, this is the best way to experience some of southern Washington's last unprotected low-elevation forest.

GETTING THERE
From the Chelatchie Prairie General Store in Amboy, drive east on NE Healy Road, which eventually turns into Forest Road 54. (Note: FR 54 is heavily buckled and prone to washouts; it's best to check road conditions at the Forest Service headquarters in Amboy first.) At 9.1 miles, bear left on FR 57. Drive 2.1 miles and, immediately after a small quarry, turn left on FR 5701. Follow this at-times potholed pavement 3.7 miles to the road's end, parking, and trailhead (elev. 1260 ft).

Chinook Falls

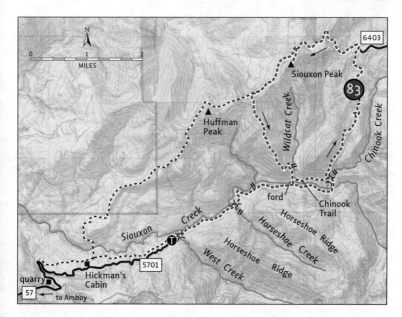

ON THE TRAIL

From the parking lot, follow the trail downhill to Siouxon Creek Trail. Turn right and follow this nearly level tread (see Hike 80 description). At 3.2 miles, go left on the Wildcat Trail for 50 yards to Siouxon Creek. If the creek is running high—as it's likely to do early in the season or after a hard rainfall—save Siouxon Peak for a later date and try nearby Horseshoe Ridge (see Hike 81) instead. If the creek ford looks manageable (you will have to ford it at the end of the summit loop), head back to the Siouxon Peak Trail and continue onward.

At 3.9 miles, cross modest 14-Mile Falls at its slickrock base. In late summer the falls can be crossed with minimal foot-soaking; in high water, scout up the creek for a log bridge.

Immediately afterward, turn left at the signed junction. Cross a sturdy wooden footbridge over Siouxon Creek's narrow chasm and parallel Chinook Creek to the outlet of the plunge pool at 50-foot Chinook Falls. Negotiate the ankle-deep crossing right at the outlet and pick up the trail. Turn right at the signed junction and begin climbing up the Chinook Creek drainage, first on seldom-used tread, then at 6 miles on ancient roadbed.

At 7.1 miles, join FR 6403 and bear left, picking up the route again at road's end. Cautiously cross a washout and pause for views of Mounts Adams, St. Helens, and Rainier. Continue on the road-trail to a clearing and stellar views of Mount St. Helens and the Swift Reservoir on the Lewis River. At the back of the clearing, pick up real trail again.

One last bit of climbing gains you the shark-fin summit ridge of Siouxon Peak at 8.1 miles. Hardy rock-garden plants entrance and, to the north, views of the southern Washington Cascades' volcanoes inspire. Round a bend and take the narrow, brushy side trail to the 4169-foot summit of Siouxon Peak. It's been well earned, with 4 miles of hiking and 3000 feet of elevation gain. From this former lookout site, spy Swift Reservoir, framed by Mount Rainier on the left and Mount Adams on the right.

Descend back to the main trail and turn left. It's an easy amble from here to Wildcat Trail at 9.3 miles. Climb to a forested knoll surrounded by ghostly snags from the Yacolt Burn and steel yourself for a knee-fatiguing descent—more than 2000 feet in 2.5 miles. Your reward, at 11.9 miles, is 225-foot Wildcat Falls. From the switchback viewpoint, descend 0.25 mile to Siouxon Creek and your knee-wetting crossing. (An alternative is to follow Chinook Trail 1.25 miles back to Chinook Falls and an easier crossing, but this adds 2.5 miles to the hike.)

Once across, climb the far bank to the Siouxon Creek Trail junction and turn right for a mellow 3.2-mile return jaunt back to the trailhead and dry clothes.

Oppostie: Tumwater Mountain from Vanson Peak

backpacking trips

While the focus of this book is on day hiking (after all that's half the book's title), we felt this volume wouldn't be complete without mentioning the following backpacking trips. Very strong hikers and trail runners can knock some of these out in a day, but you may want to consider spending a night or more in the Mount St. Helens backcountry. Note that in large portions of the national volcanic monument, backcountry camping is prohibited or restricted to just a few designated sites. So be sure to adhere to all rules, regulations, and permitting (described in the write-ups below) before setting out. Following are some suggested routes—all of which combine and extend day hikes spotlighted earlier in this book.

84 Loowit Trail

RATING/ DIFFICULTY	LOOP	ELEV GAIN/ HIGH POINT	SEASON
*****/5	32 miles	over 7500 feet/ 4850 feet	July–Oct

Map: Green Trails Mt St. Helens 332S; **Contact:** Mount St. Helens National Volcanic Monument; **Notes:** NW Forest Pass or interagency pass required. Open to bikes on south side. Dogs prohibited in restricted area from South Fork Toutle River to Windy Pass. Berry picking in season. No camping in restricted area. Water and campsites are limited. Trail prone to washing out. River, creek, and gully crossings can be dangerous; **GPS:** N 46 08.236 W 122 09.411

Although a Northwest classic, the hike around Mount St. Helens is one of the more challenging backpacking trips for its length. Difficult river, creek, gully, and lava bed crossings, as well as water and campsite scarcity, and long stretches exposed to the elements, make it a tough journey. But what a journey it is—across one of the most fascinating landscapes in the country!

GETTING THERE

You can access the Loowit Trail from several spots, but the June Lake Trail offers the shortest access. From Woodland (exit 21 on I-5), follow State Route 503 east for 29 miles to Cougar. Continue east on SR 503 (which becomes Forest Road 90) for 7 miles, turning left onto FR 83. Follow this good paved road 7 miles to the trailhead turnoff. Proceed 0.2 mile to the trailhead (elev. 2725 ft).

ON THE TRAIL

The following description is a general overview of the route. More details can be found by consulting the referenced chapters in this book. Start by following the easy June Lake Trail (Hike 40), passing June Lake (elev. 3140 ft) with good but busy camps. In old-growth forest at 1.6 miles, reach the Loowit Trail (elev. 3410 ft). Loowit is the Klickitat people's name for Mount St. Helens, and the trail circumnavigates Washington's famous volcano.

You can go either way, but here the route is described clockwise, which gets the rougher sections of trail done first. Head left and soon traverse the Worm Flows, a large, centuries-old lava flow. The going is rough, over basalt talus, and routefinding can be tough—look for metal poles marking the way. At 2.9 miles, come to the Swift Creek Ski Trail (see Hike 93; elev. 3680 ft). Cross a gully above Chocolate Falls (a snowmelt-fed cascade that flows in the afternoons) and climb above the creek.

At 3.2 miles, the Worm Flows route (used

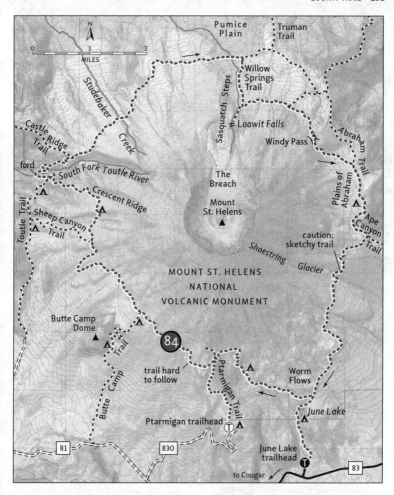

for winter climbing) diverges right. Continue left, soon passing a campsite (no reliable water) and leaving the old lava flow at 3.4 miles. Now climb steadily through beautiful old growth at the edge of the lava flows, passing several sweeping viewpoints. The way then traverses pretty alpine meadows

(elev. 4685 ft) sporting beargrass and an array of blossoms.

Reenter old-growth forest and reach a junction with the popular climbing access route (and an alternative starting point), the Ptarmigan Trail (elev. 4650 ft) at 4.9 miles. Continue straight, soon coming to a

Co-author Craig Romano negotiates a tough section of the Loowit Trail through an old lava flow.

sprawling lava flow. The going is slow here and routefinding can be challenging (look for posts) across jumbled basaltic rocks. The views up to St. Helens and out across the southern horizon are breathtaking.

The way crests a 4725-foot ridge and leaves the lava flow at 5.6 miles, entering open lodgepole pine forest. Cross a couple of small gullies (elev. 4560 ft) before resuming pleasurable hiking through forest and attractive subalpine meadows. Then bend right toward the mountain, climbing through another old lava flow. At 6.9 miles crest a 4825-foot knoll before descending to the Butte Camp Trail junction (elev. 4750 ft) at 7.2 miles.

A decent waterless camp can be found at 0.15 mile, and excellent creekside camps at 1.4 miles, left on the Butte Camp Trail. The Loowit route continues straight, traveling above timberline and hovering at about 4800–4850 feet. After crossing several gullies, including one big and challenging one at 8 miles, reach pleasant tread through pine groves and meadows. Encounter another big gully and then follow a long reroute, dropping several hundred feet to cross a deep, washed-out gully (elev. 4180 ft) at 9.4 miles.

Climb back up to where the trail once crossed what is now a canyon and crest a small ridge (elev. 4625 ft) before reaching the Sheep Canyon Trail (Hike 35) junction (elev. 4575 ft) at 10.4 miles. Continue straight across the upper reaches of Sheep Canyon to drop 100 feet into another trenched gully. Then enjoy meadows and patches of old growth before reaching a good but waterless camp (elev. 4725 ft) at 11.5 miles at the crest of Crescent Ridge.

Take in incredible views as you descend along the South Fork Toutle River trench. At

13.3 miles come to a junction with the Toutle Trail (elev. 3250 ft), where excellent creek-side campsites (elev. 3130 ft) among ancient trees can be found 0.4 mile to your left. Note that camping is restricted for the next 10 miles along the Loowit Trail.

The Loowit Trail continues right for a very challenging crossing of the South Fork Toutle River (elev. 3100 ft), the lowest point on the trail. Carefully ford the creek and clamber up the steep, loose-rock gully (a rope may be in place) embracing the river and eventually reach good tread again. Climb steeply out of the canyon to take in stunning views and reach, at 14.5 miles, the Castle Ridge Trail (elev. 3960 ft) heading west out of the monument (see Hike 85).

Now hike along the rim of the South Toutle Canyon on sandy soil. The way then bends north through meadows and new forest before entering a starker landscape. Work your way across the blast zone, crossing gullies, streams, and pumiced flats. At 16 miles, cross Studebaker Creek, which—like many of the mountain's creeks—may not be flowing until late in the day. Next, crest Studebaker Ridge (elev. 4140 ft) and then slowly descend crossing more rifts and ridges. At 18.9 miles cross a spring-fed creek before traveling across the fairly level but rocky Pumice Plain. Sections of trail here periodically wash out, making routefinding challenging. Look for cairns.

Soon afterward come to a couple of glacier-fed creeks, which must be forded and might be a little challenging later in the day. At 19.9 miles, reach the Willow Springs Trail (elev. 3865 ft). Turn right and hike toward St. Helens' crater on tiered ledges known as the Sasquatch Steps, coming to the spur (elev. 4300 ft) for Loowit Falls (Hike 57) at 20.7 miles.

The Loowit bends left to cross a couple of creeks, dips, and grassy tundra-like terrain before coming to the Windy Trail (elev. 4300 ft) at 21.7 miles. Then begin a steep climb on narrow ledges to 4850-foot Windy Pass, one of the highest points on the trail. Catch good views and cautiously descend on ledge and pumice to the Plains of Abraham (Hike 56), reaching the Abraham Trail (elev. 4475 ft) at 23.8 miles. Venture across the near-level flowering plains and come to good campsites (elev. 4325 ft) by a reliable creek at 24.6 miles. Then descend the plains, reaching the Ape Canyon Trail (elev. 4175 ft) junction at 25.4 miles.

Now continue on one of the prettiest sections of the trail, steadily climbing across meadow and pumice. Look above for mountain goats and below for elk. Cross a gully cradling the Muddy River (here a creek) and crest a 4500-foot ridge. At 26.8 miles, come to the edge of a deep and potentially dangerous trench (elev. 4375 ft) below the Shoestring Glacier. Use extreme caution here descending steep slopes where the tread frequently slides out.

Climb about 75 feet to the south rim of the trench and continue across pumice, dipping in and out of more gullies. The trail improves, traversing meadows, berry patches, Christmas tree groves, ghost forests, and an old-growth patch. On an up-and-down course, the trail eventually reaches a mudflow (elev. 4050 ft) before climbing again to a 4125-foot point with excellent views. Eventually arrive back at the Worm Flows and hop over basalt rocks as you descend to old-growth forest. Walk across a narrow rib above a creek, coming to the June Lake Trail (elev. 3410 ft) at 30.4 miles. Your vehicle and a well-deserved rest can be reached by going left 1.6 miles.

85 Castle Ridge

RATING/ DIFFICULTY	ROUNDTRIP	ELEV GAIN/ HIGH POINT	SEASON
*****/4	23.8 miles	3800 feet/ 4350 feet	July–Oct

Map: Green Trails Mt St. Helens 332S; **Contact:** Mount St. Helens National Volcanic Monument; **Notes:** NW Forest Pass or interagency pass required. Dogs prohibited. Camping prohibited on Loowit Trail through Pumice Plain and blast zone. Water scarce on Castle Ridge; **GPS:** N 46 14.935 W 122 08.169

Lonely Castle Ridge offers royal views of Mount St. Helens and all three of the grand lakes formed after the 1980 eruption. Wildflowers, wild strawberries, and wildlife are profuse on this high ridge above the South Fork Toutle River. The biggest challenge is getting there, but the views and solitude will justify any hardships along the way.

GETTING THERE

From Woodland (exit 21 on I-5), follow State Route 503 east for 29 miles to Cougar, Continue east on SR 503 (which becomes Forest Road 90) for 18.4 miles, turning left onto FR 25. Follow this good paved road 25 miles north to FR 99. (From Randle follow SR 131 south for 2 miles to where it becomes FR 25, continuing for 17.7 miles and turning right onto FR 99.) Continue on paved FR 99 for 16.2 miles to its end at the trailhead (elev. 4050 ft). Privy available.

ON THE TRAIL

There are three ways to get to Castle Ridge. The easiest and shortest is via private forest roads that are unmarked, tortuous to drive, confusing to follow, and often gated. Forget

about that option. Another access is from the south and the Toutle Trail (Hike 35) via the Loowit Trail—but this requires the difficult ford of the South Fork Toutle River and a grueling climb out of its canyon.

The recommended route to Castle Ridge is via the Loowit Trail (Hike 84) accessed from Windy Ridge. This route is longer than from the south, but eliminates the South Fork Toutle ford. Starting on the Truman Trail (Hike 29), follow this road-turned-trail hugging Windy Ridge's eastern slopes high above the Smith Creek drainage. The way climbs about 200 feet before slowly descending. At 1.7 miles, bear right at a junction (elev. 4150 ft), continuing on the Truman Trail and reaching another junction (elev. 4050 ft) at 2 miles.

Head left here on the Windy Trail and begin climbing, reaching the Loowit Trail (elev. 4300 ft) at 2.8 miles. Turn right on the Loowit Trail and cross a couple of creeks, coming to the Loowit Falls Trail (Hike 57) junction (elev. 4300 ft) at 3.8 miles. Continue right on the Loowit, descending a series of shelves known as the Sasquatch Steps to arrive at the Willow Springs Trail (elev. 3870 ft) at 4.6 miles.

Bear left here, continuing on the Loowit across the Pumice Plain. Views are excellent into the crater and of the waterfalls emanating from it. Soon come to the first of two potentially tricky creek fords. Then come to a stretch of trail in the rocky plain that often washes out. To routefind, look for cairns. At 5.6 miles, come to a spring-fed creek (elev. 3700 ft) offering silt-free water. Be sure to resupply here.

Continue, now climbing about 350 feet across a ridge. Look for horned larks nesting in this fairly barren terrain. Descend 100 feet and cross a gully where a creek cascades late

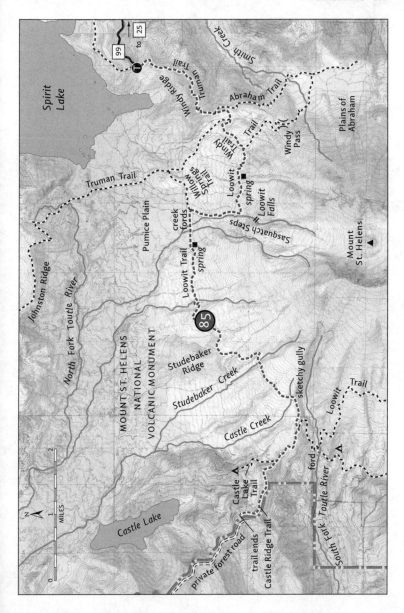

in the day. The trail then climbs and dips on its way across Studebaker Ridge (elev. 4140 ft). Descend to Studebaker Creek (elev. 3940 ft), which may be dry. Then climb up a grassy ridge sporting young trees and lots of wildflowers early in summer.

Work your way across more draws and gullies, including a pretty decent-size one that may be a little sketchy to negotiate. After cresting yet another ridge (elev. 4140 ft), start descending along the rim of the deep, impressive, and forbidding South Fork Toutle Canyon. Traverse sandy stretches lined with kinnikinnick and wild strawberries to reach a signed junction with the Castle Ridge Trail (elev. 3960 ft) at 10.0 miles.

Now continue straight on the Castle Ridge Trail (also known as the Fairview Trail), traversing the canyon rim a short distance before turning right into forest replanted shortly after the eruption. Camping is possible here, but there is no water. Continue on good tread, bending right in a meadow to begin traversing northern-facing slopes. The views are excellent down into the Castle Creek valley, which harbors a large herd of elk, and out to the Mount Margaret peaks, with Mount Rainier peeking behind them.

At 10.7 miles, come to the junction with the Castle Lake Trail (elev. 4100 ft). This trail has not been maintained in decades. It does, however, lead to good camping spots (see Extending Your Trip). The Castle Ridge Trail continues climbing rounding a small knoll with large silver snags framing Mount St. Helens. Keep hiking west across a saddle and along the ridge. Castle Lake soon comes into view—and the view of it from this trail is the best in the Monument. Coldwater Lake is also now in view, as is Spirit Lake, making this spot one of the few where all three of the big eruption-created lakes can be seen.

Below the ridge are springs and small wetlands where water can be drawn. The trail next bends right to skirt beneath ledges and craggy knolls. Wildflowers line the way. At 11.5 miles leave the Monument to enter private timberlands. At 11.9 miles reach the trail's end marked with a big rock at a rough logging road in a saddle (elev. 4350 ft). This trail access is used by locals who know their way through the maze of private roads. Chances are you'll meet no one along the way. Soak up the sweeping views out across the blast zone and along the ridge to Mount St. Helens, enjoying rare west-side views of the volcano. Then turn around and begin the long journey back or consider side trips for camping options.

EXTENDING YOUR TRIP

Option A: Return to the Loowit Trail and head right to drop 800 feet and ford the South Fork Toutle River. Now follow the Toutle Trail a short distance to excellent campsites in an old-growth forest grove. Option B: There is excellent camping, albeit without nearby water sources, along the Castle Lake Trail. Take this trail on nearly nonexistent tread off Castle Ridge, following old wooden posts. As you hike on old logging roads and across grassy slopes, the route is fairly discernible for about 0.7 mile until it reaches an old roadbed below a small saddle (elev. 3900 ft). From here the trail drops off the ridge to the Castle Creek valley, rounding the ridge in front of you reaching Castle Lake. The route can no longer be followed, being grown in and traversed by a myriad of elk trails. There are plans in the near future however for a new trail to Castle Lake from the Hummocks (see Hike 24). Plan to hike to Castle Lake then.

A trail runner darts along Castle Ridge under the watchful gaze of St. Helens.

Meanwhile, continue to the small saddle and look for a great place to camp overlooking the beautiful lake. Water can be found to the west of the saddle from springs and wetlands at the headwaters of the South Fork Castle Creek.

86 Boundary Trail

RATING/ DIFFICULTY	ONE-WAY	ELEV GAIN/ HIGH POINT	SEASON
*****/5	57.4 miles	12,200 feet/ 5690 feet	July–Oct

Maps: Green Trails Mt St. Helens 332S, McCoy Peak 333, Blue Lake 334; **Contact:** Mount St. Helens National Volcanic Monument; Gifford Pinchot National Forest, Cowlitz Valley Ranger District; **Notes:** Dogs prohibited west of Norway Pass. Berries in season. Water is limited and can be scarce in late season. Trail outside of Monument open to horses, mountain bikes, and motorcycles and is trenched in spots. Overnight permits required (and limited) and camping only permitted at designated sites within the Mount Margaret Backcountry; **GPS:** N 46 17.183 W 122 16.303

Follow the Boundary Trail (straddling the old boundary between the Columbia and Rainier National Forests, since amalgamated into the Gifford Pinchot National Forest) on an epic trip from the shadows of Mount St. Helens to the shadows of Mount Adams. Travel high ridges through meadows and old growth from the blast zone to the Dark Divide. The way is awesome, stimulating, rough, challenging, and at times discouraging.

GETTING THERE

West-end trailhead: From Castle Rock (exit 49 on I-5), follow State Route 504 east for 45.2 miles, turning right into the large parking area and trailhead for the Hummocks (elev. 2550 ft). East-end trailhead: From Randle, drive south 1 mile on SR 131. At the junction, bear left (east) on Forest Road 23 and proceed for 31.8 miles (pavement ends at 23.5 miles), turning right on FR 2334, signed for Council Bluff. Follow FR 2334 for 1.2 miles, bearing right into Council Bluff Campground. Find the trailhead (4240 ft) in 0.2 mile at the west end of the campground. Privy available.

ON THE TRAIL

Arrange a shuttle and do this hike one-way end-to-end or in sections. The following description is a general overview of the route. More details can be found by consulting the referenced chapters in this book.

Begin by following the Hummocks Trail 0.7 mile to the western start (elev. 2550 ft) of the Boundary Trail (see Hike 25). Now start climbing, winding up grassy slopes. At 3.8 miles, reach the Loowit Viewpoint (elev. 3950 ft) accessed by SR 504. Resume hiking on the Boundary Trail (signed as Trail No. 1), cresting Johnston Ridge and reaching the Johnston Ridge Observatory (elev. 4180 ft): a good spot to refill water bottles at 4.5 miles.

Continue east on the Boundary Trail, (see Hike 28), dropping 200 feet to a saddle before traversing a steep and exposed (use caution) slope. At 7 miles stay left at a junction with the Truman Trail. At 8 miles reach a junction (elev. 4400 ft) with the Harry's Ridge Trail. Continue straight, climbing steeply up a ridge granting excellent views of Spirit Lake and Mounts Adams, Hood,

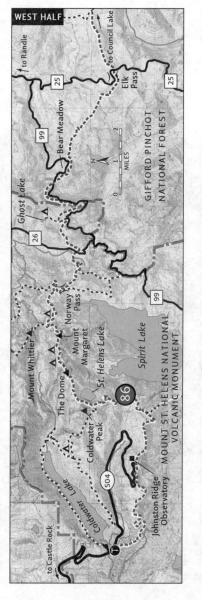

WEST HALF

to Randle

25

99

Bear Meadow

to Council Lake

Elk
Pass

25

Ghost Lake

26

GIFFORD PINCHOT
NATIONAL FOREST

N

1   2
MILES

Norway
Pass

99

Mount Whittier

Mount
Margaret

St. Helens Lake

Spirit Lake

The Dome

86

Coldwater
Peak

MOUNT ST. HELENS NATIONAL
VOLCANIC MONUMENT

Coldwater Lake

504

Johnston Ridge
Observatory

to Castle Rock

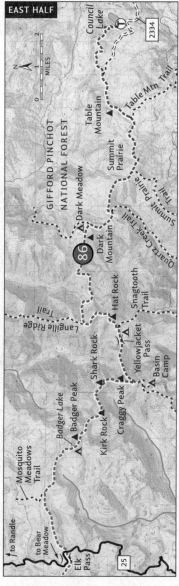

EAST HALF

Council
Lake

2334

N

0   2
MILES

Table
Mountain

Table Mtn Trail

GIFFORD
PINCHOT
NATIONAL
FOREST

Summit
Prairie

Dark Meadow

Summit Prairie
Trail

86

Dark
Mountain

Quartz Creek Trail

Hat Rock

Snagtooth
Trail

Langille Ridge Trail

Shark Rock

Yellowjacket
Pass

Basin
Camp

Badger Lake

Badger Peak

Craggy Peak

Kirk Rock

Mosquito
Meadows
Trail

to Randle

to Bear
Meadow

Elk
Pass

25

St. Helens Lake and Spirit Lake viewed from beneath The Dome

and Rainier. Attain the ridge crest (elev. 5200 ft) and pass through a dramatic natural arch before reaching a junction with the Coldwater Trail in a saddle (elev. 5070 ft) at 9.7 miles.

The next five miles or so are the most dramatic and spectacular on this route. Continue right, traversing grassy slopes beneath Coldwater Peak. At 11.2 miles, pass the spur leading to Coldwater's 5727-foot summit. Then drop into a small saddle (elev. 5025 ft) where water may be present. Traverse steep grassy slopes above sparkling St. Helens Lake while cresting a high, steep shoulder (elev. 5500 ft) of The Dome. At 12.9 miles, reach Dome Camp (elev. 5350 ft), your first camping option. Water can usually be found from a spring to the north.

More attractive Bear Camp (elev. 5390 ft), with more reliable water, is just a little farther east at 13.2 miles. From here the trail passes a 5325-foot saddle and climbs steeply to reach at 14.5 miles the short spur trail (elev. 5690 ft) to 5858-foot Mount Margaret. Now (see Hike 50) start descending (with a few short uphill sections), passing the Mount Whittier Trail and reaching at 15.7 miles the popular (reliable water) Margaret Camp (elev. 5435 ft).

Continue on a long descent, passing the Lakes, Independence Pass, and Independence Ridge Trails to arrive at the Norway Pass trailhead (elev. 3680 ft) and water at 20.1 miles. Cross FR 26 and follow the Boundary Trail (see Hike 49), reaching a 4000-foot gap at 21 miles. Then gently descend to Clearwater Creek (elev. 3730 ft) and a junction at 22 miles. Left leads 0.7 mile to Ghost Lake (elev. 3780 ft) and decent camping spots.

The Boundary Trail continues east. Keep climbing and at about 23.5 miles, leave the blast zone to enter cool, old-growth forest.

Crest a 4400-foot ridge at 24.3 miles and traverse steep ledges, passing a couple of pretty cascades and the Strawberry Mountain Trail before reaching the Bear Meadow trailhead (elev. 4100 ft) on FR 99 at 25.6 miles.

The trail, now open to motorcycles, begins an up-and-down course through gorgeous old-growth forest. At 26.6 miles, come to a tricky creek crossing (elev. 3800 ft) before passing a spur to FR 99. Then traverse deep forest occasionally interrupted by pocket meadows. The terrain is rolling, with short ups and downs. At about 30 miles, steeply climb to a 4260-foot knoll with window views north and south. Then descend, passing a spur to the Elk Pass trailhead and reaching FR 25 at Elk Pass (elev. 4075 ft) at 31.1 miles.

From the Elk Pass parking lot, cross FR 25 and continue east (see Hike 74) through widely spaced, old-growth western hemlock and true firs. At 33.1 miles, pass the junction with Mosquito Meadows Trail (elev. 4320 ft) and, at 35 miles, a short spur (elev. 4960 ft) to 5664-foot Badger Peak. Cross a small meadow and campsites at shallow Badger Lake.

From the lake, ascend a small ridge and enter back into the trees. Skirt the steep-walled north side of Kirk Rock (elev. 5000 ft) at 36.5 miles and the finlike formation of Shark Rock (elev. 5200 ft) at 37.5 miles. From Shark Rock's shoulder, descend short, steep switchbacks and across scree through open forest. Ahead juts the pinnacle of Craggy Peak (Hike 75); firs frame a nice view of Mount St. Helens to the west. Ascend a small saddle on the shoulder of Craggy Peak and then quickly descend to the junction with Craggy Peak Trail (elev. 5160 ft) at 39.1 miles (Note: some older maps show a trail

High above Dark Meadow on the Boundary Trail

traversing the north side of Craggy Peak, but this route no longer exists). Good tent sites and water can be found 0.6 mile down that trail at Basin Camp. Otherwise, traverse the top of a steep subalpine meadow and descend to the forested shoulder of Yellowjacket Pass (elev. 4320 ft) at 40.7 miles. Find campsites south of the trail near a tiny pond.

Ascend through thick timber past seldom-used Snagtooth Trail (elev. 4720 ft) at 41.2 miles. Switchback through dusty, deeply rutted tread to a rocky traverse of the north side of Hat Rock. From here, peer across Yellowjacket Creek drainage to Badger Peak and Pinto Rock. Bear right at a spur (elev. 4720 ft) at 42.9 miles and again at the Langille Ridge junction (elev. 4520 ft) at 43.1 miles.

Drop steeply along a sidehill into shady bottomland, and at 44.7 miles (elev. 3920 ft) cross closed FR 29, nearly unrecognizable now. Ascend on switchback-scarce tread through shaggy, aged hemlock before traversing a steep brushy rock face. A quick ascent attains one of the best views of the eastern Boundary Trail, with Mount Adams and the two-tiered green plateau of Dark Meadow below. Drop sharply through ruddy huckleberry slopes to Dark Meadow (elev. 4360 ft) at 46.4 miles. Camp here among elk herds—and, in July, swaths of mosquitoes. A trickle of water may be available just before of the junction with the Dark Meadow Trail.

From Dark Meadow, traverse large meadows flush with huckleberry and false azalea; maps show a large pond about a mile past Dark Meadow, but it's only seasonally wet if at all. Pass closed-to-motors Quartz Creek Trail (Hike 76) at 47.8 miles and climb to the pocket meadows of Summit Prairie (elev. 5080 ft) at 50.1 miles. Pass the Summit Prairie Trail spur and prepare for some of the worst motorcycle ruts of the route. Descend

hip-deep ruts before reaching the broad bogs near the Table Mountain junction (Hike 77) (elev. 4760 ft) at 52.1 miles.

Pass another junction with the Hike 77 route (elev. 4640 ft) at 52.7 miles and switchback down to FR 2334 at 53.9 miles. Cross the road into young firs and beargrass and climb toward the spur for Council Bluff summit (Hike 78) (elev. 4960 ft) at 56.1 miles. Now on old roadbed, descend steadily through Douglas-firs to Council Lake (elev. 4240 ft) at 57.4 miles, the end of your Boundary Trail backpacking route.

87 Lakes Trail

RATING/ DIFFICULTY	ONE-WAY	ELEV GAIN/ HIGH POINT	SEASON
*****/5	16.4 miles	3625 feet / 5200 feet	mid-July– Oct

Map: Green Trails Mt St. Helens 332S; **Contact:** Mount St. Helens National Volcanic Monument; **Notes:** NW Forest Pass or inter-agency pass required. Western 4.5 miles of trail open to bikes. Dogs prohibited. Berries in season. Overnight permits required (and limited) and camping permitted only at designated sites; **GPS:** N 46 17.530 W 122 15.979

Traverse Mount St. Helen's blast zone and pass along the shores of some of the Monument's most stunning lakes. Crest rugged ridges and high passes offering stupendous views of sparkling lakes, glistening snow-capped volcanoes, and jagged rugged peaks. And admire awesome waterfalls and slopes shrouded in brilliant blossoms.

GETTING THERE

West-end trailhead: From Castle Rock (exit 49 on I-5), follow State Route 504 east for 45

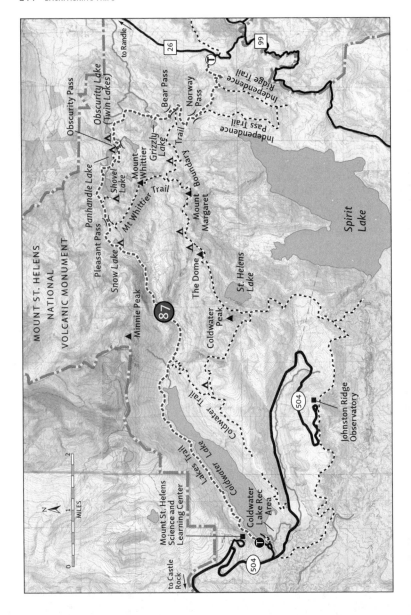

miles, turning left into the Coldwater Lake Recreation Area. Continue 0.4 mile, bearing left to the boat launch and trailhead (elev. 2510 ft). Privy available. East-end trailhead: At Norway Pass; see Hike 50 for driving directions.

ON THE TRAIL

Arrange a shuttle and do this hike one-way end-to-end. The following description is a general overview of the route from west to east. More details can be found in Hike 22 and Hike 51.

Cascading Coldwater Creek

Locate the Lakes Trail just west of the boat launch and begin your journey along massive Coldwater Lake (Hike 22). At 0.8 mile, pass the Elk Bench Trail. Continue right, soon passing a beach and backcountry compost toilet. Cross the first of many creeks, eventually coming to one donning a pretty waterfall. Next, climb across steep ledges (elev. 2600 ft), high above the lake, before descending to cross another series of creeks.

Eventually reach the more than 4-mile-long lake's marshy eastern end. Then begin paralleling Coldwater Creek. At 4.5 miles continue straight at a junction with the Coldwater Trail (elev. 2625 ft). Now on much-less-trodden tread, pass a beautiful waterfall. The trail crosses more creeks and traverses young forest groves. At 5.6 miles, come to a spectacular waterfall (elev. 2900 ft) before climbing steadily up a tight valley.

Skirt below steep ledges as you continue following thundering Coldwater Creek. There's no shade, and the going can get hot under a summer sun. Pass more waterfalls and a couple of cascading tributaries before steeply climbing above a hanging valley. Enjoy good views of Mounts Whittier and Margaret and The Dome.

The way gets brushier and the tread harder to follow. At about 7 miles, traverse steep slopes (elev. 3900 ft) that are subject to sliding out, creating potentially dangerous going (check status with the Monument office). Shortly beyond, the trail follows a creek, taking you to rarely visited Snow Lake (elev. 4700 ft) at 8 miles. Find designated campsites here.

The trail continues climbing, reaching Pleasant Pass (elev. 5200 ft) at 8.5 miles, where the Mount Whittier Trail branches right (not recommended for backpacking). Continue straight, descending through meadows

and young fir groves to a junction (elev. 5150 ft) with the Shovel Lake Trail at 8.9 miles.

If you're camping at Shovel Lake, follow the recently rebuilt trail 0.5 mile to the campsite sitting on a bluff (elev. 4800 ft) above Shovel Lake. Otherwise continue on the Lakes Trail (see Hike 51) to descend a steep open ridge with excellent views. Cross a cascading creek and reach a junction (elev. 4550 ft) at 10.1 miles. Panhandle Lake's nice campsites are 0.2 mile straight ahead.

The Lakes Trail continues right, climbing 4675-foot Obscurity Pass before descending to Obscurity Lake (also known as Twin Lakes, elev. 4350 ft) with its campsite at 11 miles. The way then drops 100 feet before traversing steep slopes on its way to Grizzly Lake (elev. 4300 ft) at 12.3 miles (no camping). Then it's a steep climb up slopes that often harbor snow late into summer to Bear Pass (elev. 4950 ft).

Enjoy the view of Mount St. Helens and start descending. At 13.3 miles, the Lakes Trail ends at a junction with the Boundary Trail. The Norway Pass trailhead and your arranged shuttle can be reached by keeping left and hiking downhill 3.1 more miles.

88 Green River— Goat Mountain Loop

RATING/ DIFFICULTY	LOOP	ELEV GAIN/ HIGH POINT	SEASON
****/4	21.5 miles	3200 feet/ 5025 feet	July–Oct

Map: Green Trails Mt St. Helens 332S; **Contact:** Mount St. Helens National Volcanic Monument, Cowlitz Valley Ranger District; **Notes:** Overnight permits/regulations: none. Trail open to horses and bicycles; **GPS:** N 46 20.946 W 122 05.095

Surveying the Green River valley from a rocky overlook

Hike through a deep glacier-carved valley draped in spectacular old-growth forest and over a high ridge at the edge of the 1980 blast zone that now bursts with wildflowers and views. Add a couple of placid subalpine lakes and an old fire lookout site to the mix and you have the makings of a wonderful adventure—and best of all, no crowds to encounter or complicated permits to vie for.

GETTING THERE
From Randle and US Highway 12, follow State Route 131 south for 2 miles to where it becomes Forest Road 25. Continue 6.7 miles. Upon crossing the Cispus River, bear right onto FR 26. Drive 12.3 miles. Turn right onto gravel FR 2612 and proceed 1.7 miles, turning left on FR Spur 027 to Green River Horse Camp. Continue 0.6 mile to the campground and trailhead parking (elev. 2875 ft). Privy available.

ON THE TRAIL
The following description is a general overview of the route. More details can be found in Hikes 59, 60, 62, 63, and 89. It's best to do this loop clockwise, allowing for a downhill

return. Follow the Green River Trail west, heading downriver through scrappy forest. Tread is good but has been relocated in many spots because the Green has jumped its banks on numerous occasions.

At 1.7 miles, just beyond crossing FR 2612 (an alternative trailhead), pass an impressive waterfall on the Green River. Continue downstream (Hike 59), passing old logging yards and abandoned mines. At about 3.5 miles, enter the national volcanic monument

and beautiful old-growth forest. At about 4.7 miles, come to a bridged crossing of a side creek. Just beyond find good riverside camps. Continue down the glacially carved U-shaped valley through magnificent primeval forest groves and across sparkling creeks.

At 6.5 miles reach a junction (elev. 2375 ft). Turn right here onto the Vanson Ridge Trail and begin climbing out of the valley. At 7.2 miles reach a ledge (elev. 2750 ft) granting excellent viewing of the verdant valley.

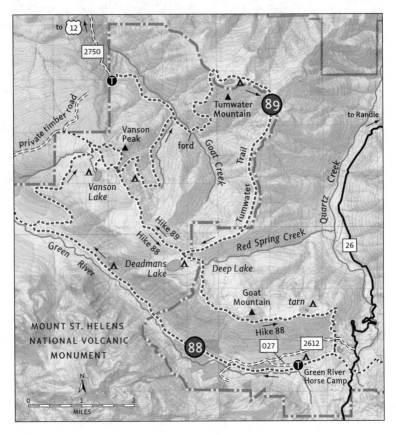

Then continue to climb steadily, crossing numerous side creeks en route. Eventually the grade eases as the trail crests a broad shoulder to reach another junction at 9.9 miles (elev. 4100 ft). Decision time—Vanson Peak or Vanson Lake?

To reach the lake, continue right, ignoring a side trail that immediately takes off right for boggy Vanson Meadows, reaching the Vanson Lake Trail in 0.2 mile. Turn right and reach the shallow grassy-shored lake (elev. 4150 ft) in 0.3 mile. Good camps can be found along its west shore.

To reach Vanson Peak, you have two options. The easier way is to hike right, passing the lake spur and reaching a four-way junction (elev. 4750 ft) in 0.7 mile. Then turn left and hike 0.5 mile to the old summit lookout site. The other option is harder but makes a loop. Head left, reaching another junction in 0.3 mile. Then head right, climbing steeply for 0.6 mile to a trail junction on a ridge crest. Head left 0.1 mile to Vanson's 4948-foot open summit for excellent views (Hike 63). Then head east on the ridge, descending 200 feet in 0.5 mile to the saddle and four-way junction. From here the trail right heads back to Vanson Lake; the trail left drops to Goat Creek (Hike 62). You want to continue straight on the Goat Mountain Trail through open forest and beargrass, climbing over several knolls with fair views north. After 2.3 miles, drop into a saddle (elev. 4400 ft) where the lonely Tumwater Mountain Trail takes off left (Hike 89). Just beyond, a short spur veers right for Deadmans Lake (elev. 4350 ft) with good albeit buggy camps.

The Goat Mountain Trail (Hike 60) continues east, passing a primitive path to Deep Lake before leaving the Monument to steeply and steadily climb to a 4930-foot saddle. The way then continues along the demarcation of the 1980 blast zone, traversing Goat Mountain's steep open southern slopes. Views of St. Helens and the Mount Margaret Backcountry peaks are excellent. Skirt below Goat's summit before reaching a 5025-foot high point beneath a knoll. Then begin another steep descent to arrive at a spur leading to a small tarn (elev. 4750 ft) with good campsites tucked in a hidden basin.

After about 1.9 miles of relentless descending, reach a trailhead (elev. 3300 ft) at FR 2612. Cross the road and continue another 0.5 mile to a junction (elev. 3000 ft) with the Green River Trail. The way left heads steeply to Strawberry Mountain. Go right 0.7 mile to close the loop.

89 Tumwater Mountain Loop

RATING/ DIFFICULTY	LOOP	ELEV GAIN/ HIGH POINT	SEASON
***/4	19.7 miles	4300 feet/ 5175 feet	July–Oct

Map: Green Trails Mt St. Helens 332S; **Contact:** Mount St. Helens National Volcanic Monument; **Notes:** Overnight permits/ regulations: none. Trail open to mountain bikes and horses. Access is via a gated private timber road that is periodically subject to closing (usually during high fire danger); **GPS:** N 46 25.763 W 122 09.289

Hike for miles along lonely ridge crests draped with ancient forests. Visit alpine lakes and pocket meadows home to elk, bear, and deer. This loop traverses some of the least-visited terrain within the Mount St. Helens National Volcanic Monument. And while it

Deadmans Lake's inviting sandy shore

comes up short on stellar views, you're assured tranquility and solitude—rare commodities in our crowded and noisy world.

GETTING THERE

From Morton, travel east on US Highway 12 for 5.3 miles, turning right at Milepost 103 onto Kosmos Road. (If coming from Randle, follow US 12 west for 12 miles to turnoff.) After 0.1 mile turn left onto the Champion Haul Road and continue 4.3 miles (passing Taidnapum Park) to a bridge over the Cowlitz River. Turn right onto a gravel forest road and, after 0.8 mile, bear left at a Y-junction onto FR 2750. Continue 4 miles to road's end and the trailhead (elev. 2400 ft).

ON THE TRAIL

Follow the Goat Creek Trail (Hike 62), crossing a couple of potentially boot-soaking creeks before coming to Cathedral Falls at 1.1 miles. Then continue on a gentle ascent before descending a little, meeting up with cascading Goat Creek. At 2.2 miles reach a junction (elev. 2550 ft). You'll be returning right—so continue straight on the lightly traveled Tumwater Trail.

Cross a creek and hike through beautiful primeval forest, along the way passing a couple of pretty waterfalls on Goat Creek. Then, at 2.8 miles, ford Goat Creek (elev. 2750 ft), which can be tricky early in the season. Fill your water bottles here: the ridge can be dry come late summer. Then traverse steep slopes shrouded in old-growth forest, coming to a viewpoint overlooking the Goat Creek valley. Continue climbing through open forest skirting ledges granting window views. Upon cresting a ridge the trail bends south and the climbing subsides. At 6 miles reach a small pond (elev. 4840 ft) surrounded by meadows beneath Tumwater

Mountain's craggy summit. This is a good spot to set up camp—but not in the fragile meadows. In the evenings, watch for wildlife. The trail beyond is dry, so fill up on water here.

The trail now swings south. Shortly after reaching a small saddle come to an easy-to-miss junction (elev. 5075 ft) at 6.7 miles. Here the spur to Tumwater's summit (Hike 64) veers sharply right, offering a nice side trip. Otherwise, continue straight along a long ridge forming the national volcanic monument border. The way climbs about 100 feet before beginning to descend, swinging around a procession of knolls along the way. The walking is fairly relaxing and mostly downhill, but count on adding about 250 cumulative feet of climbing as you progress along the ridge.

Pocket meadows awash in blossoms and rocky outcroppings granting views east and west offer respite from the emerald canopy of this forested ridge. At about 9.3 miles, reach a 4150-foot saddle and begin climbing, remaining on the ridge crest. Stop at spots offering views west to Goat and Strawberry mountains. At 10.6 miles, shortly after passing the county and Monument line, the trail skirts a knoll at 4700 feet and begins to descend again.

At 11.3 miles, reenter the Monument and come to a junction with the Goat Mountain Trail in a forested saddle (elev. 4400 ft). Left takes you to Goat Mountain and Deadmans Lake (Hike 60). (Deadmans Lake—a mere 0.2 mile away—is an excellent place to set up camp. While the lake can be buggy, by late summer it warms up nicely for a swim.) If you are not camping, continue right through pines and firs to climb along a broad ridge. Top a 4780-foot knoll—then drop 200 feet—and climb again onto a 4880-foot knoll offering views to the north.

Descend again, coming at 13.6 miles to a four-way junction on a high saddle (elev. 4700 ft). From here, the way left heads 0.7 mile to campsites at meadow-ringed Vanson Lake (elev. 4150 ft). The trail straight heads 0.5 mile to 4948-foot Vanson Peak (Hike 63); an excellent side trip with good views.

Your loop route continues right at the four-way, following the Goat Creek Trail and heading downhill. Pass wetlands and meadows where camping is possible and reliable water is available. At 15.3 miles, come to a small forest-lined pond (elev. 3800 ft) where it is also possible to camp. The trail continues descending through spectacular old growth reaching a familiar junction at 17.5 miles. Go left, heading down Goat Creek. Your vehicle is waiting for you in another 2.2 miles.

Opposite: Summit crater and blast zone from Mount St. Helens' summit

summit-climbing routes

The Cascades stretch from northern California to southern British Columbia and contain several major volcanoes. Ironically, the two mountains that had major eruptions within the last century are two of the easiest to ascend. However, while Mount St. Helens can be ascended without any technical concerns, it still is a difficult and potentially dangerous climb. Yet because of its nontechnical status, close proximity to two major metropolitan areas, and notoriety around the country, Mount St. Helens is a popular climbing destination. To protect the mountain from overuse, a permit system has been established during the warmer months, limiting the number of climbers each day. If you're physically fit, properly outfitted and prepared, and have secured your permit—go for it! The climb of Mount St. Helens is a Northwest classic, and the view from above of the summit crater and blast zone is unsurpassed.

90 Mount St. Helens Summit: Monitor Ridge

RATING/ DIFFICULTY	ROUNDTRIP	ELEV GAIN/ HIGH POINT	SEASON
*****/5	9.4 miles	4465 feet/ 8225 feet	June–Oct

Map: Green Trails Mt St. Helens 332S; **Contact:** Mount St. Helens National Volcanic Monument; **Notes:** NW Forest Pass or interagency pass required. Dogs permitted but not recommended; **Climbing notes:** All climbers going over 4800 feet must register and obtain a climbing permit (advance purchase of at least twenty-four hours required) and display it while climbing. Maximum party size is twelve. Stay back from the crater rim and note that the summit rim east

of the climbing route is closed to visitation.

From April 1 to Oct 31 secure permits at mshinstitute.org/index.php/climbing ($22 as of 2015) and pick it up in person and register at Lone Fir Resort (www.lonefirresort .com) in Cougar. From April 1 to May 14 permits are unlimited. From May 15 to Oct 31 permits are restricted to one hundred a day and sell out fast, especially on weekends. From Nov 1 to March 31 (see Hike 91 winter route); **GPS:** N 46 08.772 W 122 11.014

Hike to the top of Washington's (and the country's) most famous volcano. It's a steep, rocky, dusty, waterless, and at times hot slog up boulder fields and pumiced slopes to St. Helen's 8200-plus-foot rim. But worth the hardships! The views are breathtaking: down into the volcano's glacier-cradling crater and out across the blast zone to Spirit Lake, the Mount Margaret Backcountry, and four other impressive Northwest volcanoes in the distance.

GETTING THERE
From Woodland (exit 21 on I-5), follow State Route 503 east for 29 miles to Cougar. Continue east on SR 503 (which becomes Forest Road 90) for 7 miles, turning left onto FR 83. Follow this good paved road 3.1 miles, bearing left onto paved FR 81. After 1.7 miles, turn right onto gravel FR 830. Proceed 2.7 miles to the trailhead (elev. 3760 ft) at Climbers Bivouac Camp: a free, waterless, crowded, and unattractive car camp. Privy available.

ON THE TRAIL
While the ascent of Mount St. Helens doesn't require any technical skills, it does require scrambling skills, good conditioning, and prudence. Early in the season, it's advisable

Co-author Aaron Theisen hikes along the crater rim to St. Helens' true summit.

to bring an ice ax. After the snow melts you may want to consider gaiters for the deep pumice, and goggles and a face mask to protect yourself from blowing dust. Carry sufficient water and sunscreen and always monitor the weather, ready to turn back if conditions are adverse.

With permit displayed and an adventurous spirit in hand, begin up the well-beaten Ptarmigan Ridge Trail. Winding through a fir forest, soon enter the national volcanic monument. The way is pretty gentle at first and then gains elevation more steadily. At about 1.7 miles, pass some dry campsites. At 2 miles, reach a junction (elev. 4650 ft) with the Loowit Trail.

Continue straight, now on the Monitor Ridge climbing route. Pass a privy. Soon afterward reach the permit-only boundary and leave the forest behind. The way now becomes increasingly difficult to walk as you ascend Monitor Ridge via jumbled rocks and patches of pumice. The way braids at times. Just keep an eye on a procession of posts marking the way, which will help you stay on course.

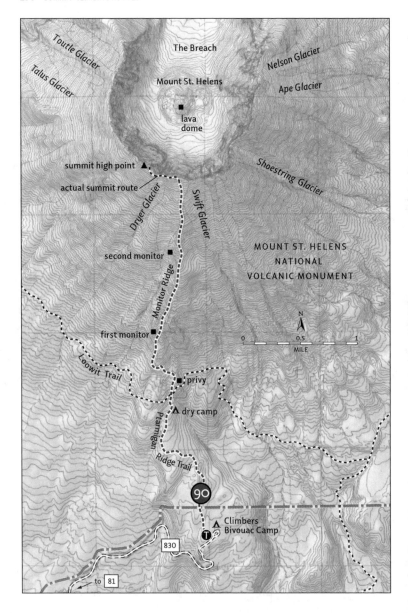

Toutle Glacier

Talus Glacier

The Breach

Nelson Glacier

Mount St. Helens

Ape Glacier

■ lava dome

summit high point ▲

actual summit route

Shoestring Glacier

Dryer Glacier

Swift Glacier

second monitor ■

MOUNT ST. HELENS
NATIONAL
VOLCANIC MONUMENT

Monitor Ridge

N

0   0.5   1
MILE

first monitor ■

Loowit Trail

■ privy

▲ dry camp

Ptarmigan

Ridge Trail

90

▲ Climbers
Bivouac Camp

T

830

to 81

At about 2.5 miles, come to the first of two spacecraft-looking monitors (elev. 5300 ft). The monitors are used to measure seismic activity on the mountain; they also answer the question of how this ridge got its name. Continue up the rocky and increasingly steep ridge, passing boulders and chunks of obsidian. With lingering snowfields on your left and the Swift Glacier on your right, continue huffing and puffing up the mountain. At about 3.8 miles, come to the second monitor (elev. 6900 ft).

Notice the plants working hard to colonize these barren upper slopes. After negotiating one more rocky section, the way heads up a sandy and pumice-laden ridge. The going is quite laborious, tantamount to hiking up a steep sand dune. At 4.7 miles, reach the 8225-foot summit rim. After congratulating yourself, savor the incredible views out to Mounts Rainier and Adams in Washington and Hood and Jefferson in Oregon. And marvel at St. Helens' crater below (being sure to safely stay far back from the rim and its cornice in early season), where a glacier continues to grow—one of the few glaciers in the Cascades that is not receding. Look too across the blast zone and try to imagine what it was like here before the top blew off on May 18, 1980.

Most hikers will stop here, content on reaching the "summit." But the actual summit lies just to the west. If conditions are good, experienced and equipped scramblers can seek it (see below); otherwise bask in your accomplishment and prepare your knees for the jarring descent.

EXTENDING YOUR TRIP

To reach the actual summit, hike west 0.4 mile along the ridge, following a fairly well-defined scramble path. Crest an 8250-foot knob and descend on ledge and loose rock (using extreme caution) to a saddle (elev. 8125 ft) wedged between the Dryer Glacier (named for Thomas J. Dryer who in 1853 became the first person to ascend St. Helens) and steep snowfields clinging to the crater rim. Once beyond this sketchy section, it's a pretty straight shot up pumice to the 8365-foot summit.

91 Mount St. Helens Summit: Worm Flows Winter Route

RATING/ DIFFICULTY	ROUNDTRIP	ELEV GAIN/ HIGH POINT	SEASON
*****/5	11.6 miles	5700 feet/ 8287 feet	Dec–May

Map: Green Trails Mt St. Helens 364S; **Contact:** Gifford Pinchot National Forest, Cowlitz Valley Ranger District; **Notes:** NW Forest Pass or interagency pass required. Sno-Park Pass required. Dogs permitted; **Climbing notes:** All climbers going over 4800 feet must register and obtain a climbing permit (advance purchase of at least twenty-four hours required) and display it while climbing. Maximum party size is twelve. Between November 1 and March 31, climbers must self-register at either the Climber's Bivouac or Marble Mountain Sno-Park climbers registers. There is not fee for the permit during this period. Stay back from the crater rim and note that the summit rim east of the climbing route is closed to visitation. For details, see Appendix II, Contact Information; **GPS:** N 46 07.844 W 122 10.296

Bag a Cascades peak sans rope and harness on this ascent of the most volatile volcano in North America. Its nontechnical

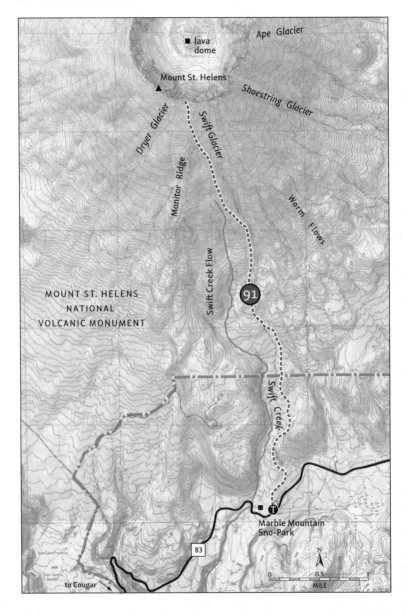

A flamingo-toting climber on the annual Mount St. Helens Mother's Day Climb

nature makes Mount St. Helens perfect for first-time climbers and an annual tradition for seasoned mountaineers. Whether it's your first ascent or fiftieth, the view from the summit—across the corniced crater rim to Mount St. Helens' snow-covered volcanic cousins in their winter finery—will rival that of any in the Cascades.

GETTING THERE

From Woodland (exit 21 on I-5), follow State Route 503 east for 29 miles to Cougar. Continue east on SR 503 (which becomes Forest Road 90) for 7 miles, turning left onto FR 83. Follow this good paved road 6 miles to the Marble Mountain Sno-Park (elev. 2660 ft). (In winter and early spring, FR 83 is gated just past the sno-park.) Privy available.

ON THE TRAIL

A nontechnical climb perfect for first ascents, the winter route of Mount St. Helens is in many ways easier than its summer counterpart (Hike 90). Snow masks the massive piles of pumice, and gone is the fine dust that can coat throats and eyes. However, be aware that fickle winter weather conditions—particularly a low fog deck that can obscure the route—can quickly overwhelm even well-seasoned climbers. If the forecast calls for storms, save bagging the peak for another day.

Beginning at Marble Mountain Sno-Park, warm up on the westward portion of Swift Creek Trail (Hike 93) in cool forest. Huckleberry shrubs grace the way. At about 2 miles, leave the forest behind for bare rock gullies carved by rivers of lava for which the Worm Flows Winter Route received its name. Wooden posts mark the way up to about 4800 feet.

Now above treeline, begin the "climb." Although technical mountaineering gear and know-how are not required, climbers should bring an ice ax—and with it the ability to self-arrest—in addition to snowshoes, crampons, or other traction devices. Expect to take eight to twelve hours round-trip, depending on your mode of descent; skis and glissade chutes will save time spent post-holing down the mountain.

After two steadily steep pitches, reach the false summit at 8287 feet. Hardy hikers will want to curve around the crescent-shaped summit cornice to reach the actual summit, but most climbers will be content with calling this the top. Take care to stay well away from the edge of the summit cornice: a peek into the crater at the still-growing Crater Glacier will have to wait for summer. But the views in all directions should be ample reward: Mount St. Helens' volcanic siblings—Mounts Rainier, Adams, and Hood—sit upon their own cloudbeds, and Spirit Lake sparkles below. On a clear day, Oregon's Mount Jefferson in the central Cascades shimmers in the distance.

EXTENDING YOUR TRIP

Consider participating in the annual Mother's Day Climb of Mount St. Helens. For nearly thirty years, climbers and skiers have taken advantage of Mother's Day weekend—the last weekend before the mountain's summer permit quotas take effect—to make a Mardi Gras–like party out of the nontechnical ascent, donning dresses and wigs to honor mothers everywhere atop North America's most famous volcano.

Opposite: Mount St. Helens viewed from an old lava flow north of Redrock Pass

cross-country skiing
and snowshoe trails

The Mount St. Helens National Volcanic Monument contains an excellent well-maintained and signed network of cross-country skiing and snowshoeing trails. Located on the Monument's southern side, the trails originate from two sno-parks (Cougar and Marble Mountain) reached by paved Forest Roads 83 and 90 from the Lewis River valley. Many of the trails are family-friendly and most of the terrain traversed is free of avalanche concerns. The trails, however, are located at a relatively low elevation. While this makes driving to them less challenging, during periods of low snowfall or high snowpacks, conditions can be less than optimal or not conducive at all to winter recreation. However, the Kalama, Swift Creek, June Lake, and Sasquatch Trails can also be hiked when snow-free.

92 Kalama Ski Trail

RATING/ DIFFICULTY	ROUNDTRIP	ELEV GAIN/ HIGH POINT	SEASON
***/3	22.2 miles	2660 feet/ 3350 feet	Dec–Apr

Map: Green Trails Mt St. Helens 332S; **Contact:** Mount St. Helens National Volcanic Monument; **Notes:** Sno-Park Pass required; **GPS:** N 46 07.121 W 122 12.379

One of the nicest ski trails in the region, the Kalama Ski Trail travels more than ten miles through deep forest and across old lava and mud-flows. Most of the going is mellow, with gentle climbs and long, near-level stretches with a handful of decent views out to Mount St. Helens. Ski the whole trail or short loops via the Bear Trails.

GETTING THERE
From Woodland (exit 21 on I-5), follow State Route 503 east for 29 miles to Cougar. Continue east on SR 503 (which becomes Forest Road 90) for 7 miles, turning left onto FR 83. Follow this good paved road 3.1 miles, bearing left onto paved FR 81 and immediately coming to the Cougar Sno-Park (elev. 2350 ft).

ON THE TRAIL
While the Kalama Ski Trail (no. 231) is open to both skiers and snowshoers, it is primarily used by skiers. If you're snowshoeing, remember not to walk on the ski tracks. Once the snow is gone, the western half of the trail can easily be walked, allowing for loop options when combined with nearby hiking trails. Parts of the eastern half of the trail however are brushy.

Follow the trail (marked with blue diamonds) along the edge of a bluff above the West Fork Swift Creek. Be careful here, as the drop-off to FR 83 below is steep. At 0.2 mile, reach a junction (elev. 2425 ft) with the Baby Bear Trail (no. 231A), which leads a couple hundred feet west to FR 81 (closed in winter and skiable). Continue straight along the bluff before turning northwestward and winding up a thickly forested ridge.

At 0.7 mile, reach a junction (elev. 2600 ft) with the Mama Bear Trail (no. 231B), which leads 0.1 mile west to FR 81. The way then winds gently through forest, reaching, at 1.2 miles, the junction (elev. 2700 ft) with the Papa Bear Trail (no. 231C), which heads 0.1 mile west to FR 81. Continue right past a hunters camp before traversing beautiful old-growth forest.

Now climbing, cross the West Fork Snowmobile Trail at 2.3 miles and FR 830

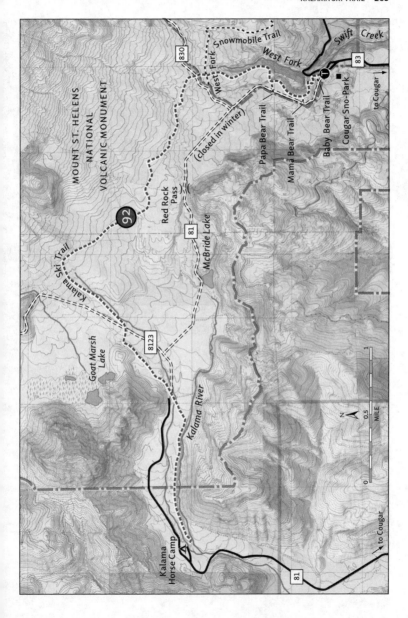

The Kalama Ski Trail offers miles of peaceful forest wandering.

(elev. 3140 ft) at 2.6 miles. Then continue, following old skid roads through old harvest units and old-growth pockets. After climbing to 3350 feet, the way descends through an open outwash area with good views of St. Helens. Be careful not to lose the trail here: the way bends right, reentering forest and, at 4.5 miles, arrives at the Toutle Trail (elev. 3225 ft). Continue straight, dropping about 175 feet before gradually climbing again.

Traverse pine and fir groves, old lahars and lava flows, which provide views of St. Helens and out to Cinnamon Peak and Goat Mountain. After reaching a 3260-foot high point at about 6.5 miles, the way bends southwest, passing the Blue Lake Horse Trail to start a long descent. At 7.5 miles, cross FR 8123 (closed in winter). Still descending, pass the Goat Lake Marsh Trail and come to FR 81 at 8.6 miles.

Cross the road and at 9.1 miles turn right, the trail now following the Toutle Trail (see Hike 32). Now, following on a high bluff above the Kalama River, continue descending through attractive forest, reaching the Kalama Horse Camp and trailhead (elev. 2040 ft) at 11.1 miles. When snow levels are low, the trail can be accessed from this spot, allowing for a one-way if you can set up a shuttle. Otherwise, you've just hit the halfway mark. Enjoy the trip back to the Cougar Sno-Park!

93 Swift Creek— June Lake Loop

RATING/ DIFFICULTY	LOOP	ELEV GAIN/ HIGH POINT	SEASON
****/2	4.9 miles	800 feet/ 3140 feet	Dec–Apr

Map: Green Trails Mt St. Helens 332S; **Contact:** Mount St. Helens National Volcanic Monument; **Notes:** Sno-Park Pass required; **GPS:** N 46 07.839 W 122 10.286

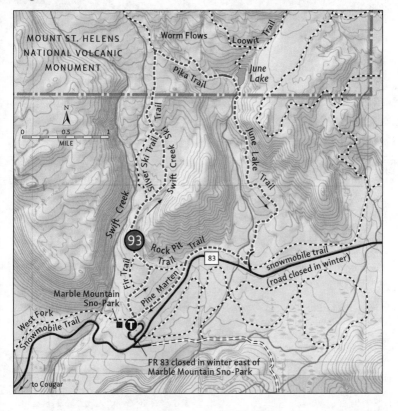

A snowshoer explores the Worm Flows.

June Lake makes for a *wonderful kid-friendly snowshoeing trip. This loop crosses old lava flows, offering excellent views of Mount St. Helens.*

GETTING THERE

From Woodland (exit 21 on I-5), follow State Route 503 east for 29 miles to Cougar. Continue east on SR 503 (which becomes Forest Road 90) for 7 miles, turning left onto FR 83. Follow this good paved road 6 miles to the large Marble Mountain Sno-Park (elev. 2650 ft). Privy available.

ON THE TRAIL

Start by heading north on the wide and popular Swift Creek Ski Trail. You'll be sharing the path with backcountry skiers and climbers heading to Mount St. Helens' summit (Hike 91). At 0.15 mile, cross the West Fork Snowmobile Trail. At 0.3 mile the Fir Trail diverges left. Climb steadily through old-growth forest to reach the Rock Pit Trail (elev. 2800 ft) at 0.5 mile, which crosses an old rock pit on its way to the Pine Marten Trails (Hike 94).

Continue your forest climb on the bench above Swift Creek. At 0.6 mile pass the upper junction of the Fir Trail. At 1 mile, the Silver Ski Trail diverges left and meets up again with the Swift Creek Trail at 1.5 miles. As you head higher up the trail, the forest thins, providing good views of Mount St. Helens.

At 2 miles, come to a junction with the Pika Trail (elev. 3400 ft). Turn right here, cresting a small ridge before traversing an old lava flow with more good St. Helens views. This section can be difficult when the snowpack is light because of the jumbled and jagged basalt rocks. At 2.6 miles, come to June Lake (elev. 3140 ft), a pretty sight with its feeding waterfall. Now turn right and follow a wide path gently downward, reaching a junction (elev. 2680 ft) with the Pine Marten Trail No. 245 at 3.9 miles. Turn right and follow this trail 1 mile back to your start.

EXTENDING YOUR TRIP

Continue on the Swift Creek Trail for another 0.6 mile and explore the Worm Flows, a series of sprawling lava flows hundreds of years old. Remember that a climbing permit is required if you go above 4800 feet.

94 Pine Marten Trails

RATING/ DIFFICULTY	LOOP	ELEV GAIN/ HIGH POINT	SEASON
**/1	up to 7 miles	up to 200 feet/ 2775 feet	Dec–Mar

Map: Green Trails Mt St. Helens 332S; **Contact:** Mount St. Helens National Volcanic Monument; **Notes:** Sno-Park Pass required. Trails may be difficult to travel with low snowpack; **GPS:** N 46 07.877 W 122 10.216

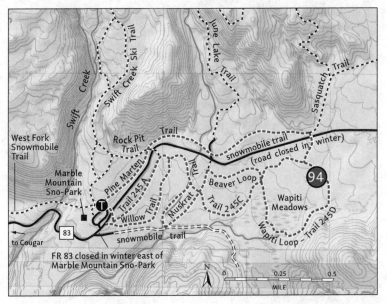

Spend an hour or all day on a series of easy, interconnecting, family-friendly winter trails. On snowshoes or skis, loop through forest groves and wetland meadows and enjoy an occasional St. Helens view or perhaps an elk or other critter sighting.

GETTING THERE

From Woodland (exit 21 on I-5), follow State Route 503 east for 29 miles to Cougar. Continue east on SR 503 (which becomes Forest Road 90) for 7 miles, turning left onto FR 83. Follow this good paved road 6 miles to the large Marble Mountain Sno-Park (elev. 2650 ft). Privy available.

ON THE TRAIL

The Pine Marten Trails are fairly gentle, with just small ups and downs, a network of looped routes perfect for winter recreationists of all ages and abilities. These wide trails are open to both skiers and snowshoers (though if you're snowshoeing, be sure not to walk in ski tracks), with plenty of room for both pursuits. Note that FR 83 (bisecting the Pine Marten Trail system) and FR 8312 (bordering the area to the south) are both open to snowmobiles. You'll want to steer clear of those routes. And what's a pine marten? A very cute member of the weasel family—look for them: you might see them, especially in the trees.

From the humongous Sno-Park lot, head east on Pine Marten Trail No. 245, immediately crossing the West Fork Snowmobile Trail. At 0.5 mile, come to a junction with the Marble Loop Trail (no. 245A), which loops back 0.5 mile to the Sno-Park.

Pine Marten Trail continues straight to a junction with the Rock Pit Trail (no. 244A, which climbs left 0.3 mile to meet the Swift Creek Trail). Continue forward again, reaching the popular June Lake Trail (see Hike 92) at 1 mile from your start. Here you can also go right on the Muskrat Trail (no. 245G) to the Willow Trail (no. 245B) and return 1.6 miles to the Sno-Park.

The Pine Marten Trail continues straight to eventually cross a meadow with views of Mount St. Helens before making a bridged crossing over a creek. At 1.8 miles, arrive at a junction (elev. 2775 ft) with the Sasquatch Trail (see Hike 95). You want to go right, crossing FR 83 and coming to another junction (elev. 2735 ft) at 2 miles. Now, either head left for a 1.2-mile loop through wetland meadows and forest on the Wapiti Loop (no. 245D) or head right to reach the Beaver Loop (no. 245C) at 2.3 miles. Go left or right for 0.5 mile on the Beaver Loop to meet the Muskrat Trail (no. 245G). It is then another 1.3 miles back to the Sno-Park via the Muskrat Trail loop or 0.9 mile back via the more direct Willow Trail (no. 245B). You have many travel options on this wonderful winter trail network.

95 Sasquatch Loop

RATING/ DIFFICULTY	LOOP	ELEV GAIN/ HIGH POINT	SEASON
***/3	9.9 miles	1000 feet/ 3475 feet	Dec–Apr

Map: Green Trails Mt St. Helens 332S; **Contact:** Mount St. Helens National Volcanic Monument; **Notes:** Sno-Park Pass required; **GPS:** N 46 07.877 W 122 10.216

Opposite: The Pine Marten Trails network consists of miles of easy routes.

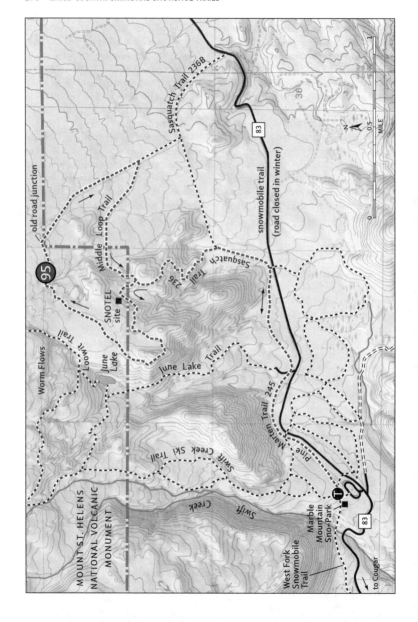

Traverse open forest on a bluff at the base of Mount St. Helens. Catch good glimpses of the nearby snowy volcano as well as other volcanoes and peaks in the distance. Enjoy some good dips too to add more kick to your ski kick and glide.

GETTING THERE

From Woodland (exit 21 on I-5), follow State Route 503 east for 29 miles to Cougar. Continue east on SR 503 (which becomes Forest Road 90) for 7 miles, turning left onto FR 83. Follow this good paved road 6 miles to

A snowshoer checks out the SNOTEL site on the Sasquatch Trail.

the large Marble Mountain Sno-Park (elev. 2650 ft). Privy available.

ON THE TRAIL

While the Sasquatch Trails are open to both skiers and snowshoers, they'll probably appeal more to skiers—until warming, spring conditions make them more favorable for snowshoeing. And if you're snowshoeing, remember not to walk in the ski tracks. The trails are fairly wide, so there's plenty of room for everyone, including Sasquatches.

From the humongous parking lot, head east on Pine Marten Trail No. 245 (Hike 93) or on the open-to-snowmobiles FR 83 for 1.8 miles to the start of the Sasquatch Trails Network. (elev. 2775 ft). Go left on Sasquatch Trail (no. 236) following on old road track and coming to a junction (elev. 2875 ft) at 2.2 miles. You can go right here for 0.7 mile on an old road track to meet back up with the Sasquatch Trail (no. 236) before continuing on Sasquatch Trail (no. 236B) another 0.9 mile to end at FR 83. But it's more interesting (and challenging) to go left at this junction.

Start climbing and reach another junction (elev. 3300 ft) at 3 miles. You'll be returning right—so head left (west) through open forest, enjoying views to St. Helens and the Indian Heaven Wilderness country. Pass the June Lake SNOTEL site (elev. 3440 ft), one of many stations throughout the American West used for measuring snowpacks and forecasting water supplies. Continue west through meadows before swinging north with a good view of St. Helens. The way then bends east, traversing pocket meadows and reaching an elevation of about 3475 feet before gently descending.

Round a creek basin and continue through mature forest to reach an old road junction at 5.1 miles. It's possible to follow this old track left toward the Worm Flows. Your route keeps right through an old timber harvest area, bending around before reaching a junction (elev. 3125 ft) at 6 miles. You can go straight for 0.3 mile to the old road track and a right-hand return to the first junction with the Sasquatch Trail. But it's more interesting to turn right here onto the Middle Loop Trail (no. 236A) instead.

Gradually ascend through open forest and wetlands, passing some decent views of Mount St. Helens and one good view of Mount Adams. At 6.9 miles, reach a familiar junction (elev. 3300 ft). Turn left and enjoy the downhill back to the Sno-Park, retracing the first 3 miles of your route.

Wildflowers paint the Pumice Plain in an array of colors.

Appendix I
Contact Information

**Charles W. Bingham Forest
Learning Center**
www.weyerhaeuser.com/Sustainability
/People/Communities/EducationAnd
Outreach/MountSaintHelens

City of Castle Rock Parks
(360) 274-7478
http://ci.castle-rock.wa.us/parks.htm

City of Longview Parks Department
(360) 442-5400
www.mylongview.com

Cowlitz on the Move
www.cowlitzonthemove.org

Gifford Pinchot National Forest
Cowlitz Valley and Mount St. Helens
Ranger Districts
(360) 891-5000
www.fs.usda.gov/main/giffordpinchot

Lewis County Community Trails
www.lewiscountytrails.org

Lewis and Clark State Park
(360) 864-2643
www.parks.wa.gov

Lone Fir Resort
www.lonefirresort.com

**Mount St. Helens National Volcanic
Monument**
US Forest Service, Gifford Pinchot
National Forest
www.fs.usda.gov/main/mountsthelens

**Mount St. Helens National Volcanic
Monument and Surrounding Area
Headquarters**
(360) 449-7800
www.fs.usda.gov/recarea/giffordpinchot
/recarea/?recid=32340

**Mount St. Helens Science
Learning Center**
www.mshslc.org

PacifiCorp
(503) 813-6666
www.pacificorp.com/about/or
/washington.html

Port of Kalama
(360) 673-2325
http://portofkalama.com/recreation

Seaquest State Park
3030 Spirit Lake Highway
Castle Rock, WA 98611
(360) 274-8633
www.parks.wa.gov/581/Seaquest

US Army Corps of Engineers
Portland District
www.nwp.usace.army.mil/Home

**Washington State Department of
Natural Resources**
Pacific Cascade Region (Castle Rock)
www.dnr.wa.gov

Washington State Parks
www.parks.wa.gov/519/Ike-Kinswa

Appendix II
Conservation and Trail Organizations

Cascadians
P. O. Box 2201
Yakima, WA 98907
http://cascadians.org

Chehalis River Basin Trust
www.chehalislandtrust.org

Columbia Land Trust
1351 Officers' Row
Vancouver, WA 98661
(360) 696-0131
www.columbialandtrust.org

Friends of Seminary Hill
(360) 266-0568
chehalisbrian@gmail.com

Mazamas
527 SE 43rd Ave
Portland, OR 97215
(503) 227-2345
www.mazamas.org

The Mountaineers
7700 Sand Point Way NE
Seattle, WA 98115
(206) 521-6001
www.mountaineers.org

Mount St. Helens Club
P. O. Box 843
Longview, WA 98632
(360) 636-4575
www.mtsthelensclub.org

Mount St. Helens Institute
42218 NE Yale Bridge Rd
Amboy, WA 98601
(360) 449-7883
www.mshinstitute.org

Nature Conservancy
Washington Field Office
1917 First Avenue
Seattle, WA 98101
(206) 343-4344
www.nature.org

Pacific Crest Trail Association
1331 Garden Highway
Sacramento, CA 95833
(916) 285-1846
www.pcta.org

Rocky Mountain Elk Foundation
www.rmef.org

Spring Trust for Trails
5015 88th Ave SE
Mercer Island, WA 98040
http://springtrailtrust.org/

The Trust for Public Lands
www.tpl.org

Washington Trails Association
705 Second Avenue, Suite 300
Seattle, WA 98104
(206) 625-1367
www.wta.org

Appendix III
Recommended Reading

Asars, Tami. *Day Hiking Mount Adams and the Goat Rocks.* Seattle: Mountaineers Books, 2014.

Carson, Rob. *Mount St. Helens: The Eruption and Recovery of a Volcano,* 20th ed. Seattle: Sasquatch Books, 2000.

Egan, Timothy. *The Big Burn: Teddy Roosevelt and the Fire that Saved America.* Boston: Houghton Mifflin Harcourt, 2009.

Gordon, David George. *The Sasquatch Seeker's Field Manual: Using Citizen Science to Uncover North America's Most Elusive Creature.* Seattle: Mountaineers Books, 2015.

Manning, Harvey, and Bob and Ira Spring. *Mountain Flowers of the Cascades and Olympics,* 2nd ed. Seattle: Mountaineers Books, 2002.

Mueller, Marge and Ted. *Exploring Washington's Wild Areas,* 2nd ed. Seattle: Mountaineers Books, 2002.

———. *Washington State Parks: A Complete Recreation Guide,* 3rd ed. Seattle: Mountaineers Books, 2004.

Pyle, Robert Michael. *Where Bigfoot Walks: Crossing the Dark Divide.* Boston: Mariner Books, 1997.

Romano, Craig. *Day Hiking Columbia River Gorge.* Seattle: Mountaineers Books, 2011.

Whitney, Stephen R., and Rob Sanderlin. *Field Guide to the Cascades & Olympics,* 2nd ed. Seattle: Mountaineers Books, 2003.

Index

1% for Trails—
Outdoor Nonprofits
in Partnership

Where would we be without trails? Not very far into the wilderness.

That's why Mountaineers Books designates 1 percent of the sales of select guidebooks in our *Day Hiking* series toward volunteer trail maintenance. Since launching this program, we've contributed more than $14,000 toward improving trails.

For this book, our 1 percent of sales is going to **Washington Trails Association** (WTA). WTA hosts more than 750 work parties throughout Washington's Cascades and Olympics each year, with volunteers clearing downed logs after spring snowmelt, cutting away brush, retreading worn stretches of trail, and building bridges and turnpikes. Their efforts are essential to the land managers who maintain thousands of acres on shoestring budgets.

Mountaineers Books donates many books to nonprofit recreation and conservation organizations. Our 1% for Trails campaign is one more way we can help fellow nonprofit organizations as we work together to get more people outside, to both enjoy and protect our wild public lands.

If you'd like to support Mountaineers Books and our nonprofit partnership programs, please visit our website to learn more or email mbooks@mountaineersbooks.org.

Author Craig Romano

Author Aaron Theisen (photo by Elizabeth Cole)

About the Authors

Craig Romano grew up in rural New Hampshire, where he fell in love with the natural world. He has traveled extensively, from Alaska to Argentina, Sicily to South Korea, seeking wild and spectacular landscapes. He ranks Washington State, his home since 1989, among the most beautiful places on the planet, and he has thoroughly hiked it, over 17,000 miles' worth, from Cape Flattery to Puffer Butte. An avid runner as well, Craig has run over twenty-five marathons and ultra runs, including the Boston Marathon and the White River 50 Mile Endurance Run.

An award-winning author and coauthor of thirteen books, his *Columbia Highlands: Exploring Washington's Last Frontier* was recognized in 2010 by Washington secretary of state Sam Reed and state librarian Jan Walsh as a *Washington Reads* book for its contribution to Washington's cultural heritage. Craig writes for numerous publications, tourism agencies, and Hikeoftheweek.com, and is also a columnist for *Northwest Runner* and *Outdoors NW*.

When not hiking, running, or writing, he can be found napping with his wife, Heather, son, Giovanni, and cats, Giuseppe and Mazie, at his home in Skagit County. Visit him at http://CraigRomano.com and on Facebook at "Craig Romano Guidebook Author."

Aaron Theisen is an accomplished outdoors and travel writer and photographer. His work has appeared in numerous publications, including *Northwest Travel*, *Montana*, *Distinctly Montana*, *Montana Outdoors*, *Adventures NW*, *Sandpoint Magazine*, and *Out There Monthly*. He is a member of the Board of Directors of the Washington Trails Association.

His photographs have been featured in galleries and solo exhibitions throughout Eastern Washington, in calendars for organizations such as the Washington Native Plant Society and Montana Wilderness Association, and in magazines such as *Western Byways* and *Bugle*. In addition to being a full-time outdoors and travel writer, Aaron is a consultant medical writer and has written or edited hundreds of publications for some of the world's premier genetics journals.

When Aaron is not traipsing around the backcountry he can be found in Spokane with his wife, Kristi, son, Owen, and cat, Pudding. Visit him at http://aarontheisen.com and on Facebook at "Aaron Theisen Writer and Photographer."

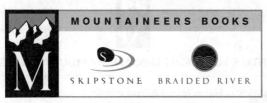

MOUNTAINEERS BOOKS

SKIPSTONE   BRAIDED RIVER

recreation · lifestyle · conservation

MOUNTAINEERS BOOKS is a leading publisher of mountaineering literature and guides—including our flagship title, *Mountaineering: The Freedom of the Hills*—as well as adventure narratives, natural history, and general outdoor recreation. Through our two imprints, Skipstone and Braided River, we also publish titles on sustainability and conservation. We are committed to supporting the environmental and educational goals of our organization by providing expert information on human-powered adventure, sustainable practices at home and on the trail, and preservation of wilderness.

The Mountaineers, founded in 1906, is a 501(c)(3) nonprofit outdoor activity and conservation organization whose mission is "to explore, study, preserve, and enjoy the natural beauty of the outdoors." One of the largest such organizations in the United States, it sponsors classes and year-round outdoor activities throughout the Pacific Northwest, including climbing, hiking, backcountry skiing, snowshoeing, bicycling, camping, paddling, and more. The Mountaineers also supports its mission through its publishing division, Mountaineers Books, and promotes environmental education and citizen engagement. For more information, visit The Mountaineers Program Center, 7700 Sand Point Way NE, Seattle, WA 98115-3996; phone 206-521-6001; www.mountaineers.org; or email info@mountaineers.org.

Our publications are made possible through the generosity of donors and through sales of more than 600 titles on outdoor recreation, sustainable lifestyle, and conservation. To donate, purchase books, or learn more, visit us online:

MOUNTAINEERS BOOKS
1001 SW Klickitat Way, Suite 201 · Seattle, WA 98134
800-553-4453 · mbooks@mountaineersbooks.org · www.mountaineersbooks.org

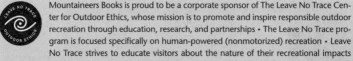

Mountaineers Books is proud to be a corporate sponsor of The Leave No Trace Center for Outdoor Ethics, whose mission is to promote and inspire responsible outdoor recreation through education, research, and partnerships · The Leave No Trace program is focused specifically on human-powered (nonmotorized) recreation · Leave No Trace strives to educate visitors about the nature of their recreational impacts and offers techniques to prevent and minimize such impacts · Leave No Trace is best understood as an educational and ethical program, not as a set of rules and regulations · For more information, visit www.lnt.org, or call 800-332-4100.

OTHER TITLES YOU MIGHT ENJOY FROM MOUNTAINEERS BOOKS

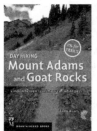

Day Hiking Mount Adams and Goat Rocks
Tami Asars
81 enticing hikes explore Washington's
stunning southern Cascades

Day Hiking Snoqualmie Region, 2nd edition
Dan Nelson and Alan Bauer
135 gorgeous hikes close to the Puget
Sound region—includes the Alpine Lakes

Day Hiking Eastern Washington
Craig Romano and Rich Landers
125 sunny hikes on the
dry side of the Cascades

Day Hiking the San Juans and Gulf Islands
Craig Romano
136 hikes on two dozen islands—plus Victoria,
Anacortes, Tsawwassen, and Point Roberts

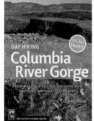

Day Hiking Columbia River Gorge
Craig Romano
100+ fabulous hikes in and around the
Columbia River Gorge Scenic Area—
plus the Portland region

www.mountaineersbooks.org